MW01114721

The Efficient Market Hypothesists

Great Minds in Finance
Series Editor: Professor **Colin Read**

This series explores the lives and times, theories and applications of those who have contributed most significantly to the formal study of finance. It aims to bring to life the theories that are the foundation of modern finance, by examining them within the context of the historical backdrop and the life stories and characters of the 'great minds' behind them.

Readers may be those interested in the fundamental underpinnings of our stock and bond markets; college students who want to delve into the significance behind the theories; or experts who constantly look for ways to more clearly understand what they do, so they can better relate to their clients and communities.

Titles include:

THE LIFE CYCLISTS

THE PORTFOLIO THEORISTS

THE RISE OF THE QUANTS

THE EFFICIENT MARKET HYPOTHESISTS

The Efficient Market Hypothesists

Bachelier, Samuelson, Fama, Ross, Tobin, and Shiller

Colin Read

First published 2013 by
PALGRAVE MACMILLAN

Palgrave Macmillan in the UK is an imprint of Macmillan Publishers Limited, registered in England, company number 785998, of Houndmills, Basingstoke, Hampshire RG21 6XS.

Palgrave Macmillan in the US is a division of St Martin's Press LLC, 175 Fifth Avenue, New York, NY 10010.

Palgrave Macmillan is the global academic imprint of the above companies and has companies and representatives throughout the world.

Palgrave® and Macmillan® are registered trademarks in the United States, the United Kingdom, Europe and other countries.

ISBN 978–0–230–27421–1

This book is printed on paper suitable for recycling and made from fully managed and sustained forest sources. Logging, pulping and manufacturing processes are expected to conform to the environmental regulations of the country of origin.

A catalogue record for this book is available from the British Library.

A catalog record for this book is available from the Library of Congress.

10   9   8   7   6   5   4   3   2   1
22 21 20 19 18 17 16 15 14 13

Printed and bound in the United States of America

Contents

List of Figures   vii

Preface to the Great Minds in Finance *series*   viii

1   Introduction   1

Section 1   Louis Bachelier: The First Physicist Financial Theorist

2   The Early Years   7

3   The Times   14

4   The Theory   24

5   Discussion and Applications: Einstein and Bachelier   33

6   Life and Legacy   44

Section 2   Paul Samuelson's Random Walk

7   The Early Years   55

8   The Times   65

9   The Theory   75

10   Discussion and Applications   82

11   The Nobel Prize, Life, and Legacy   87

Section 3   Eugene Fama's Efficient Market Hypothesis

12   The Early Years   93

13   The Times   98

14   The Theory   102

15   Discussion and Applications   107

16   Life and Legacy   116

Section 4   Stephen Ross and Arbitrage Pricing Theory

17   The Early Years   121

18   The Times   128

19   The Theory   130

20   Discussion and Applications   134

21   Life and Legacy   139

Section 5   James Tobin and a New Policy

22   The Early Years   147

23   The Times   153

24   Tobin's Efficient Market Paradigm   158

25   Discussion and Applications   163

26   The Nobel Prize, Life, and Legacy   170

Section 6   Robert Shiller and Irrational Exuberance

27   The Early Years   177

28   The Times   184

29   The Theory   189

30   Discussion and Applications   193

31   Life and Legacy   195

Section 7   What We Have Learned

32   Combined Contributions   201

33   Conclusions   205

Glossary   207

Notes   213

Index   219

List of Figures

2.1   The family tree of Louis Bachelier (1870–1946)   8

7.1   The family tree of Paul Samuelson (1915–2009)   57

7.2   The family tree of Marion Crawford (1916–1978)   63

12.1 The family tree of Eugene Fama (1939–)   94

17.1 The family tree of Stephen Ross (1944–)   123

17.2 The family tree of Carol Frost (1944–)   125

22.1 The family tree of James Tobin (1928–2002)   148

27.1 The family tree of Robert Shiller (1946–)   179

27.2 The family tree of Virginia Marie
      (Faulstich) Shiller   182

Preface to the *Great Minds in Finance* series

This series covers the gamut of the study of finance – from the significance of financial decisions over time and through the cycle of one's life to the ways in which investors balance reward and risk; from how the price of a security is determined to whether these prices properly reflect all available information – we will look at the fundamental questions and answers in finance. We delve into theories that govern personal decision-making, those that dictate the decisions of corporations and other similar entities, and the public finance of government. This will be done by looking at the lives and contributions of the key players upon whose shoulders the discipline rests.

By focusing on the great minds in finance, we draw together the concepts that have stood the test of time and have proven themselves to reveal something about the way humans make financial decisions. These principles, which have flowed from individuals, many of whom have been awarded the Nobel Memorial Prize in Economics for their insights (or perhaps shall be awarded some day), allow us to see the financial forest for the trees.

The insights of these contributors to finance arose because these great minds were uniquely able to glimpse a familiar problem through a wider lens. From the greater insights provided by a more expansive view, they were able to focus upon details that have eluded previous scholars. Their unique perspectives provided new insights that are the measure of their genius. The giants who have produced the theories and concepts that drive financial fundamentals share one important characteristic: they have developed insights that explain how markets can be used or tailored to create a more efficient economy.

The approach taken is one taught in our finance programs and practiced by fundamentals analysts. We present theories to enrich and motivate our financial understanding. This approach is in contrast to the tools of technicians formulated solely on capitalizing on market inefficiencies without delving too deeply into the very meaning of efficiency in the first place. From a strictly aesthetic perspective, one cannot entirely condemn the tug-of-war of profits sought by the technicians, even if they do little to enhance – and may even detract from – efficiency. The mathematics and physics of price movements and the sophistication of computer algorithms is fascinating in its own right. Indeed, my appreciation for technical analysis came from my university studies toward a Bachelor of Science degree in physics, followed immediately by a PhD in economics.

However, as I began to teach economics and finance, I realized that the analytic tools of physics that so pervaded modern economics have strayed too far from explaining this important dimension of human financial decision-making. To better understand the interplay between the scientific method, economics, human behavior, and public policy, I continued with my studies toward a Master of Accountancy in taxation, an MBA, and a Juris Doctor of Law.

As I taught the economics of intertemporal choice, the role of money and financial instruments, and the structure of the banking and financial intermediaries, I recognized that my students had become increasingly fascinated with investment banking and Wall Street. Meanwhile, the developed world experienced the most significant breakdown of financial markets in almost eight decades. I realized that this once-in-a-lifetime global financial meltdown arose because we had moved from an economy that produced things to one in which, by 2006, generated a third of all profits in financial markets, with little to show but pieces of paper representing wealth that had value only if some stood ready to purchase them.

I decided to shift my research from academic research in esoteric fields of economics and finance and toward the contribution to a better understanding of markets by the educated public. I began to write a regular business column and a book that documented the unraveling of the Great Recession. The book, entitled *Global Financial Meltdown: How We Can Avoid the Next Economic Crisis*, described the events that gave rise to the most significant economic crisis in our lifetime. I followed that book with *The Fear Factor*, which explained the important role of fear as a sometimes constructive and at other times destructive influence in our financial decision-making. I then wrote a book on why many economies at first thrive and then struggle to survive in *The Rise and Fall of an Economic Empire*. Throughout, I try to impart to you, the educated reader, the intuition and the understanding that would, at least, help you to make informed decisions in increasingly volatile global economies and financial markets.

As I describe the theories that form the foundations of modern finance, I show how individuals born without great fanfare can come to be regarded as geniuses within their own lifetime. The lives of each of the individuals examined in this series became extraordinary, not because they made an unfathomable leap in our understanding, but rather because they looked at something in a different way and caused us all thereafter to look at the problem in this new way. That is the test of genius.

1
Introduction

This book is the fourth in a series of discussions about the great minds in the history and theory of finance. While the series addresses the contributions of significant individuals to our understanding of financial decisions and markets, this entry in the series describes a paradigm that was almost universally accepted by finance scholars upon its inception in the mid-1960s and questioned by financial practitioners ever since. We will describe the controversial efficient market paradigm and attempts by the finance discipline to make our financial models more realistic.

We begin with a description of one of the most profound contributions to finance in the twentieth century. Astoundingly, while this contribution was made more than a century ago at the very beginning of the twentieth century, the work of Louis Bachelier remained almost unknown for another 60 years until the finance discipline matured sufficiently to appreciate his insights. Many now acknowledge Bachelier as the father of modern finance, even though he never enjoyed such recognition in his lifetime.

We briefly covered some of Bachelier's work in volume 3 of this series entitled *The Rise of the Quants*. However, while we noted that Bachelier also presaged the famous Black-Scholes equation by almost three-quarters of a century, he made another related contribution that was even more profound. He presented to us the random walk. Our realization of his contribution subsequently gave rise to a related concept, the efficient market hypothesis.

One of the reinventors of Bachelier's work, the great mind Paul Samuelson, recognized the profound implications of the random walk and produced the theoretical justification of what we now call the efficient market hypothesis. While he qualified the usefulness of this hypothesis, later more empirically motivated commentators, especially the great mind Eugene Fama, were less circumspect. From it, Fama established for finance a mantra that has been quoted ever since – the principle that "security prices reflect all information."

Others subsequently built upon the three-legged stool of the random walk, the efficient market hypothesis, and the notion of arbitrage upon which both arguments depend. For instance, the great mind Stephen Ross understood the interdependencies of these relationships to develop a more complete and useful extension of the Capital Asset Pricing Model (CAPM), now known as arbitrage pricing theory. However, these new methodologies and paradigms, while intellectually rich, were inadequate to explain all the dynamics and gyrations of modern financial markets. The challenges of market bubbles and their collapses forced a new set of scholars, led by James Tobin and Robert Shiller of Yale University, to question conventional wisdom through both intuition and empiricism.

The final chapters on the efficient market paradigm are only now being written, though. These great minds have given us much intuition and many methodologies, and have motivated a whole new body of current and future research into behavioral finance. While this new field of behavioral finance will be left for a future volume, we cover in this volume the theories and criticisms of great minds in finance in informing the current cadre of scholars and practitioners alike. We will first cover the early life, and then the times, of these great minds because their life experiences informed their great insights. We will then describe their significant theory and insights into our financial decisions, followed by the various ways their insights were applied to benefit and, at times, challenge others. Each part will conclude with the reasons why various illustrious groups have recognized their contributions and their place in financial history.

In 1776, Adam Smith (1723–1790) published a treatise that created the discipline of economics. His *Inquiry into the Nature and Causes of the Wealth of Nations* defined the notion of the invisible hand of economic activity. According to this paradigm, the enlightened self-interest of myriad independent producers and consumers provides the signals for production and consumption and allows market prices to adjust to equate these two sides of the market. Should there be a surplus, enlightened agents rid themselves of this excess by lowering prices, while shortages are addressed by a fictitious auctioneer who raises prices until more production is forthcoming and some consumption is curtailed.

Smith never described the actual dynamic process by which these prices adjust or how supply or demand is expanded or curtailed to establish or re-establish equilibrium. Indeed, the precise dynamics of this process remains vague to this day. However, the story Smith could tell was a simple one that entailed the entry of new producers when supply is short and their exit when there is excess supply.

All economists and finance students are schooled in this familiar story. The pursuit of profits drives such entry and exit until all profit opportunities are usurped. The great mind Kenneth Arrow's proof of the existence of such a competitive equilibrium, and his extension of this concept to financial markets contingent on various future states of the world, forever enshrined this paradigm and has remained perhaps the most complete, robust, and widely accepted concept in all of finance and economics.

An analogy to this concept inevitably found its way into the theory of financial markets, even though it is inconceivable that financial markets could rise to the perfectly complete and competitive standard that Arrow envisioned. Instead of trading tangible goods between producers and consumers, traders of financial instruments are trading pieces of paper called securities with the expectation that the purchaser secures the right to a future flow of profits.

We shall see in this volume that there are extensions from the free market paradigm that make sense, and others that are much more subtle. It turns out that the concept of allocative efficiency in markets for tangible goods and services does not have a direct parallel in the information efficiency assumed in financial markets.

However, the compelling attractiveness of the argument that a financial security price should incorporate all available information through the twin forces of competition and arbitrage remains a cornerstone of modern finance, if not explicitly for some, then at least implicitly by most who cannot fathom the alternative. If securities prices do not incorporate all relevant information, the free entry of financial entrepreneurs, called arbitrageurs, would buy or short sell the mispriced assets under the premise that the market would eventually "get it right" and bestow upon these arbitrageurs profits for their courage and insight.

This logic is compelling. The discipline of finance assumes markets are information-efficient because to be otherwise would imply that there really is such a thing as a "free lunch," a reward without the creation of anything substantial. Under the discipline of this logic, securities prices must logically reflect all available information, and any further fluctuations in prices must arise from unknown and reasonably unknowable factors influencing securities.

This logic spawned a great deal of subsequent empirical research which verified that any remaining price movements, once arbitrage has taken its course, must be random and indiscernible, as one would surmise if markets were informationally efficient.

Of course, some financial traders never troubled themselves with this financial logic. These chartists, or technical analysts, were too busy trying to glean tendencies in stock prices and realizing profits for their efforts – or at least so they would say. Practitioners of the other ilk, the fundamentalists, were trying to glean information unknown by others on the true underlying value of individual firms. These practitioners, too, believed that their creation of such private information, intelligence, or intuition was also rewarded with profits. Financial practitioners, divided into these two camps of the chartists and the fundamentalists, were united in their suspicion of the academicians who argued that both practitioner groups were claiming to earn profits that could not be earned in theory.

This is the story of the lives, times, insights, criticisms, and legacies of the great minds that created and fueled the debate over the efficient market hypothesis. We begin with the father of modern finance, and one who most students of finance know little about.

Section 1
Louis Bachelier: The First Physicist Financial Theorist

In the decades following the beginning of the Cold War, economics began its period of intense mathematization. Suddenly, with Harry Markowitz's development of the Modern Portfolio Theory, and the extensions through the CAPM and the Black-Scholes equation, finance, too, became much more mathematics-intensive, just as physics had two centuries earlier. The end of the Cold War, the Space Race, and the arms race created a lull in the demand for rocket scientists and physicists and saw these theoreticians drawn toward finance and economics. The resulting drawing of physicists from a Space Race won by the Americans in the 1960s created a race for mathematical sophistication in finance in the 1970s. Many consider the 1970s to be the demarcation point for the foray of physics into finance. However, many now appreciate that the first mathematical physicist to contribute to modern finance was a Frenchman, Louis Bachelier 70 years earlier, at the tail end of the nineteenth century.

We begin with this first theorist who was able to translate the insights of those who came earlier with the mathematical rigor that would allow us to convert rhetoric and logic into science and mathematics.

2
The Early Years

There is some mystery surrounding the early life of Louis Jean-Baptiste Alphonse Bachelier. Our culture documents in great detail the lives of the famous, influential, and powerful. Less is known about scholars whose contributions are not recognized until long after they have passed. Bachelier's story was further obscured because a fire destroyed some archives, because he departed early from the traditional upbringing of scholar prodigies when he was thrust into independent adulthood at too young an age, and because his life was punctuated by the chaos of two wars.

This we do know though. At an early age, Bachelier seemed destined for a prosperous and successful life. He was born into a family of some wealth. His maternal grandfather, Jean-Baptiste Fort-Meu, was a well-known banker and director of the bank *la Compagnie des Caisses d'Escompte* in Le Havre, and a minor poet. He raised a daughter, Louis' mother, Cecile Gabrielle Adelaide Fort-Meu (1845–1889). Cecile was an articulate and educated woman who fell in love and married Louis' father, Alphonse Bachelier, who was five years her senior, born on August 3, 1840 in Libourne, in the province of Gironde. Alphonse and Cecile married in 1867.

The young married couple settled in Le Havre, in the northwestern Haute-Normandie region of France at the mouth of the River Seine, where Alphonse maintained a successful family business. Then, as now, Le Havre was a bustling seaport, originally with the rest of Europe and then more broadly as trade routes expanded toward the West Indies and Central America. Alphonse was a wine merchant who represented the renowned Champagne vintner Mumm de Reims and the Bordeaux region vintner Balaresque in the export of their wines. He also acted as the director of the consulate on behalf of Venezuela. The family

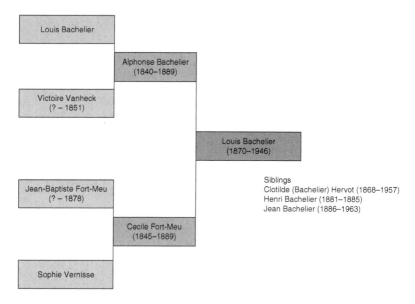

Figure 2.1   The family tree of Louis Bachelier (1870–1946)

was well-to-do and there was an expectation that their first son, Louis Jean-Baptiste Alphonse Bachelier, would continue the family name, tradition, and business.

Louis Jean-Baptiste Alphonse Bachelier was born on March 11, 1870 in Le Havre. His first name was taken from his paternal grandfather, and his middle names from his maternal grandfather and his father. Louis was preceded by his sister, Marie Louise Sophie Clotilde, and was followed by a brother, Henri, 11 years later and another brother, Jean Henri Etienne Francis, 16 years later. Henri died in 1885 at the age of four.

The family offered young Louis a stimulating upbringing. His father was an amateur scientist and shared with him an interest in mathematics and physics. Louis went on to study at high school (called the lycée in France) at nearby Caen, the capital of Basse-Normandie.

Louis graduated from high school in October 1888, just three months before his father's death on January 11, 1889.[1] Still reeling with the immense responsibility, at the age of 18, of maintaining his father's business, Louis' mother died less than four months later, on May 7, 1889. As the elder son, he was left to run the family company Bachelier Fils and to support himself, his older sister, and his three-year-old brother.

Louis juggled these premature burdens for more than two years before he was called to mandatory military service. The French had been concerned about the growing power and influence of the German Empire and had established compulsory military service in 1872. Military indoctrination was also common in public schools, and Louis was called to national duty at the age of 21. Some more affluent and influential families could arrange for their sons to avoid such service. However, young Louis had little such influence following the death of his father.

At the end of his military service, Bachelier enrolled at the Sorbonne in Paris. Meanwhile, he supported himself with various jobs that exposed him to the workings of the Paris Stock Exchange. Three years later, in what must have been an intense combination of study and self-support, he completed his Bachelor of Sciences degree at the Sorbonne. He continued his studies at the Sorbonne and completed a Certificate in Mathematical Physics less than two years later. He defended a thesis in applied mathematics less than three years after that, just after his thirtieth birthday.

Clearly, Bachelier was brilliant, but his studies were unconventional. He did not have the luxury of strict devotion to study without any material worries, as had many of his colleagues. On the other hand, he also gained a working knowledge of the function of one of the world's leading financial markets, which was an appreciation none of his colleagues in mathematical physics could have gleaned.

From the academic record, it is clear that Bachelier struggled to garner the focus necessary to excel in mathematical physics in an era in which his chosen field was beginning a rapid acceleration in terms of sophistication. He had the opportunity to study underneath the brilliant French mathematician Jules Henri Poincaré, but he had to repeat at least one major progress exam in mathematics a number of times before barely passing it. Eventually, he managed to pass all the predicate exams and was afforded the opportunity to defend his thesis.

Many commentators have suggested the quality of his thesis defense as being at the root of his academic obscurity. However, the truth is more complex. In the French higher education system at the time, each mathematical physics program had two chaired professors – one steeped in the tradition of partial differential equations and the other more squarely in the study of physics. A thesis is usually more deeply immersed in one field or the other, and Bachelier proceeded accordingly. However, he had to also defend his understanding of the alternate topic not encompassed in his thesis. As stated earlier, he struggled in some areas and may not have excelled in this second part of his thesis. In grading his work, the thesis committee granted him the distinction of 'honorable', not the 'tres honorable' reserved for an excellent defense in both areas. However, his dubious distinction was not a comment on his innovative thesis.

This modest slight became significant because of the academic reality in France at the time that since each program had only two permanent chairs, new academic positions became available only through retirement. Without the thesis distinction of 'tres honorable', subsequent academic appointment would be difficult and academic obscurity in France at that time would be the more likely result.

We shall return to Bachelier's lifelong frustration at a lack of academic recognition in his later life. With regard to the quality of the thesis itself, we find no such clues as to why his work would go unrecognized for generations. As he prepared for his thesis, he had taken the required instruction in the various areas of mathematical physics, including calculus, mechanics, and astronomy. He likely came under the tutelage of Jules Henri Poincaré first through Poincaré's renowned course in celestial mechanics. However, Bachelier did not have any requisite exposure to the nascent field of probability theory, as the major innovations in such areas as measure theory, by Frenchmen such as Félix Édouard Justin Emile Borel (1871–1956), had yet to be formulated. Bachelier would have been exposed to the heat diffusion process and probably began to make the connection between the diffusion of heat in physics and the diffusion of information in financial markets. He would need to develop and refine the necessary mathematics to perform this transformation, and his work in the application of information diffusion to instruments on the Paris Stock Exchange became the admittedly unconventional subject of his thesis in mathematical physics.

The blessing and the curse of Bachelier's academic philosophy was his apparent unconventionality shared by all great minds who are ahead of their time. He had held a lifelong scholarly interest in games of chance and subsequently wrote academic papers on game theory. He also became accomplished in the new field of probability theory. In the creation of his thesis, he had relied on the work of the famed French mathematician and statistician Pierre-Simon, Marquis de Laplace (1749–1827), who, in combination with the work of Johann Carl Friedrich Gauss (1777–1855), had helped to establish what we now know of as the normal distribution that describes the collection of independent random variables. Bachelier was influenced by the early probability theorists well before others understood the implications of random motion as described by probability distributions. He felt that a model of random motion might equally well explain the movement of prices for a popular investment tool in France during that era, the perpetuity bond.

Robert Brown's motion

Actually, seemingly random motion had intrigued scientists and philosophers for millennia. The observation of microscopic random motion had even caused some to postulate the existence of small invisible particles that we deduce exist only through the result of their collision with observable particles. For instance, the Roman Lucretius wrote a poem "On the Nature of Things" in 60 B.C., in which he postulated:

> Observe what happens when sunbeams are admitted into a building and shed light on its shadowy places. You will see a multitude of tiny particles mingling in a multitude of ways ... their dancing is an actual indication of underlying movements of matter that are hidden from our sight ... It originates with the atoms which move of themselves [i.e., spontaneously]. Then those small compound bodies that are least removed from the impetus of the atoms are set in motion by the impact of their invisible blows and in turn cannon against slightly larger bodies. So the movement mounts up from the atoms and gradually emerges to the level of our senses, so that those bodies are in motion that we see in sunbeams, moved by blows that remain invisible.[2]

In 1827, the botanist Robert Brown (1773–1858) further observed the jiggles and jolts of pollen suspended in water under a microscope, a phenomenon the Dutch chemist Jan Ingenhousz (1730–1799) had earlier noticed in 1785 in coal dust suspended in alcohol. We now know this jiggling motion as Brownian motion, perhaps because Ingenhousz and Lucretius motion is a bit too problematic to pronounce.

While this Brownian impingement of random forces on a particle defied theoretical explanation, a Danish mathematician, Thorvald N. Thiele (1838–1910), had described in a paper in French in 1880 how independent variables could be summed to produce a distribution that followed the Laplace and Gaussian distributions.[3] Thiele's first paper on the subject of the least squares methodology included a description of Brownian motion that showed increments in positions that are normally distributed, with a variance that is proportional to time. Thiele's advances clearly hinted at what we now know as Brownian motion and martingales. Given that his paper was available in French and was likely to have been accessible to Bachelier at the Sorbonne, it is plausible that Bachelier could have relied on Thiele's traditional work for his own very unconventional treatment of prices in financial markets.

Poincaré's predicament

Bachelier's decision to model mathematically and then fit his model to the movement of option prices for perpetual bonds on the Paris Stock Exchange is probably the most unusual successfully defended thesis Poincaré ever supervised. Academics often abhor non-conventionality because it forces scholars to stretch and to reject old and closely held ideas for new ideas that have not stood the test of time. Such conventionality threatens the value of the tools scholars invest in over their careers.

Poincaré must also have been concerned about the application of pure science and mathematics to the impure speculation on what many regarded as vulgar money markets. Two centuries earlier, Sir Isaac Newton (1642–1727) had already concluded that the laws which govern celestial bodies could not be applied to the folly of human decision-making. These academic obstacles did not deter Bachelier, though, and nor did it deter Poincaré, to his credit. In fact, following Bachelier's presentation of his thesis, Poincaré, as the lead arbiter on a panel of three mathematical physicists charged with judging Bachelier's thesis, declared:

> The subject chosen by Mr. Bachelier is somewhat removed from those which are normally dealt with by our applicants. His thesis is entitled "Theory of Speculation" and focuses on the application of probability to the stock market. First, one may fear that the author had exaggerated the applicability of probability as is often done. Fortunately, this is not the case. In his introduction and further in the paragraph entitled "Probability in Stock Exchange Operations", he strives to set limits within which one can legitimately apply this type of reasoning. He does not exaggerate the range of his results, and I do not think that he is deceived by his formulas.[4]

Poincaré also praised Bachelier in his novel derivation of Gauss' distribution in a discrete mathematical form. He added that he thought the thesis was:

> very original, and all the more interesting in that Fourier's reasoning can be extended with a few changes to the theory of errors … It is regrettable that M. Bachelier did not develop this part of his thesis further.[5]

While the praise may seem faint, Poincaré subsequently helped Bachelier to publish his paper on speculation in one of France's leading journals, the *Annales Scientifiques de l'Ecole Normale Superieure* and later in the *Journal de Mathématiques Pures et Appliquées*. At that time in France, there was a wide gulf in status between professors and their students. It was not the eminent Poincaré's obligation to assist Bachelier. While he may not have embraced Bachelier's application, he certainly appreciated Bachelier's methods, insights, and intelligence.

With a successful thesis defense from the prestigious Sorbonne University in hand, Bachelier was faced with the significant challenge of finding an academic position. Yet, with only a rank of 'honorable' on his thesis that appeared entirely unconventional, he had pursued a risky academic strategy. We shall see that his risky venture did not pay great dividends.

3
The Times

The mystery of Louis Bachelier is why he has remained relatively obscure within the finance literature until his "discovery" by Paul Samuelson in 1964. To better understand why results so fundamental today remained almost unknown for three generations, we must peer into the nature of scientific research before the emergence of English as the de facto international language of academia.

The Renaissance man

The archetypal Renaissance man Leonardo da Vinci (1452–1519) was a renowned painter, sculptor, engineer, physicist, astronomer, and inventor who helped usher in a new era of scientific and artistic enlightenment. At the time, Spain, Italy, France, Portugal, the Netherlands, China, and others all vied for global prominence, or perhaps dominance, as the world began to realize the advantages of global trade.

This era spawned the great wealth created by trade, the cultural and intellectual exchanges that inevitably occur when diverse peoples and ideas are brought together, and the creation of a marketplace for power and ideas. With the expansion of the economic pie through trade, those who created and hence earned great wealth soon realized that affluence allowed for the quick satiation of material needs. These icons of international influence soon discovered that patronage of the arts and sciences could create a new avenue for their influence and hence their prominence. The Medici House, a wealthy dynasty of traders and bankers in the Tuscan region of Italy, helped found and fund the creative outburst from the minds of Leonardo da Vinci and others from the fourteenth century onward.

Part of the tradition of the Renaissance man was in a command of the languages of literature at the time. It was expected that young scholars would be fluent in the varied languages of Europe that flowed from Latin. There was an appreciation by Italians of the works of the French and the Spanish, the Dutch, and the emerging English. Ideas among scholars were exchanged through extensive multi-lingual correspondences. These exchanges were remarkably efficient in an era before the widespread use of academic journals. Some scholars shared their results within their close-knit academic circles, while others shared their work in anagrams whose meaning could only be discerned by scholars in the know who were able to decipher their cryptic messages. Two leading scholars of their day, Sir Isaac Newton and Gottfried Leibniz (1646–1716), both transmitted their work in such cryptic messages that it induced centuries of controversy over the true originator of calculus as a consequence of their less than efficient methods of scholarly publication.

In fact, royal patrons at the time in the House of Brunswick supported Leibniz's scientific work and its eventual publication in one of the world's first scholarly journals, the *Acta Eruditorum*. However, a competing journal closely allied to Isaac Newton subsequently accused Leibniz of stealing Newton's work on the mathematics of calculus, even though each scholar had approached calculus from a different direction and each made important contributions consistent with their differing approach.

These early tensions pointed to a number of controversies and inefficiencies. Correspondence between individual scholars was obviously too tedious if knowledge was to expand more rapidly. The learned societies of the day could facilitate the dissemination of ideas locally, but only the printing press could carry ideas easily across borders and learned societies.

The first research journals were simply the transactions of these learned societies. This more efficient dissemination of ideas was actually problematic in itself. In fact, famed sociologist Robert King Merton (1910–2003), the father of the great mind in finance Robert Merton, noted that 92 percent of scientific discoveries were simultaneously claimed by at least two scholars and ended up in dispute in the eighteenth century.[6] Publication at first created controversy because one could finally discover that "discoveries" were not necessarily new or unique. However, as journals became more accepted, simultaneous discoveries became less controversial.

Learned societies and the transactions and journals they produced certainly helped to disseminate scientific discovery. Among Renaissance men, the appreciation of diverse European languages facilitated such scholarly exchange. The more efficient form of communication permitted by printed journals had allowed scientific inquiry to expand at a dramatic exponential rate that inevitably created a bottleneck. Just as Thomas Malthus (1766–1834) noted with the creation of fits of feast and famine when the population increases geometrically while food sources only expand arithmetically, publications soon outstripped the ability for scholars to absorb the rapidly occurring innovations.

By the mid-nineteenth century, there began to be a scholarly retrenchment among national lines, with German and Austro-Hungarian scholarship remaining unknown to English scholars, and French scholarship remaining obscure to the Italians and the Russians. The Gilded Era in the USA and its development of very strong intellectual circles and universities in the nineteenth and twentieth centuries within a melting-pot culture centered around American English further contributed to this balkanization of scholarship, at least until English emerged as the informal language of scholarship in the twentieth century.

Caught squarely in this unfortunate tendency toward the nationalization of scholarship was the work of Louis Bachelier in the early twentieth century, and, for that matter, the great mind Bruno de Finetti (1906–1985) a little later. The work of both of these brilliant scholars remained abstruse both for reasons of language and for the advanced nature of their mathematical and philosophical discoveries in the field of probability. Frank Plumpton Ramsey (1903–1930) also suffered a similar fate in the 1920s not for reasons of language, as he wrote in English, the *lingua franca* of finance and economics by then, but for demonstrating a mathematical sophistication so far ahead of anybody else writing at that time. Like a tree falling in the woods, the ideas flowing from these great minds failed to inspire because their works could not be understood. Failures in communications, both in the medium and in the comprehension of sophisticated subject matter, delayed academic progress.

While the works of all these great minds are now better appreciated, the much-delayed appreciation of their brilliance and discovery delayed the development of finance by generations.

Financial insights in France in the mid-nineteenth century

There have been heroes of financial innovation in many countries over the past two centuries. In previous volumes of this series, we have referred to Sir Isaac Newton's forays as a financier and his eventual losses in the South Sea Company, following which he stated that, despite his brilliance in calculating movements in the cosmos, he "could not calculate the madness of people."[2] We have observed the insights of the Canadian Scotsman John Rae (1796–1872) on the role of interest rates and the innovations of the Austrian School's Eugen von Böhm-Bawerk (1851–1914). These scholars helped form the brilliance coalescing of thought by the American great mind Irving Fisher in the early part of the twentieth century regarding the role of the interest rate in financial decision-making. By the 1920s, it was widely regarded that Irving Fisher's work was the most sophisticated and rigorous financial theory at the time. Lost until recently was knowledge of the sophistication of an obscure French financial theorist in the latter half of the nineteenth century.

As fate would have it, the sophisticated financial innovation Bachelier studied arose as a consequence of the French Revolution. The Revolution forced many French aristocrats to seek exile for fear of their lives. With the resolution of the Revolution, the exiles returned and were offered reparation for their property that had been seized. To fund this, the French government issued a new type of bond that offered interest payments in perpetuity with no return of capital (or return of capital at a date infinite). These perpetuities offered the holder an annual "rente" and created "rentiers," a class of income recipients that earned their income from the bond perpetuities.

The value of these bonds of course depended on the attractiveness of these rentes. It is a simple exercise to calculate such a present value p as a function of the interest payment r they earn each year, compared to the interest payment r* at which they could borrow to buy such a perpetuity, or lend out and earn should they sell such a perpetual bond. Arbitrage should force the price of these bonds to adjust to make either alternative transactions unprofitable. In essence, the present value of an existing perpetual bond then adjusts to align itself to the value of a newly issued bond at the prevailing interest rate.

Consider a newly issued perpetual bond of face value $1 at the prevailing interest rate r*. Then, the present value of the bond, discounted by the prevailing interest rate, is given by:

$$p = \int_0^\infty re^{-r^*t}dt = \frac{r}{r*}$$

If the bond interest rate r is twice that of the prevailing discount rate, the market price of the bond is twice its face value. The bond market at the Paris Bourse quickly grasped both the simplicity of valuation of such perpetual bonds and the inherent richness in the factors that affect their pricing. First, one must determine the expected fair market interest rate r*. Then, one must incorporate any default risk for these perpetuities and adjust the time horizon of the bond accordingly. For instance, if the instrument is expected to default at a date T, followed by a complete default, the calculation becomes:

$$p = \int_0^T re^{-r*t}dt = \frac{r}{r*}(1 - e^{-r*T})$$

This expression includes an additional term if, at the time of default, the holder can expect a liquidation payment of a fraction k of a bond of nominal face value $1:

$$p = \frac{r}{r*}(1 - e^{-r*T}) + ke^{-r*T}$$

Notice that this expression is not a simple linear function of either the prevailing interest rate r* or the expected default date T, even if it is linear in the annual return r and the liquidation proportion k.

French financiers of the nineteenth century quickly grasped the richness of these simple instruments. Prices of perpetuities issued in the past adjusted efficiently as the prevailing interest rate and the French government's fiscal circumstances changed. There was active trading in these perpetuities and a very liquid market grew around them. Those who required greater income could sell them, others could purchase them as a store of value of excess income, and the instruments were often passed from generation to generation. Some without heirs passed them to universities to permanently endow chairs or to generate income for research grants. In fact, Louis Bachelier himself benefited from some of these grants up to the period just after the First World War when the French government defaulted and the franc collapsed, making the perpetual bonds worthless.

Before the collapse of the French perpetuities following the First World War, the Paris Bourse was the primary market for pricing any information that would affect interest rates, market liquidity, and the default risk of government bonds. Those who did not want to buy or sell bonds directly could also buy or sell options on these bonds. One would exercise an option to buy such a bond at a predetermined date if the price of the bond at that date was higher than the strike price, or pre-agreed-upon price, of the bond. Alternately, one would lose the purchase fee for such an option if the strike price exceeded the going value of the bond at the settlement date, just as the purchase of an insurance policy forfeited the regular premiums if the event insured against did not occur.

The pricing of these options that derived their value on the underlying bond price added one additional dimension to the valuation exercise. While the random movements, up or down, of a bond were immaterial for one who purchased such a bond as a long-term investment, those who dealt in the option derivatives had a vested interest in the day-to-day fluctuations of the bond.

The French have a tradition of profound philosophy, and commentators on the Paris Stock Exchange followed this national tradition. One notable financial philosopher and financial analyst was Jules Regnault, who, in 1863, waxed philosophical in a book entitled *Calcul des chances et philosophie de la bourse* about the nature of seemingly random movements in the price of a bond or its derivate option.[8]

Regnault had an early life remarkably similar to that of Bachelier. Born on February 1, 1834, in France's Départment du Nord, he suffered the death of his father just before his twelfth birthday. He was subsequently supported by his brother as he studied advanced mathematics in Brussels, and then moved with his brother to Paris to become a financial broker. He died on December 9, 1894, but not before he amassed a sizable fortune through his investment in bonds as a rentier.

Regnault also produced the earliest financial theory of the dispersion of securities prices over time. He argued that while the mean value of a financial instrument may converge to some expected value, it was seemingly buffeted up or down by myriad external and subtle forces. Robert Brown had observed this same buffeting in nature earlier in the century. Let us call such buffeting a random walk of prices. Regnault postulated that steps in such a random walk in one dimension, up or down, over time should cancel each other out on average, leaving one's expectation of the price of the position unchanged. However, if a step could be made in any direction on a two-dimensional plane, the possible area for which a series of steps is confined would increase linearly over time, like an ever-expanding circle. In a stroke of profound insight and analogy, Regnault then observed that the distance between the end position and the starting position, or the radius of the circle, increased proportional to the square root of the area, and hence the square root of time. He then set about testing his new financial hypothesis, and indeed observed that the price of financial instruments seemed to drift with the square root of the observed time span. French financial commentators following Regnault accepted his square root deviation rule.

Regnault was neither a mathematician nor a physicist. He postulated a financial relationship and he empirically verified the rough accuracy of his rule. His was a rule of thumb that was the hallmark of the art of finance until the rise of the quants in the 1960s. He had, most probably by luck, stumbled upon a result known to physicists at the time in their study of compounding errors. He had derived the correct relationship of drift over time, but perhaps through an incorrect analogy.

We now know that the phenomenon that Regnault discovered (as did Bachelier and Fischer Black later on) was a simple diffusion process that physicists had developed to model the migration of heat in a material.

Random walks in time

Let us look at some mathematics of a random walk as Regnault postulated in his rough analogy. Assume that a random walker can take one step either left or right, depending on the flip of a fair coin. Then, on average, we should expect the position to be unchanged over time. In finance, we would expect accordingly that a security buffeted randomly should approximately reside at its true fundamental value. This notion underpins the efficient market hypothesis.

Consider the random walk further. If, for simplicity, each step is of unit length, but could be left or right depending on the flip of the coin, we can calculate the expected distance away from our fundamental starting point over time in the way that physicists typically measure distance rather than position. To ensure that all distances remain positive, we square all the possible endpoints to the left and to the right, multiplied by their respective (and symmetric) probabilities, and we take the square root of the sum. This is called the root-mean-square distance, or RMS for short.

A simple example demonstrates our scenario. If we flip the coin once, we will end up at +1 or −1 with equal probability 1/2. Then, our average distance away from the starting point is:

$$x_{rms} = \sqrt{2 * \left(\frac{1}{2}\right) * 1^2} = \sqrt{1} = 1$$

After three flips, we could end up at +3 or −3 with a probability of 1/8 each. We could end up at +1 or −1 with equal odds of 3 out of 8 in either direction and we cannot end up at the +2 or −2 position. We end up on average a distance from the starting point:

$$x_{rms} = \sqrt{2 * \left(\frac{1}{8}\right) + 2 * \left(\frac{3}{8}\right) * 1^2} = \sqrt{3}$$

If we flip a coin five times and thus take five such steps, it is possible that we could end up five steps to the left or five steps to the right, each with a probability of $1/2^5$ or $1/32$. There is no possibility that we would end up either four steps or two steps to the left or right in a five-step random walk. We will find ourselves three steps to the left of right in 10 out of 32 trials, and we will find ourselves one step to the left or right 20 times out of 32. Then, our average RMS distance is:

$$x_{rms} = \sqrt{2 * \left(\frac{1}{32}\right) * 5^2 + 2 * \left(\frac{5}{32}\right) * 3^2 + 2 * \left(\frac{10}{32}\right) * 1^2} = \sqrt{5}$$

This simple analogy demonstrates that Regnault was correct. If there is a step of b length every time period, we find ourselves a distance $b\sqrt{t}$ after t iterations. Financial securities buffeted by random and equal-sized shocks tend to drift over time by an amount proportional to the square root of the elapsed time.

This pattern can be generalized by noting that, after T flips, we could end up a certain number of steps forward or backward to end up at a position n such that:

$$n_{forward} + n_{backward} = T$$

$$n_{forward} - n_{backward} = n$$

Then:

$$n_{forward} = (T + n)/2,$$

$$n_{backward} = (T - n)/2$$

We can then calculate the total number of ways we could find ourselves at a position n, out of 2^T possibilities, to yield the probability P(n) of ending at a position n:

$$P(n) = \frac{T!}{2^m n_{forward}! \, n_{backward}!}$$

$$= \frac{T!}{2^n \left(\dfrac{T+n}{2}\right)! \left(\dfrac{T-n}{2}\right)!}$$

James Stirling (1692–1770), a contemporary of Sir Isaac Newton, developed such an approximation that is helpful in calculating the above expression. The Stirling approximation applied in this case shows that:

$$Ln(P(n)) \approx P(n)ln(P(n)) - P(n) + \frac{\ln(2\pi n)}{2}:$$

$$\approx -n^2/2T + \frac{\ln(2\pi n)}{2}$$

Then, the probability P(n) that the process finds itself n steps away from the mean yields the familiar expression we now know as the Gaussian normal distribution, which is given by:

$$P(n) = \frac{1}{\sqrt{2\pi T}} e^{-n^2/2T}$$

We see that the drift of random walks over time is dictated by the law of large numbers and the central limit theorem, which states that the mean sum of a large number of independent random variables of finite mean and a given variance can be approximated by a normal distribution. Regnault and Bachelier both postulated that financial securities buffeted by random forces can be described by the same mathematics and physics of many physical processes. These methods were also used in physics to describe the total effect of a large number of gas molecules that defy description on a molecule-by-molecule basis.

By the early twentieth century, innovations by mathematicians and physicists in probability theory were beginning to spread into finance. This mathematical physics of probability was rapidly unfolding, following the insights of the great mind Daniel Bernoulli (1700–1782), who, in 1738, first formulated the mathematics of probability.

Game theory and the martingale

As mathematical physics increasingly contemplated and incorporated probability theory, the French scholars of the eighteenth and nineteenth centuries became fascinated by gambling and the analysis of games of chance. One such game, a Martingale, was a betting strategy in eighteenth-century France. One strategy in a game of repeated coin flipping has the player doubling his bet after every loss, a strategy gamblers now call double or nothing. This strategy allows the gambler to recoup the loss of the previous round and earn him an equal profit. If the gambler is all in at every turn in this double-or-nothing strategy, he could always leave the game with a sizable profit, which means the martingale strategy is eventually a sure thing. Of course, a string of bad luck continues to double the stakes, at which time the winner on the other side of the gambler's losses could also decide at any time to quit the game and book his gains. Thus, he would deprive the gambler of such a sure thing.[9]

While the mathematics of martingales was not more fully explored until the latter half of the twentieth century, by the end of the nineteenth century, French mathematical physicists and financial philosophers had the tools and many of the insights into probability that we still use today. By 1859, James Clerk Maxwell (1831–1879) had developed the first statistical laws of gases at about the same time that Regnault was developing his rule of thumb for the random walk of financial securities on the Paris Stock Exchange over time. Missing was a holistic synthesis that could bring together these insights into a coherent theory of securities pricing. Louis Bachelier's model provided that insight.

4
The Theory

Louis Bachelier had an interest in the theories of games of chance that had intrigued French scholars before him and, most significantly, following him for a long time. Bachelier's formal training in mathematical physics at the Sorbonne University under Jules Henri Poincaré also exposed him to the diffusion theory of heat and gases. However, before Bachelier, no scholar had made the profound connection between mathematical physics and the decision-making sciences, even if many have done so since.

Bachelier's big idea

We have discussed the derivative put and call options written on the government perpetual bonds called rentes and bought and sold on the Paris Stock Exchange since the 1850s. Bachelier wanted to model the trajectory of the price of these options randomly bumped up and down in absolute terms. He hoped to create a science in the analysis of prices that, up to that point, was considered an art.

Conventional wisdom might deem that financial instruments buffeted by random and uncorrelated shocks should maintain a balance at about their mean fundamental value. After all, a shock in one direction should be cancelled out by an equal and opposite shock over time, in the absence of correlation or something that might cause the fundamental value to drift over time.

However, such a "random walk" is not neutral in movement. In fact, if a shock pushes an instrument one step upward, there is then a 50/50 chance that a second shock will move it still higher or cause it to revert to the mean. A financial instrument buffeted by forces may find itself near its fundamental value on average, but may also drift away from this value with a probability according to a Gaussian distribution. This was Bachelier's first insight.

Actually, Bachelier may have missed the significance of his walk of compounding errors in additional application to physics. Poincaré likely saw the beauty and utility of Bachelier's idea in explaining Brownian motion in physical processes. Bachelier had the physics right, but was limited in his application solely to financial markets.

There are reasons why Bachelier may have failed to see the broader implications and applications of his discovery. As a relatively young and inexperienced scholar, his academic mind may well have been immature in 1900. He was in a field of mathematical physics in which scholars typically do their best work in their late twenties. Bachelier had been diverted by wars and deaths in his family during his most formative mathematical years. Moreover, he had just turned 30 when he defended his thesis. By that age, more seasoned minds have either become narrowed by doctrine and academic dogma or widened by a great curiosity in the developments of parallel discovery. Great minds often have or develop such a curiosity and ability to make connections, create extensions, and develop academic innovations. Bachelier's initial foray was brilliant, but he was robbed of a platform to make it the first result in a profound career in probability theory.

Others certainly saw the beauty and applicability of a model of Brownian motion. They did so without knowledge of Bachelier's insights, for reasons of language and of his application to finance rather than physics. Yet, Bachelier was the first to model interactions as Brownian motion, to describe the resulting position distribution function over time for what we now call a Wiener stochastic process, and to link the process to the standard second-order partial differential equation that was, by then, a well-known description of diffusion processes. Five years later, Albert Einstein (1879–1955) used the same reasoning in physics and went a step further by calibrating the model and the resulting diffusion rate to determine the size of atoms. One of Bachelier's Sorbonne colleagues, the chemical physicist Jean Baptiste Perrin (1870–1942), subsequently performed the experiments that verified Einstein's results.

There is another parallel between the work of Bachelier in 1900 and Einstein in 1905. Both scholars were iconoclasts, Einstein perhaps with some disregard or disinterest for those who came before him or those who taught him, and Bachelier for his circumstances that distracted him equally.

The respective literatures of finance and physics both regard these works for their outcomes. Einstein applied the familiar Fourier diffusion process to the movement of his molecules and was able to both estimate the mass of particles unseen and prove that matter is made up of discrete units, or atoms, as the only explanation for the discrete Brownian motion of molecules. And, since the work of the great minds in finance Paul Samuelson, Fischer Black, Myron Scholes, and Robert Merton, we have rediscovered the formula that Bachelier developed to price an option. Their more recent Nobel Prize-winning work differed from his in that Bachelier modeled the absolute movement of options prices as a consequence of the density óf random shocks, while the modern literature instead modeled relative price changes, or absolute changes in the logarithm of prices. Nonetheless, Bachelier is now properly recognized as the originator of the first sophisticated formula of derivatives pricing, in a form that is remarkably similar to the Black-Scholes option pricing formula we use today. Indeed, were Bachelier still alive, there is no doubt he too would have jointly received the Nobel Prize earned by Black and Scholes in 1997 for their famous formula.

Both these results – of atomic structure by Einstein and of options pricing by Bachelier – are fortunate byproducts of the fundamentally important methods of each scholar. We leave physicists to weigh the importance of Einstein's conclusions, and the previous volume of this series documents the utility of Bachelier's options pricing formula. The more important result, though, is the application of the random walk methodology in finance and physics respectively.

However, while Einstein's work remains well known and widely cited, Bachelier's major development is now attributed to another. His Wiener process is credited to the American statistical theorist Norbert Wiener (1894–1964). While the statistician William Feller, in his 1951 paper "The Asymptotic Distribution of the Range of Sums of Independent Random Variables,"[10] properly credited Bachelier's great insight and the now-familiar process as the Bachelier-Wiener stochastic process, the nomenclature has unfortunately not become standard.

Bachelier's other principles that have since diffused throughout finance theory and theoretical physics, and are attributed to others, are the theory of Brownian motion and random walks, and, especially for finance, the parallel principle that a price reflects all information currently known and incorporated. This information integration characterizes equilibrium, while arbitrage is the force that causes the market to converge toward equilibrium.

While Einstein was an incredible physics entrepreneur, able to take a few simple and revolutionary postulates, like the quantum nature of light, the Brownian motion of particles, and the absolute speed of light for all relative motion, and spin from them dozens of revolutionary implications that defied conventional wisdom, Bachelier was almost clumsy and naïve in his inability to "spin" his innovations to great success. Others had spotted his brilliance, though. His work pre-dated Wiener, Andrey Kolmogorov (1903–1987) in 1931, Kiyoshi Itô (1915–2008), a contemporary of John von Neumann, and Black, Scholes, and Merton in 1973. The slights Bachelier suffered for a life-time continued even after his death. In Itô's *New York Times* obituary, it was noted that his development of stochastic calculus built upon the foundations of Einstein and Wiener, but failed to mention Bachelier, whose discovery predated the insights of both these pioneers.[11]

A random walk in Bachelier's thesis

Bachelier's then-underappreciated innovation is now commonly under-stood and applied in finance theory. Let us first describe his innovation as translated from his own words. His thesis opened with the following passage:

> The factors that determine activity on the Exchange are innumerable, with events, current or expected, often bearing no apparent relation to price variation. Beside the somewhat natural causes for variation come artificial causes: The Exchange reacts to itself, and the current trading is a function, not only of prior trading, but also of its relationship to the rest of the market. The determination of this activity depends on an infinite number of factors: It is thus impossible to hope for math-ematical forecasting. Contradictory opinions about these variations are so evenly divided that at the same instant buyers expect a rise and sellers expect a fall.
>
> The calculus of probability can doubtless never be applied to market activity, and the dynamics of the Exchange will never be an exact science. But it is possible to study mathematically the state of the market at a given instant – that is to say, to establish the laws of probability for price variation that the market at that instant dictates. If the market, in effect, does not predict in fluctuations, it does assess them as being more or less likely, and this likelihood can be evaluated mathematically.[12]

This now broadly accepted statement was profound in its day. Observers of markets then, likely including Bachelier's thesis supervisor, saw stock markets as little more than high-priced gambling. Yet, Bachelier was asserting that prices should be modeled as without memory, reflected all available information, and buffeted by random forces of various strength, which he would go on and describe as characterized by a Gaussian distribution. If one could accept this characterization of the market, then Bachelier described the stochastic process and used the resulting random walk of prices to determine the probability a financial instrument will exceed a defined bound.

He was also saying something equally profound. While some may view the function of financial markets as a game of chance at worse, or an art of exchanging risk at best, few would argue that its workings functioned with the beauty and the regularity of a science. Nonetheless, Bachelier argued that even a market buffeted by unknown and unknowable forces can be described with scientific tools. In his mind, the emerging laws of probability govern its evolution of prices. Having established the predictions from the tools of probability he developed, Bachelier then reasoned how the prices of options traded on the French Stock Exchange roughly followed his predictions.

Indeed, while his was the first analysis in finance to model returns and risk scientifically, Bachelier made no effort to understand the forces that give rise to the random shocks that buffet stock and options prices. Such an analysis would just be too difficult and wrought with uncertainty. Instead, he modeled the evolution of a price as a fair game. In other words, just like a coin toss, the game is not rigged and no player has any advantage over another. All information is known, and any past history will not impinge upon the future price trajectory beyond its starting point. He also reasoned that perhaps the volatility of the stock is a reflection of the strength of myriad past random shocks and can hence calibrate our expectation of the strength of future shocks.

To better understand the meaning of a fair game of the type Bachelier modeled, contrast the analogy with chess and the card game poker. A game of chess can be resumed at any time by any player without disadvantage. All observers of a snapshot of the chess board have all the available information. The past history of moves and captures is immaterial. The only relevant issue is the position of the chess men at any moment. However, in poker, even if one could observe all hands at a time t or have all inside information belonging to each player at a given stage of the game, past history remains important. The composition of the pile of cards that have been discarded and swapped are only partially known, and only to individual players. And even if one were to know the cards they discarded, and hence had some idea of the cards remaining in the deck or in the hands of others, the information is imperfect. In fact, poker is an imperfect game of insider information, while chess or coin tossing are games that are informationally perfect, as Bachelier and the proponents of efficient markets have assumed of financial markets ever since.

The efficient market hypothesis

This notion of history independence is now integrated into what we call the "efficient market hypothesis." All available information at time t is incorporated into the security price at that time. However, it is not possible to determine such shocks in advance, or *ex ante*. All market participants have equal knowledge of past events, and the current prices each presumably exhibit an identical lack of foresight of future events, hence the observed price is assumed to be correct, if only perhaps as a matter of financial philosophy or faith.

Through the influence of random shocks, prices are jostled and the resulting history independent random path we now call a random walk. However, Bachelier did not use that term himself. Actually, it did not arrive for another five years, when a letter from Karl Pearson to the journal *Nature* asked its readers to help him with what he called "The Problem of the Random Walk." He asked if one could predict the probability that a person would be within a distance r of a starting point as a function of time in a process in which he takes a step of equal length but in any direction once in each unit of time.[13] Interestingly, John William Strut, 3rd Baron Rayleigh (1842–1919), the noted physicist and 1904 Nobel Physics Prize winner, responded to Pearson's intellectual query with the solution of compounding errors developed by Gauss a century earlier. He forever immortalized the random walk when he characterized a solution and concluded "a drunk on a random walk can be expected to be found at his starting point." This random walk has since been labeled on occasion as a drunkard's walk.

Actually, Bachelier's specification of the random walk differed from the Pearson specification in one important way. Bachelier allowed the effect on the price of the information that arrives at a constant average rate to differ in strength. The probabilistic distribution of the resulting drift is described by a normal distribution and will hence yield a Gaussian random walk.

With the result that a random walk, driven by many jolts unobservable in advance, generates a Gaussian distribution of positions, Bachelier was able to bring to bear the by-then well-established tools of Gaussian statistics. Most significantly, he argued that the Gaussian drift of a price could be likened to the diffusion of heat, as derived by Joseph Fourier (1768–1830), which generates the same statistical properties. He could have concluded, before Einstein, that heat transfer is driven by mysterious random collisions from one molecule to another in any direction over time. This was the idea that Einstein employed in his argument that Brownian motion arises from the interaction of particles too small to observe directly. Bachelier's supervisor, Poincaré, likely saw this greater applicability when he lamented that Bachelier could have teased from his analysis much more important and fundamental results had he applied the tools he had developed to a more conventional topic.

Theoretical economists typically carry out the econometrics necessary to verify, or at least not rule out, their theories. Physics operates in a similar manner. Einstein produced his hypothesis and, as is typical for physics theorists, left it to an experimentalist to prove. Bachelier's Sorbonne colleague Jean Baptiste Perrin took up this challenge on Einstein's behalf. Theoretical physicists are rarely also experimental physicists. However, in finance there is a somewhat greater expectation for theory to be accompanied by testable hypotheses that are also put to the test by the theory's originator. Bachelier, as the world's first modern financial theorist, helped to establish this tradition. He calibrated his model and determined the probability that an options call buyer had a 40 percent chance of exercising the option and earning a profit. The model's apparent predictive success went far beyond any reasonable expectation. He then analyzed data from the Paris Bourse and observed that profits on the Paris Stock Exchange were actually earned on average at a rate of 39 percent, which is remarkably close to Bachelier's predicted probability of 40 percent[14]

Subtleties in probabilities

Perhaps Bachelier's most subtle innovation is one of great significance in finance, but one that is not pondered enough. In games of chance, a probability is a rather obvious concept. There is a 50/50 chance that a tossed coin will land heads. There is a 1/52 probability that a freshly drawn card from a full deck will be the queen of hearts. In fact, early probability theory, as developed by the Bernoullis and others, was based on these scientifically determinable likelihoods that could be measured or calculated with all necessary precision.

However, the probabilities that Bachelier surmised for the market described random variables were unknowable and impossible to predict. These were not risks that occur by chance, which can be measured from past experience; rather, they are the uncertain expectations of the unknown, at best. Later, Frank Knight (1885–1972) discerned between objective and knowable risks and the more subjective uncertainties of the unknown.

Certainly, the probabilities an analyst applies to a future financial event include some small degree of knowable chance. For instance, futures market traders closely watch the probability of rain to predict the quality and quantity of crops. These are the objective probabilities that can be described within scientific functions.

More typically, though, the collective group of traders on a financial instrument determines a subjective expectation of a future price shock just like gamblers might wager on either side of a football game and collectively determine in advance a point spread for which there is then an even probability that either betting side will "beat the spread." These are the subjective or personal probabilities subsequently defined by Bruno de Finetti in the 1930s and Leonard Jimmie Savage in the 1950s.

In this case, the price of a call option is bid up if the collective belief is that the price of the underlying stock will rise. Every speculator makes a personal assessment of the various probabilities that the price is too high or too low, and their subsequent, and presumably rapid, bidding quickly aligns the price to a collective sense of the market's assessment. Bachelier noted that: "It seems that the market, the aggregate of speculators, at a given instant can believe in neither a market rise nor a market fall, since for each quoted price there are as many buyers as sellers." From this neutral expectation, the instrument remains a fair game, even if it followed a rising or falling trend to arrive at the true price. When the security is in equilibrium, subsequent second-guessing is irrelevant, until expectations change on the creation of new information. We now call this the "reflection principle" because all available information is reflected in the price. The past is irrelevant, the present is transparent, and only the future need be discovered.

Bachelier's options also have another quality. He observed that options "price" volatility. A more volatile stock will increase both the price to purchase a call, or a right to buy the stock at a given price, and the price of a put, or the right to sell at a given price at a future certain date. Options prices are hence market-determined prices on expected volatility and should then be correlated to the measure of volatility in the respective Gaussian distribution, the second moment, or variance, or its square root, the standard deviation.

By the 1930s, Jacob Marschak (1898–1977) and others firmly established measures of the first moment, or the price of an instrument, and the second moment, its variability, as the relevant parameters that finance has adopted ever since. However, these measures began first with Bachelier. In the case of options, increased volatility raises put and call prices, while an upward price trend in the underlying stock, perhaps due to a change in its fundamental value, moves these prices for puts and calls in opposite directions.

5
Discussion and Applications: Einstein and Bachelier

Louis Bachelier's narrow application of a powerful mathematical insight to the then-obscure financial markets explained his inability to gain recognition within the mathematical physics community. Not all contemporaries faced this same limitation, though.

Bachelier shared with Albert Einstein a number of important qualities. Both struggled at times as students in mathematical physics, perhaps for similar reasons. Both had distractions in life that made it difficult for them to tolerate the tedious re-proving of the results of others before them. This learning method worked well to establish the style and significance of discoveries by those who preceded them. However, both Einstein and Bachelier seemed intent on driving ahead while looking forward, not looking through a rear-view mirror.

Their ignorance and irreverence was actually a virtue rather than a curse. Each scholar was sufficiently well versed to understand the problems and recognize gaps in theory, but both were also sufficiently open-minded to pursue avenues that others before them had deemed unfruitful or risky. Einstein and Bachelier were consummate academic risk-takers and hence were destined to be regarded as either brilliant or academic quacks. They were academic revolutionaries among many who were evolutionaries at best.

In fact, Bachelier's result in 1900 was almost identical to an insight developed by Einstein in a different context just five years later. 1905 was the year scientific historians call the "annus mirabilis." In a tremendous flourish, in just three months, Einstein published four papers that each should have earned him a Nobel Prize in Physics. One, his first major paper, in March 1905 was on the photoelectric effect. It was also his paper on the smallest of all scales in physics. His paper, in which he described quantum effects, showed how light could be represented by photons that can be considered discrete units of energy.

In that same year, Einstein later published a pair of papers that represented two parts of the same problem. In his April paper, he derived the equations of Brownian motion in a way that was strikingly similar to Bachelier's argument of the cumulative effects of random shocks on financial instruments. However, rather than the creation of a model of options prices, Einstein described how the momentum of atoms impinging on other particles can help predict the mass of atoms. In turn, he provided support for the very existence and mass of atoms.

Einstein followed this with his paper on the special theory of relativity that demonstrated how mass and length must rise or contract as speeds approach the speed of light, at least if we want to preserve an absolute measure for the speed of light regardless of the speed of the measurer. He closed off his miracle year by combining his results in the big and the small, which allowed him to conclude that energy and mass are made equivalent through the equation $E = mc^2$.

Let us look more deeply into the argument of Einstein on Brownian motion so that we can see the similarities between his groundbreaking work and the work of Bachelier before him.

Einstein's second paper of 1905 provided a theory for the movement of particles suspended in a liquid, just as Robert Brown and Jan Ingenhousz had described more than a century earlier. Einstein first asked how far a particle would move in a given amount of time if bombarded by random collisions from any direction. He postulated a density of such particles at a point x and a time t, and used a diffusion equation to model how the density will diffuse over time and distance.

Einstein then sought to calculate how far a particle suspended in a fluid could travel in a given period of time. Given the large number of collisions impinging on a particle, a deterministic calculation is impossible using classical mechanics. Instead, he used statistics to measure the collective effect of these bombardments. He demonstrated that if $\rho(x,t)$ is the density of Brownian particles at point x at time t, then ρ satisfies the diffusion equation.

If the density function $\rho(x,t)$ evolves according to the traditional diffusion equation:

$$\frac{\delta \rho}{\delta t} = D \frac{\delta^2 \rho}{\delta x^2}$$

Then it was widely understood at the time that the solution must be given by:

$$\rho(x,t) = \frac{1}{(4\pi Dt)^{\frac{1}{2}}} e^{-x^2/4Dt}$$

Einstein could then integrate this density function and combine it with the result known to Bachelier that the first integration (the first moment) must impose on the solution that particles must remain stationary over time on average. This was the symmetry result from Bachelier that so impressed Jules Henri Poincaré, and was based on the premise that Bachelier's financial instrument was as likely to move up in price as it was to fall.

The second moment, a measure of the variance of the particle's position, or its root mean square, Einstein discovered to be given by:

$$\overline{x}^2 = 2Dt.$$

We can take the square root of this expression to derive what Bachelier had also discovered five years earlier and that Regnault postulated before both of them. Displacement of Brownian motion is proportional to the square root of time.

By all regards, Einstein never saw Bachelier's groundbreaking results, even if his derivation and conclusions were identical. In fact, some note that Einstein's derivation was clumsier and less detailed than that offered by Bachelier. Einstein was brilliant in his creativity, but many believe he was ill-prepared for the mathematics that came easier to Bachelier and to Einstein's first wife, Mileva Marić (1875–1948).

In 1921, Einstein won a Nobel Prize for his work in 1905. However, it was not for his development of the random walk and Brownian motion in physics; rather, it was for his paper on the photoelectric effect in that same year. His other groundbreaking work in that miracle year might have earned him a second and third Nobel Prize in Physics as well. However, the Academy does not offer multiple awards in the same field to the same recipients.

Applications of Bachelier's discoveries

The third volume of this series documented the significance of the mean-variance approach to finance theory, from Jacob Marschak's establishment of the conditions that justify such a mean-variance two-parameter description to the use of Gaussian distributions in the CAPM, the option pricing model, and their extensions. We commented on the limitations and constraints of the two-parameter characterization and discussed the subsequent relaxation of its assumptions by the extension to other families of probability distributions.

Bachelier, the mathematician, physicist, and statistician, did not understand or follow over his career the significance of his innovation in the yet-to-be-developed discipline of finance. Beyond his comparisons of the model's predictions with some data from the Paris Stock Exchange, there was little activity until the 1920s or 1930s in testing the predictions of his model. Meanwhile, he moved on to other research topics.

When scholars and financial analysts began to turn their attention to Bachelier's work, it was not initially in the predictability of his option pricing formula. Rather, many scholars in the late 1950s and early 1960s first began to explore whether markets were truly efficient.

The lull in research activity in this area for more than six decades was not surprising. There was little or no theoretical work on the pricing of securities of any kind until a financial analyst Harvard-trained as a chemist returned to Harvard and its MBA program so that he could hone his intuition on fundamental analysis. John Burr Williams' work on the discounted present value of future earnings finally allowed analysts to determine the true long-run price of a security based on its discounted future flow of profits. However, even this relatively primitive measure of asset value was not extensively applied. It was not until the CAPM of William Sharpe, the computing algorithms of Harry Markowitz and others, and the computing power of the International Business Machines Corporation (IBM) in the 1960s that analysts could regularly scour the data for stocks that appeared to be mispriced. With the CAPM tool in hand, researchers such as Paul Samuelson sought out pricing tools for more complicated securities like options and soon discovered that the solution had been around for more than 60 years. It took a significant reinvention of the wheel before anybody realized that the solution they derived was almost identical to the discovery of an obscure French mathematical physicist at the turn of the century.

Bachelier's other significant hypothesis was that securities can be modeled as if they followed a memoryless random walk. This became the primary testable prediction of the efficient market hypothesis. His subtle assumption was that the price of a security at any time should be considered the starting point to a fair game. All known information is incorporated into that price and perhaps its observed variability. If such an assumption is valid, any one properly priced security should perform over time no better and no worse than the overall market. Alternately, there is no reason for one to go to great lengths to manage a portfolio of stock, presumably at some cost, when any stock, or a portfolio of stock, is merely fair game from which the investor cannot profit.

Such an information-efficient market should not give rise to a speculative bubble unless it suffers from the widespread simultaneous upward bias of personal probability assessments. As we shall see from the work of Robert Shiller later in this volume, such irrational exuberance occurs at times and, during those times, there is little interest in or appetite for discussions that could pop the bubble. Once the bubble bursts, though, there is often a period of great introspection. This period began with the Wall Street Crash in 1929 and the ensuing global depression over the next decade.

A prediction that markets can be characterized as exhibiting irrational exuberance on occasion is certainly a testable hypothesis. However, while there was a great supply of data to be analyzed as economic activity ratcheted up following the First World War, there was little demand for such analyses. The post-war economy was growing rapidly, and stock markets and returns were growing even quicker. If there was any academic interest in the seemingly unending dramatic growth in returns in the speculative bubble of the Roaring Twenties, it would be in pondering just how much quicker the market could accelerate rather than just how rigged the game could be.

During the 1930s, researchers increasingly turned their attention to tests of market dysfunction and discovered what Bachelier had postulated. Markets appear to be efficient, at least in the sense that stock prices appear just as the model of a memoryless fair game assumed.

These delays were understandable. Following Bachelier's work, few statisticians in that newly developed discipline had the tools to analyze markets, and even fewer economists, just coming to grips with the new mathematical methods of the 1930s, had the econometric tools to analyze markets. Finally, any analysis that was being done was applied to markets that people perceived mattered most. Bond and commodity markets seemed to deserve greater attention than the activities in the dens for gamblers at the major stock exchanges. The tools necessary to treat bonds were well understood and commodity market prices were dictated by the supply and demand in other less speculative intermediate goods markets. However, stock and derivatives markets were considered more speculative and hence less amenable to scientific analysis, at least until Bachelier produced his results.

Once the appropriate econometric tests began in the 1930s, scholars and analysts could test two implications of the random walk model. First, tests could be conducted to see if the walk was memoryless and if price movements were indeed random, and not serially correlated with other recent movements.

Beyond such tests for independence, researchers could also explore whether the variability of the price movements in practice obeyed those specified by the Gaussian distribution. Many of these early confirming analyses were conducted by Alfred Cowles III.

The Cowles Commission

Alfred Cowles III (1891–1984) was an affluent and eclectic financial analyst from Colorado who took upon himself the goal of increasing the rigor in financial analytics.

A graduate of Yale University in 1913 and a member of its infamous but secretive Skull and Bones society, he was a grandson of the founder of the *Chicago Tribune* newspaper empire, Alfred Cowles Sr. He was also a product of the American manufacturing revolution of the first part of the twentieth century. By the Roaring Twenties, manufacturing expansion had exhausted the easy growth from scale economies, monopolization and abundant industrial expansion opportunities by Gilded Age entrepreneurs, and surmised that future expansion would require more scientific methods of production. This new scientific revolution provided the world with electrification, mass production, aviation, and other innovations. It also established a new approach to business that considered management a science rather than an art.

Cowles was frustrated with the relatively slow adoption of more scientific methods in economics and finance. He was also frustrated by the profession's inability to predict the Great Crash of 1929. To rectify these shortcomings, he helped found and fund the Econometrics Society, which publishes the journal *Econometrica*, and the Cowles Commission.

The Cowles Commission was a grand experiment to see if a group could catalyze an entire discipline. For more than two decades, from its founding in Colorado Springs, Colorado, in 1932, through its move to Chicago in 1939 to its move to Yale in 1955, the Cowles Commission for Economic Research became the world's premier institute for the integration of mathematics, the scientific method, and economics and finance. The creation of extensive stock market databases and the development of improved econometric techniques were both hallmarks of the Commission.

The Cowles Commission colleagues pioneered new econometric techniques and sophisticated general equilibrium modeling as represented by the work of the Cowles scholars and great minds Kenneth Arrow and Gerard Debreu, both of whom were later honored with Nobel Prizes, as were other Cowles scholars such as Trygve Haavelmo, Lawrence Klein, Harry Markowitz, Franco Modigliani, Herbert Simon, James Tobin, and the early Cowles Commission director Tjalling Koopmans.

Cowles himself produced significant original work on tests of the random walk and early exploration of the efficient market hypothesis. While Cowles' results were mixed, he demonstrated that shocks appeared to be slightly correlated over short time periods. He also observed that these correlations seem to largely disappear over longer time periods. In a retrospective paper in 1960 that summarized his work over the 1930s and 1940s, Cowles concluded that there were slight autocorrelations in the residual errors. However, in the conclusion of his paper, he concluded that some autocorrelation did not matter, using an argument that, by then, had already become a hallmark of the Chicago School of economic and financial thought. He adopted the reasoning of former Cowles Commission director Tjalling Koopmans and noted:

A positive first-order serial correlation in the first differences has been disclosed for every stock price series analysed in which the intervals between successive observations are less than four years. When allowance is made for brokerage costs, however, there is nothing in this situation to indicate that the stock exchange is not functioning as a free competitive market in which theoretically any such tendency toward correlation would be eliminated. Professor Tjalling C. Koopmans has suggested that, if the persistence in stock price movements were sufficient to provide capital gains appreciably in excess of brokerage costs, professional traders would presumably be aware of this situation and through their market operations would inadvertently wipe out the persistence in price movements from which they were attempting to profit. Whether or not this has actually occurred, the fact remains that, while our various analyses have disclosed a tendency towards persistence in stock price movements, in no case is this sufficient to provide more than negligible profits after payment of brokerage costs.[15]

Cowles concluded that small degrees of serial correlation are insufficient to be arbitraged away, given the transaction costs of arbitrage exchanges that might capitalize on these imperfections. Since his work, a number of scholars have verified his conclusions. We shall turn later on to more recent challenges to these conclusions that were broadly accepted through the 1960s.

However, there was a growing recognition that the resulting distribution of shocks allow for larger changes than the Gaussian distribution predicts. These observations take on two dimensions. The first description of a more appropriate distribution came from the American astrophysicist Matthew Fontaine Maury Osborne (1916–2003).

Osborne's extension

To see Osborne's insight that has since been broadly adopted among finance theoreticians, let us look at the version of Bachelier's random walk that the American MIT Mathematics Professor Norbert Wiener formulated in the early 1920s. He specified that:

- a random real valued continuous function W(t) as a function of time on the probability space [0;1) such that
- W(0) = 0,
- for each t > 0, W(t) is Gaussian with mean zero and variance t, and
- if the intervals $[t_1; t_2]$ and $[u_1; u_2]$ do not overlap, then the random variables $W(t_2) - W(t_1)$ and $W(u_2) - W(u_1)$ are independent.

This specification is now known as a Wiener process, despite Bachelier's earlier specification and William Feller's insistence that it should be known as the Bachelier-Wiener process. If the time interval dt is a small positive number, then the increment W(t + dt) – W(t) is Gaussian with mean zero and variance dt. This gives rise to the result that its mean is of an order of magnitude $\sqrt{dt}$, which yields the familiar interpretation that dispersion is at a rate proportional to the square root of time.

Diffusion processes

We can generalize this simple process to allow for drift, the mean value to change, and the variation to depend on the state S(t) and time. This generalized version is called a diffusion process because the probabilities for the path's position diffuse over time:

$$dS(t) = \mu(S(t),t)dt + \sigma(S(t),t)dW(t)$$

This more generalized form still retains the independence property that is labeled the Markov property after its formulator, the brilliant Russian mathematician Andrey Markov (1856–1922). The evolution of the position S(t) depends only on its current position and time, not on any history that brought S to its current position. Other scholars, most notably Kiyoshi Itô, have included the past path in their treatments, now known as Itô processes.

By the 1950s, economics and finance had discovered Wiener processes, but were yet to discover Bachelier's work. However, the great mind Leonard Jimmie Savage had been researching a new approach to probability theory based not on the known and objective probabilities of John von Neumann (1903–1957) and Oskar Morgenstern (1902–1977) and their expected utility hypothesis, but on the subjective probabilities each of us calculate to govern our personal actions. In his research on an entirely new approach to statistics based on personal probabilities, he had come across Bachelier's discussion of "true prices." He began to circulate a number of postcards to contemporaries asking if any of them knew about his work. None had, but a few people found his postcard sufficiently intriguing to begin to explore his original thesis. The physicist Osborne was the first to extend Bachelier's model to provide a better fit of financial data.

Osborne proposed that the Wiener-Bachelier process would fit financial data better if it were converted to a log-normal function. The reasoning was that prices are normalized. There cannot be negative prices. In addition, investors typically relate to the percent change of prices (the price is discounted 20 percent, for instance) rather than absolute price changes. This allows us to compare price movements between any item or instrument, and maintains the neutrality of our results for stocks that undergo splits. For instance, if a share in a particular stock valued at $100 rises or falls by $5 and it splits into ten shares, we expect the changes to be $0.50. The five percent price movements are maintained.

To do so, Osborne converted the Wiener process as follows:

$$d \ln(S(t)) = \mu_0 \, dt + \sigma_0 \, dW(t),$$

or:

$$\frac{dS(t)}{S(t)} = \mu_0 dt + \sigma_0 dW(t),$$

and:

$$dS(t) = \mu_0 S(t)dt + \sigma_0 S(t)dW(t).$$

This log-Gaussian formulation actually performed better than Bachelier's formulation. Since then, many scholars have proposed modifications to allow for more realistic distributions that predict occasional large movements, often called fat-tailed distributions. However, these alternative specifications are often problematic to apply and do not retain the simplicity of the log-Gaussian approach. Theorists and practitioners alike prefer the overly simplistic but tractable approach to others that may be more accurate but difficult to apply.

This latter log-Gaussian process requires only a minor modification of Bachelier's option pricing formula based on the heat diffusion solution. It was the log-Gaussian respecification that Fischer Black and Myron Scholes used in their now-standard Black-Scholes option pricing formula.

One last technical point that was not fully appreciated by Bachelier was subsequently resolved by a later nemesis-turned-ally, Paul Lévy (1886–1971). From a mathematical perspective, the expectations of both the mean and variance of the diffusion position must exist. In other words, we now say that the random variable must be square-integrable if the central limit theorem is to apply to Bachelier's Gaussian formulation.

The search for Bachelier

Savage's intriguing postcard and Osborne's argument for a log-Gaussian form piqued renewed interest in the logarithmic random walk in which relative price changes follow a random walk. Work by Arnold Larson (1960),[16] Holbrook Working (1960),[17] Hendrick Houthakker (1961),[18] Sidney Alexander (1961),[19] Paul Cootner (1962),[20] Chicago PhD student and Eugene Fama colleague Arnold Moore (1962),[21] and Sir Clive W.J. Granger and Oskar Morgenstern (1963)[22] all supported Osborne's intuition.

These studies explored various tests of the reformulated model. Some tested for serial correlation, as discussed earlier. Others explored whether there was a momentum effect, measured to determine if run-ups or persistent declines occur, as a stronger form of serial correlation. The third avenue explored whether simple rules could outperform the buy and hold strategy recommended by the efficient market hypothesis and the random walk. Finally, there were explorations as to whether the size of a change is correlated to the size of recent exchanges, as might occur with bandwagon effects or periods of shifting volatility.

Still other studies confirmed the efficient market approach, at least based on the reformulation by Cowles in 1960 that allows for some persistent mispricing but on a scale that is sufficiently small to prevent arbitrage. For instance, in 1933, Cowles had concluded that boards of directors of major insurance companies were unable to predict the direction of the market. This allowed him to conclude that if the captains of industry could not determine the direction of the market, the employment of professional fund management might be a poor investment decision because they could not outperform the market with a sufficiently wide margin to cover their fees. This exploration of whether the returns on managed funds, net of fees, could "beat the market" has remained a topic of interest in finance ever since.

A persistent controversy

Bachelier's hypothesis first piqued the interest of the discipline of finance. Subsequently, his thesis has increased in controversy. His simple random walk analogy and its closely related extension to the efficient market hypothesis described in the next section have divided the finance discipline into two camps. One camp subscribes to the efficient market hypothesis, even if it might employ variants of the log-Gaussian form to maintain its basic tenet. Their message, accepted by most financial theorists and academics, at least on some level, is that there is little that can be done to beat the market in a systematic manner. This argument rests critically on the observation that, if one could, one would trade until all such profit opportunities are arbitraged. If this process works relatively quickly, then prices would quickly adjust to incorporate any such information gaps and renew efficiency.

However, the professional financial management discipline is at philosophical odds with the efficient market hypothesis. Financial practitioners spend hundreds of billions of dollars a year globally to manage financial securities portfolios to earn a better than average return, the efficient market hypothesis aside. These professionals often use technical analysis designed to regularly beat the market by taking advantage of the collective market psychology.

There is a joke among financial theorists that can actually cut two ways. When a University of Chicago finance student points out to his professor that there is a $100 bill on the ground, the professor recommends that he doesn't bother picking it up because, if it were real, someone would have already grabbed it. However, the professional financial management technicians could equally point out that it is worth keeping a sharp eye out for $100 bills on the ground before others see them. At least they do not have to worry about racing to beat the efficient market proponents.

6
Life and Legacy

There are only a handful of scholars in any discipline that spark a movement. In this instance, Louis Bachelier never fully comprehended the role his thesis would play and, for that matter, nor did the discipline. However, Bachelier's life after his thesis remained surprisingly controversial.

Much of this controversy flowed directly from the circumstances that seemed to cause Bachelier to be in the right place but often at the wrong time. His unconventional education, followed by an unconventional thesis, culminated in an unconventional and frustrating career. He simply did not have the pre-ordained academic trajectory reserved for those favored sons and daughters of scholarly benefaction.

Bachelier's first posting

It is well known in academia that a career follows a trajectory that is, for the most part, defined by one's first academic position. It is difficult to be placed in a good position if one does not graduate from a top school. It is also rare to successfully move to a top school from a substantially inferior school. This first placing and those first few years are of paramount importance.

Bachelier faced a couple of challenges, though. He viewed himself as a mathematician, but his thesis was not in pure mathematics. Rather, it was a novel application of probability theory to a financial market that many pure mathematicians or physicists could not imagine could be characterized by objective probabilities. Now, we recognize that the probabilities of financial markets are not those objective probabilities coolly calculated by mathematicians, but instead are the subjective probabilities arrived at by a consensus of market participants. Not until more than half a century later, with the development by Leonard Jimmie Savage of axioms of personal probabilities, could one formally argue that the treatment of subjective probabilities was a valid approach. And while Jules Henri Poincaré saw the insightful product from his student with a less-than-stellar educational pedigree, he may have been unwilling to exercise considerable political capital to place his student well. He did work to help Bachelier access good journals, but that appears to be the extent of his intervention.

Bachelier apparently worked where he could over the first decade of the new century. He applied for and earned a number of research grants offered by French universities from endowments from the perpetual bonds bequeathed to them for which the options written upon these bonds he had studied in his thesis.

At the end of the decade following the completion of his thesis, Bachelier was already turning 40. Many view pure mathematics as a field for young and agile minds. Scholars in this field are expected to do their best work before the age of 30, but he had only just defended his thesis at that age. He recognized that he would have to pay exceptional dues to get his delayed career back on track, and even taught for free at the Sorbonne to build up his résumé. Poincaré had helped Bachelier publish in journals that could only be accessed by the recommendation of someone of his stature. However, by 1912, Bachelier's academic benefactor had died, and Bachelier was not yet established himself in a permanent position at a university.

Bachelier served in the French army during the First World War and reached the rank of lieutenant. Immediately before and after the War, he had secured a few minor academic positions, mostly as a visitor to fill in for chaired professors on leave. In the interim, he married Augustine Jeanne Maillot on September 14, 1920, but was not married long before she died.

In this period before and after the First World War, Bachelier had a fair amount of success in publishing reasonably good work and, at least in one body of work, of a quality that may have matched his brilliant thesis of 1900. For instance, in 1912, he authored a book entitled *Calcul des probabilités*, followed up in 1914 by one of the first books on game theory, entitled *Le Jeu, la Chance et le Hasard*.[23] The latter book, one of the first works on the theory of games, became quite popular and sold many thousands of copies when most academic books might sell many hundreds at best. The title referred to games, probability, and randomness, and differentiated between chance, of known odds, and risk, of unknown odds. His treatment was the most thorough and groundbreaking at the time, and predated the University of Chicago Professor Frank Knight's subsequent work on the differentiation between known risk and unknowable uncertainty.

Yet, his colleagues ignored him, or pretended to do so. At the time at the Sorbonne, the premier young mathematician was Émile Borel (1871–1956). Borel was born just a year after Bachelier, but completed his doctorate six years before Bachelier's defense. He was offered a position at the Sorbonne at the age of 25, four years before Bachelier defended his thesis there. Borel was considered a rising star among French mathematical elite and clearly understood the politics of elitism. He had married the daughter of the Dean of the Sorbonne's Faculty of Sciences and embarked upon an illustrious career in which he made great strides in the calculus of probability and in game theory. He well understood the contributions in the theory of probability made by the Frenchman Joseph Bertrand (1822–1900), who died just as Bachelier defended his thesis, and by the great mind John Maynard Keynes (1883–1946). As were his contemporaries, Borel was interested in the philosophical distinction between objective and subjective probabilities. He also supervised students in physics, including Jean Baptiste Perrin, who went on to prove experimentally Einstein's hypothesis on Brownian motion.

Borel also established some early results in the theory of two-person games early in the 1920s. At the same time, though, he was increasingly drawn into French politics, which culminated in his retirement from public service in 1940 as Minister of the Navy.

In his research, Borel described constant-sum games, which can include the winner-take-all games such as checkers and chess, and had analogies to war, and economics and finance. In his first major treatise in 1921, Borel noted in "La théorie du jeu et les équations intégrales à noyau symétrique gauche" that:

> The problems of probability and analysis that suggest themselves concerning the art of war, or economic or financial speculations, are not without analogy with problems concerning games, though they generally have a higher degree of complication.[24]

In a subsequent paper, he later elaborated:

> It seems to me that the study of games in which chance and the skill of the players simultaneously intervene might furnish the opportunity for mathematical investigations, the applications of which go

beyond the limits of the restricted domain to which this first study is limited. They might extend to numerous questions in which psychological unknowns figure simultaneously with algebraic unknowns; but before thinking of this extension, it is appropriate to work first on the serious study of the simplest particular cases.[25]

In the 1921 paper, Borel developed what we now know as a mixed strategy in game theory, which allowed randomness in what each player would do. By permitting such strategies, Borel reasoned that each player in a symmetric game could receive no more and no less than even odds of winning in a two-person game. He went on to extend his determination of equilibrium based on symmetric solutions to mixed strategies to games with more players, first with three, then with five and, by 1927, seven.

Borel believed that there could not be a general solution to an arbitrary number of students. However, in 1938, he helped guide one of his students, Jean Ville (1910–1989), to an elegant proof of the concept of a minimax strategy that the brilliant Hungarian great mind John von Neumann had already developed in 1928.

This work by Borel and Ville actually motivated von Neumann and Oskar Morgenstern to complete their great work, *The Theory of Games and Economic Behavior*, in 1944. By chance, Morgenstern came across Ville's simplified proof of von Neumann's minimax strategy and introduced the approach to von Neumann. Within a couple of years, von Neumann and Morgenstern completed their revolutionary work on games.

Borel's work is often cited in the founding of game theory, but Bachelier's earlier work in game theory, or his work on the calculus of probabilities, for which Borel is so well known, was disregarded. It would be incredible to imagine that Borel had no knowledge of Bachelier's work in an area of mathematics for which Borel would go on to be well known. They were of the same age and both worked at the same institution, Borel as the eminent chaired professor and Bachelier as one who offered his services for free to the Sorbonne. Borel had refereed a number of research grant applications that Bachelier successfully submitted to the Sorbonne for work in probability theory. Moreover, Borel had guided Perrin in his work on Einstein's Brownian motion, a theory that Bachelier established. Yet, while Borel was well established in the academic elite, Bachelier continued to watch from outside.

At the end of the First World War, Bachelier obtained an academic position of lecturer at the University of Besançon, then moved to

Dijon (1922) and subsequently to Rennes (1925). He finally earned a permanent position at Besançon, where he remained only for ten years before he retired, probably as a mandatory retirement based on age. He died less than a decade later, on April 28, 1946.

Accolades too late

Others also took note of Bachelier's work, most notably the eminent Russian statistician Andrey Kolmogorov, who credited Bachelier with the early insights on the Markov process and attempted to significantly raise awareness of Bachelier's work in the statistics and mathematics community. Kolmogorov's famous paper, which established modern stochastic processes theory and which credited Bachelier's groundbreaking work three decades earlier, "Uber die analytischen Methoden in der Wahrscheinlichkeitsrechnung," was published in 1931. By then, though, Bachelier was 60 years old and nearing retirement.

Bachelier had suffered, in part, because he was of a school of science caught between two eras. Those who came before the scholars of the latter half of the nineteenth century and the first years of the twentieth century maintained some of the hand-waving and incomplete proofs in the margins for which their predecessors were notorious. It was expected that a good scholar should be able to fill in the blanks. In fact, French professors at the time were notorious for expecting their brilliant students to fill in the blanks or complete their proofs. This approach, of leaving some details to the reader, left Bachelier vulnerable.

A little later, the sciences began to evolve toward an axiomatic approach, as championed first by David Hilbert (1862–1943) in mathematics, then by his prodigy John von Neumann in physics, economics, and finance, and then by Leonard Jimmie Savage in statistics. Soon, rigor was expected, and errors of omission in proofs became unusual.

However, Bachelier became caught up in some academic politics when he applied for a position for which one of his potential future colleagues had preferred another candidate over him. At one of the universities where Bachelier had worked as a visiting professor, the University of Dijon, a permanent chair became available in 1926. The other chair in the department, Maurice Gevrey, preferred another candidate and set about to discredit Bachelier's work. He thought he discovered a fundamental error in one of Bachelier's papers and sent a complaint and an excerpt out of context to Lévy, who was then a 40-year-old professor at the École Polytechnique in Paris.

The complaint referred to a part of Bachelier's thesis from 26 years earlier, and a later paper. Bachelier had developed a geometric approach to his solution that demonstrated that the mean distance of the random walk from the origin rises proportionally to the square root of time. With increased steps and time, Bachelier showed a convergence, but the wording extracted by Gevrey for Lévy's review seemed to suggest that Bachelier thought the relationship between distance and time was constant. Lévy correctly noted that this relationship was not constant, which of course Bachelier, and all other experts by 1926, knew. Bachelier complained to Lévy, but Lévy was initially defensive and unapologetic.

Like Borel, Lévy was a pioneer in stochastic processes from his highly respected chair at the École Polytechnique. Just as it seems impossible or impossibly ignorant that Borel was unfamiliar with Bachelier's work, it is equally improbable that Lévy was unfamiliar with Bachelier, especially since Bachelier had written three books and more than a dozen papers in the area.

In fact, Lévy, who had helped develop the axioms of Markov processes, was introduced to Bachelier's groundbreaking contributions to probability theory through the endorsements proffered by Kolmogorov. A few years after their unfortunate misunderstanding, Lévy apologized to an embittered Bachelier, and Bachelier accepted the apology from the, by then, eminent Lévy. In retrospect, Lévy's entire reputation was built upon work that Bachelier had initiated. Indeed, Bachelier, during the Second World War, and after he retired to live with his sister in Brittany near their birthplace, wrote to Lévy to note that a few instances of Lévy's work and the presumably original work of others were identical to work he had published much earlier. Lévy had others explore whether there were indeed oversights in priority and discovered that Bachelier was correct. However, Lévy argued that he would not have made the mistake of neglecting Bachelier's work if Bachelier had not made a mistake in his less than rigorous writing.

The reconciliation between Lévy and Bachelier occurred well after Bachelier's career was over. In the end, Bachelier's career within French mathematical circles never earned the respect it deserved.

Bachelier's reputation among financial theorists

The most significant and well-known work of Kolmogorov, in Russian and German, was motivated by Bachelier. Kolmogorov took the discrete event work of all those before him, including Bachelier, and created the axioms of modern continuous-time stochastic process theory that finally offered rigor to Bachelier's work. Kolmogorov wrote:

> In probability theory, one usually considers only schemes according to which any changes of the states of a system are only possible at certain moments $t_1, t_2, \ldots t_n, \ldots$ which forms a discrete series. As far as I know, Bachelier was the first to make a systematic study of schemes in which the probability $P(t_0, x, t, \varepsilon)$ varies according to time t ... Here we note only that Bachelier's constructions are by no means mathematically rigorous.[26]

Of course, Kolmogorov was inspired by Bachelier's work, but he noted that Bachelier's work was of an era and in a field (of physics) with a different standard for rigor. Kolmogorov's results were much better integrated and absorbed in the United States, where academics did not suffer from the elitism that held back Bachelier's research in France. Followers of Kolmogorov's 1931 work began to recognize Bachelier's work. For instance, in 1946, Paul Erdös and Mark Kac published a paper on proofs of the central limit theorem, in which they referred to Bachelier's 1937 recasting of previous work in his *Les lois des grands nombres du calcul des probabilitiés*. In their reference to a number of pieces of work in Bachelier's book, Erdös and Kac wrote: 'This book contains no proofs but it gives reference to earlier papers.'[27]

This rather abstruse recognition in the USA began before Bachelier died, but accelerated significantly about a decade later. The practitioners of finance were not interested in the esoteric theories of turn-of-the-century mathematical physicists, but an American physicist in the late 1950s had an interest in finance. This earliest acknowledgement of Bachelier's great contribution to finance came from Matthew Fontaine Maury Osborne in 1959. Osborne, a physicist working at the Naval Research Laboratory in Washington, DC, had written a manuscript on the modeling of financial instruments. He wrote:

> I believe the pioneer work on randomness in economic time series, and yet most modern in viewpoint, is that of Bachelier ... Bachelier proceeds, by quite elegant mathematical methods, directly from the assumption that the expected gain (in francs) at any instant on the Bourse is zero, to a normal distribution of price changes, with dispersion increasing as the square root of the time, in accordance with the Fourier equation of heat diffusion. The theory is applied to speculation on rente, an interest-bearing obligation which appeared

to be the principal vehicle of speculation at the time, but no attempt was made to analyze the variation of prices into components except for the market discounting of future coupons, or interest payments. The theory was fitted to observations on rente for the years 1894–98. There is a considerable quantitative discussion of the expectations from the use of options (puts and calls). He also remarked that the theory was equally applicable to other types of speculation, in stock, commodities, and merchandise. To him is due credit for major priority on this problem.[28]

Meanwhile, in the 1950s, the great mind Leonard Jimmie Savage accomplished his goal of creating an axiomatic approach to personal probabilities. In the process, he came across references by another great mind, John Maynard Keynes, in Keynes' famous *A Treatise on Probability*, to the work of Bachelier.[29] Savage wrote to dozens of his American colleagues with his intriguing postcard asking them if they were familiar with Bachelier's work. One recipient was Paul Samuelson. We will turn to his story next.

Since the awarding of the Nobel Prize in Economics to Fischer Black and Myron Scholes for their options pricing formula, there has been a renewed interest in Bachelier's thesis. An International Bachelier Society has been formed. Every year or two, the Society meets at a conference to discuss the work of Bachelier and recent extensions to the breakthroughs he created.

It is now recognized that Bachelier established the foundations of modern finance, in rigor, in empiricism, in the pricing of derivatives, in the random walk, and in the efficient market hypothesis through arbitrage. However, this recognition came only after others reinvented each of these innovations, as much as a half century or more later. Bachelier's story was a remarkable example of an unlikely great mind.

Section 2
Paul Samuelson's Random Walk

There are a few avenues for great academic success. One is through a brilliant mind that is able to synthesize complex problems down to simple solutions that lend themselves to further empirical analysis. This approach requires tremendous insights into the problem and a great command, or an ability to command up, the techniques necessary to treat the problem. These often result in breakthroughs that subsequently produce wide bodies of subsequent scholarship for others. We may call those who accomplish such revolutionary academic feats the visionaries.

A second approach describes what these others do with breakthrough ideas. They take the ideas of great minds and extend them in one direction or another, one step at a time. These scholars are the evolutionaries.

The third group is the revolutionaries. They take visions and evolutions and create something that is greater than the sum of its parts. The Nobel Prizes are typically awarded to this latter category. Albert Einstein is a classic example of this category of great minds.

Occasionally, a scholar comes along who is visionary, evolutionary, and revolutionary. Such scholars are capable not only of seeing the forest for the trees, but also of understanding how one tree is an extension of or grows in parallel to another. For instance, John von Neumann was a scholar who was well read, well schooled, and well regarded in many disciplines of pure and applied mathematics, including economics and finance. These individuals are boundary spanners and act like academic bees by pollinating many disciplines with the insights of others. Another example might be Richard Feynman (1918–1988), the famous physicist called in to help discover why the US Space Shuttle *Challenger* exploded soon after takeoff.

Within economics and finance, Paul Samuelson best fits into this latter category of rare scholars who can contribute to many sub-disciplines in their lifetime while lesser scholars toil away within the narrowest confines.

7
The Early Years

The subtext of Bachelier's career-long plight and lifelong pursuit for academic recognition was the French penchant at the time of intellectual style over substance. An elitist academic climate meant that scholarship of value could only come from elite scholars and that one need not read works in other languages, especially when so much good work was presumed to be done by French scholars. Such academic provincialism ultimately serves no greater purpose. Yet, it preserved the status quo and the vaunted position of those admitted to the club of the scholarly elite.

In fact, this elitism often reaches its pinnacle a little after the apex of the body of accomplishments that give rise to the arrogance in the first place. Academic communities sometimes fall into this trap, just as nations do. For instance, empires thrive and rise in power based on a better model, a grander vision, or a greater synergy, and then decline once they take a manifest destiny and superiority too much to heart. The Roman Empire came and went, and the British Empire, fueled by the Industrial Revolution and the colonial model, also reached its apex and unraveled as less arrogant and more inclusive national models emerged. Someday, too, these new empires will decline, at least if they cannot recognize their strengths and ameliorate their own weaknesses.

The first half of the twentieth century saw Europe engulfed in national conflict and balkanized by language. Academic communities, too, suffered from this balkanization, and many scholars, especially Jewish academics, sought academic refuge in the United States, just as others had sought economic liberation in the USA ever since the seventeenth century. The US academic community became the entrepreneurial engine of global scholarship and the melting pot of scholarly ideas. This model of liberation helped establish the English language as the language of academia, even if finance, mathematics, and physics also used the language of mathematics as a universal language.

It is within this model of scholarly liberation and the high valuation of academic entrepreneurship that we cast the career of Paul Samuelson. In such a paradigm, his family pedigree is rich, but, as we shall see, it is by no means unique. We find that the great minds who met with great success in their careers often had family members who could trace their roots back to the first settlers of America, and others who brought the old land to the new in a wave of immigration from Central and Southern Europe from 1880 to 1920. Their heritages were eclectic and entrepreneurial rather than ensconced in academic privilege and elitism.

In search of freedom

The Samuelson name was brought to the USA from Raczik, Poland, then part of the Prussian Empire before the Second World War. Paul Samuelson's grandfather, Leo Samuelson, and his grandmother, Jennie Epstein, were part of a Jewish community that saw waves of immigrants come to the USA in the latter half of the nineteenth and the beginning of the twentieth centuries. Their son, Frank Samuelson (1886–1939), had married Ella Lipton and they immigrated to the USA in 1908 to build a pharmacy business in Gary, Indiana. Frank's older brother Herman also emigrated from Poland and started up a furrier business in the area, along with Frank's other brother Charles.

The Samuelson family was very entrepreneurial in the booming steel-making town of Gary, about 25 miles southeast of Chicago, Illinois, on the shores of Lake Michigan. Now part of the Chicago metropolitan area, Gary was then a distinct community with a very large proportion of working-class Midwesterners and immigrants.

Gary was a town that had reached its heyday in the run-up to the First World War. Its new, state-of-the-art steel mills were running full bore to produce the armaments that the Allied nations needed to prepare for war. The plants and the factories were staffed by immigrants and refugees from the same Austro-Hungarian Empire nations that were drawn into the other side of Europe's conflicts. Then, with the end of the War, a post-war recession struck the USA while labor strife struck Gary. The formerly bustling city was beset with strikes, and immigrant strike-breakers were brought in from Mexico.

Frank and Ella Samuelson's pharmacy was reasonably prosperous over these years, partly because local families could not afford either the expense or the time off work to visit doctors. Instead, they relied on the

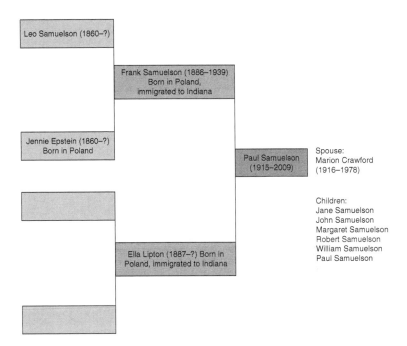

Figure 7.1   The family tree of Paul Samuelson (1915–2009)

pharmacist's advice for their health care. The family also took in boarders to their home to raise some additional income. Any surplus income went into the booming Roaring Twenties financial and investment markets. By the middle of the decade, Paul's father had deeply invested in the same Florida real estate that also attracted the type of investors as had the Bostonian confidence man Charles Ponzi, whose pyramid schemes placed his name in infamy to this day. The Samuelsons' relatively comfortable upbringing also afforded the Samuelson boys, Charles, the elder son, born in 1913, Paul Anthony, born on May 15, 1915, and the younger brother, Robert, born in 1922, an opportunity to escape the heat and pollution of Gary and Chicago in summer and spend parts of their summers in a nearby farm community or to take trips with the family to Florida.

Like many Jewish immigrant families, the Samuelson family valued the education of their three boys highly. Frank and Ella decided to move to nearby Chicago so that their sons could attend Hyde Park High School in the exclusive Woodlawn neighborhood. The neighborhood was then the home of those who had helped build the 1893

Chicago World's Columbian Exposition, and many of the professors who worked at the nearby University of Chicago. The High School was then one of the top schools in the Chicago area and is now known as the Hyde Park Career Academy. Graduates in that era included the famed aviation pioneer Amelia Earhart and many world-class musicians.

Before the Samuelson family lost a fair bit of their wealth in Florida real estate in the latter half of the Roaring Twenties, Paul and his brothers would also enjoy summers in vast Florida housing projects that would be left unfinished once the economy turned. With the looming Great Depression ahead of him and his cross-country summer jaunts behind him, Paul instead turned his attention to his studies, and especially to an interest in math that was augmented by his interest in his high school algebra teacher. By his own admission, he was an under-achiever in high school, in contrast to his precociousness up to that point. However, he was precocious in his early interest in finance. He would help his algebra teacher choose stock, as many middle-class households were wont to do in the Roaring Twenties. With the Great Crash of 1929, both his teacher and his family lost small fortunes.

The Chicago years

Two years later, in 1931, Samuelson applied to the local school for Chicago's best, the University of Chicago. Already by then, under Frank Knight's influence and his almost blind faith in the free market, the emerging Chicago School of economic thought, had remained enamored with faith in laissez-faire economics, despite the deepening Great Depression by 1931 and 1932. This contrast between economic doctrine and reality made a great impression on the young Samuelson and created in him a lifelong interest in the workings and failings of markets.

Following Samuelson's early graduation from high school at the young age of 16 in 1931, he enrolled at the University of Chicago with a notion that he wanted to study mathematics. However, he was almost immediately enticed into economics following his attendance of a lecture, at 8:00 am on January 2, 1932, on the nineteenth-century economist Thomas Malthus, for whom the economics discipline was named "the dismal science" because of Malthus' prophecy that the world would be plagued by cycles of feast and famine. Samuelson later related that the lecture changed his life.

Samuelson's first exposure to Malthus' dismal prophecy that, despite humankind's best intentions, booms and busts will buffet our economies rang true to him. He saw in his own life experiences fortunes made and lost, labor strife, and long unemployment lines. These experiences created in the young economics student a life lesson that economies were driven by animal spirits that could cause wild market gyrations and great human sorrow at times. By the time he began attending the University of Chicago in January 1932, the nation had plunged into the Great Depression. While his own family had lost much in the stock market themselves, university attendance seemed opportune because unemployment was high and thus the opportunity cost to attend school was low. However, he set himself ambitious academic goals and succeeded in graduating with his Baccalaureate degree in Arts by 1935 just as he turned 20.

Even then, under the direction of such eminent economic personalities as Knight, the University of Chicago had created for itself a distinct school of economic thought. This philosophy, within which Samuelson was immersed, was formed by the founders of the Chicago School, which also included notable Chicago colleagues at the time such as the noted Canadian economist Jacob Viner (1892–1970) and Henry Calvert Simons (1899–1946).

The Chicago School was built upon an almost zealous faith in the beauty of free and unfettered markets. Knight, in particular, was grappling with the role of information and uncertainty in the price system. He attributed the term "risk" to the category of unknown events for which we cannot know their probabilities in advance. Such risk is in opposition to the known probabilities of games of chance. However, past realizations may allow us to estimate the costs of risk, and, in doing so, insure against them. In this respect, the costs of indemnifying the decision-maker against risk became part of the cost of doing business. Knight stated:

> Uncertainty must be taken in a sense radically distinct from the familiar notion of risk, from which it has never been properly separated ... The essential fact is that "risk" means in some cases a quantity susceptible of measurement, while at other times it is something distinctly not of this character; and there are far-reaching and crucial differences in the bearings of the phenomena depending on which of the two is really present and operating ... It will appear that a measurable uncertainty, or "risk" proper, as we shall use the term, is so far different from an unmeasurable one that it is not in effect an uncertainty at all.

Such subtle underpinnings of the free market, as espoused by the Chicago School, fascinated Samuelson. Meanwhile, job opportunities remained scarce by the time Samuelson graduated, and his family had not yet recovered from the Depression. Fortunately, his success at the University of Chicago was sufficient to earn him a nationally competitive scholarship, but with the provision that recipients did not attend graduate school at the same school where they had completed their undergraduate degree. Instead, he applied to and was accepted into graduate economics studies at Chicago's rival school, Harvard University. One year later, by his twenty-first birthday, Samuelson had earned a Master's degree in economics. He earned his PhD three years later, just before the USA entered the Second World War.

With the tools of price theory gleaned directly from the minds of the masters, Samuelson found himself in the den of liberal economic thought at Harvard. While the Chicago School would invariably favor non-interventionist policies, even in the light of the Great Depression at that time, Harvard's scholars typically maintained a much more interventionist approach to markets and economic policy. At Harvard, Samuelson was exposed to some of the great economists of the day, including Joseph Schumpeter, Wassily Leontief, and a most able and skilled mathematical economist, Edwin Bidwell Wilson (1879–1964). He spent six years under their tutelage, which may seem like a fairly long time to complete a Masters and a PhD in economics. However, his skill and economic intelligence had earned him the exceptional award as a junior fellow of the Harvard Society for three of those six years. This fellowship included a generous stipend and offered its recipients an opportunity to study anything they wished, without a requirement to teach or act as a research assistant for senior faculty members. This fellowship afforded him a tremendous luxury of time to develop a new axiomatic theory of economics and finance.

Samuelson became especially well versed in the complex systems approach to equilibrium that was the hallmark of the work of some of the discipline's first heavily mathematical scholars: Wilson and Leontief. Samuelson mastered the emerging state of mathematics in economics and produced a very strong graduation thesis.

His interest in the study of equilibrium was one on which his Chicago colleagues placed little importance because they assumed the economy consistently finds itself in an equilibrium that fully employs available resources. In the Chicago world, there could be no persistent unemployment because prices, particularly wages in this example, would adjust to ensure that any excess labor was absorbed.

Initially, Samuelson accepted this explanation. However, during the Great Depression, he could not find summer work and believed it even pointless to search. He began to accept the Harvard interventionist economic philosophy and developed an appreciation for the need to better understand economic equilibrium and market failure.

An economic prodigy

While at Harvard, Samuelson was immediately recognized for his brilliance, perhaps especially for his bold statement about his goal to produce a sweeping thesis that would recast economics into a much more mathematically rigorous foundation. These were strong statements from an impetuous young graduate student who had a penchant for criticizing those senior faculty who rested on their academic laurels or who could not offer explanations as to why an economy could remain in peril for so many years and why economics seemed to have so little to offer as a solution. He apparently had a particularly contentious relationship with the department's chair, Harold Hitchings. However, despite Hitchings' fervent protestations, upon publication of this thesis, he won the prestigious John Bates Clark Medal, given by the American Economic Association for the most promising economist under the age of 40. When he graduated from Harvard, he was 26 years old.

In fact, Samuelson's PhD thesis was a tour de force in the development of modern economics and finance as a social science, based on the scientific principle and employing the mathematical tools of the sciences. He began his thesis with a statement from J. Willard Gibbs (1839–1903) that "Mathematics is a language"[30] and went on to set the tone for his treatise:

> The existence of analogies between central features of various theories implies the existence of a general theory which underlies the particular theories and unifies them with respect to those central features. This fundamental principle of generalization by abstraction was enunciated by the eminent American mathematician E. H. Moore more than thirty years ago. It is the purpose of the pages that follow to work out its implications for theoretical and applied economics.[31]

Samuelson developed two simple concepts in his thesis and his subsequent book *Foundations of Economic Analysis*, published shortly after the

War in 1947. He insisted that economic theory should be based on the principle that one should:

- retain in the analysis the fewest number of variables and economic relationships necessary to prove the premise; and
- use the method of constrained optimization as the primary methodological technique of economic modeling.

Given his immense early recognition, it might be imagined that Harvard might want to retain the brilliant young scholar. Unfortunately, Harvard has a history of hiring only well-established scholars, and most academic institutions are reticent to employ their own graduates. Instead, Samuelson had to seek employment at the other end of Cambridge Avenue, at the Massachusetts Institute of Technology (MIT). In 1940, the year before he graduated from Harvard, he was offered an Assistant Professor position at MIT, followed with tenure and associate rank just four years later in 1944. He later reflected that he felt cast out of Harvard, as had many other brilliant scholars at the time, many of whom were of Jewish descent. He actually rejoiced in joining the likes of other prominent and brilliant Harvard castaways who found their way to MIT, such as Norbert Wiener, one of the founders of modern stochastic processes. Samuelson relished in enjoying a spectacular career post-Harvard. He remained at MIT until he retired as a Professor Emeritus in 1986.

Family life

There was one other fortunate aspect of Samuelson's Harvard experience: he met Marion Crawford, a Radcliffe economics student who shared some classes with him. She was working on her PhD thesis with the famous economist Wassily Leontief and was subsequently credited by Samuelson for her assistance in his tour-de-force book that flowed from his thesis. They married in 1938. One year later, Samuelson's father Frank died in Chicago on May 8, 1939, just as Paul was completing his fellowship at Harvard.

With the onset of the Second World War, one of Samuelson's first assignments at MIT was at the Radiation Laboratory. There he gained experience in the methods of engineering physicists and in the emerging field of computing. He and his wife started a family once the War and his obligation to MIT's war-related Radiation Laboratory ended.

By all accounts, Samuelson's fellow PhD economist and life partner Marion Crawford was instrumental in his academic life. He gave her special credit for her advice and collaboration in his writing of his groundbreaking thesis and subsequent book. He brought to these projects his brilliance and inventiveness. She brought to him perspective and confidence based on a heritage very different from his own.

Born in Wisconsin in 1916, the year after Samuelson's birth, Marion Crawford could trace her family right back to the first settlers from Europe in the Americas. While her maiden name Crawford traces back to John Crawford, who arrived in the USA following his birth in Ireland in Ballebay, Monighan, on October 18, 1812, Marion's paternal grandmother, Laura Givens Selleck, had relatives who dated back to the first settlement ships that arrived in the Americas in the seventeenth century.

The first American patriarch of the family was David Selleck. He was born in Middlesex, England in 1610, but had settled in the Massachusetts

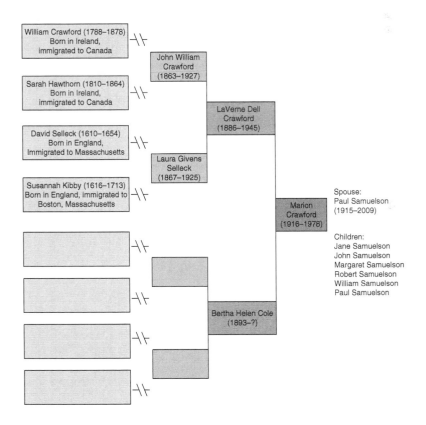

Figure 7.2   The family tree of Marion Crawford (1916–1978)

area and died while on an exploratory expedition to the American Virginias in 1654.[32] Selleck's settlement was part of the Massachusetts Bay Colony, a very early English settlement on the east coast of North America near present-day Boston. It was founded by the Massachusetts Bay Company and investors from the Dorchester Company who began briefly settling the area in 1624 and then more extensively beginning in 1628. Selleck arrived on the shores of Weymouth, in the Colony of Massachusetts, on July 24, 1633 on a ship with 85 passengers and 12 cows. Their crossing took three months, including a brief stay at a set of islands so that the Portuguese crew could secure a leak in the hull. Eight years after his arrival, Selleck moved north to Boston and started up his own company as a "Soape boyler," ship-owner, and importer-exporter.

Selleck was a freeman, which meant he could own land and was able to vote. In fact, he voted, on December 7, 1641, to pay a direct tax that would be used to establish a free public school for the town's children. He had four sons, including a ship's captain, a military major, John Selleck, Marion Crawford's great-great-great-great-great-great-great-great-great-grandfather, and three daughters with his wife, Susannah Kibby, who also came over from Middlesex in the same era.

Marion brought to the family her own good grasp of the subject of economics and an established New World ancestry, while Samuelson benefited from the entrepreneurial and intellectual zeal so characteristic of first- and second-generation Americans of Eastern European descent. Together, they had six children, the last three of whom were triplet boys: Jane, Margaret, William, Robert, John, and Paul.

If Samuelson's heritage was shared by many new immigrants who took a risk to forge a new life for their family, so did his wife's family 300 years earlier. He was immersed in a heritage of consummate academic entrepreneurs and scholarly energy that was able to toss away the convention before it so that new wisdom could be fresh and progressive. This is often the hallmark of a great mind.

8
The Times

Paul Samuelson arrived not only to MIT but also to a profession that was undergoing a metamorphosis. In the early 1930s, the American economist Irving Fisher had extended his earlier work on the role of the interest rate in intertemporal decision-making. He was considered by many to be the best and most sophisticated economist of his day, and was regarded as the first popularly known financial theorist. However, his discipline was economics and finance based primarily on rhetoric rather than on the compact language of mathematics almost universally employed in the hard sciences.

Physics had been going through a similar metamorphosis following Einstein's magnificent year in 1905. However, even Einstein's work, while it employed some sophisticated mathematical tools, was written in a very different style and a lower level of formalism and rigor than scientists would expect today.

In the 1920s, a pure mathematician named David Hilbert and his prodigy John von Neumann set about making mathematics and physics more rigorous through an axiomatic approach to modeling. The concept can be likened to using building block modules to assemble a model in finance. Each module, based on a set of axioms and the conclusions that flow from these axioms, can be linked to other modules in a combination that creates an entire model. Then, if each component is developed in a rigorous manner, so is the assembly of axioms which, when taken to their logical conclusions, constitute a theory.

This axiomatic approach is now almost universally used. The idea of a series of strong foundations upon which all theory will be built, and a set of guiding principles based on the maximization of each agent's objective function, was the philosophy that Samuelson brought to finance and economics as espoused in his dissertation. It turned out that his approach was also amenable to the tools of calculus, which has been employed ever since.

Samuelson was not alone in championing the use of the scientific method and the compact language of mathematics. Certainly, John von Neumann was also doing so for economics and finance over the 1930s and 1940s, although he relied primarily on set theory rather than calculus in his game-theoretic approach. In addition, others who followed Samuelson, perhaps most notably his brother-in-law by marriage, Kenneth Arrow, added still further rigor to the Samuelson foundations. Yet, Samuelson's *Foundations of Economic Analysis* textbook is still considered the starting point to modern economics and finance, and is still the recommended reading for any graduate student preparing for comprehensive examinations.

This new scientific approach was by no means uncontroversial, though. Both Harvard and the University of Chicago had built up entire schools of economic thought on a tradition of rhetorical hand-waving in their respective economic belief systems. However, without powerful mathematical tools, they could not establish a proof of the existence of their economic guiding principles. Instead, they subscribed to their respective department-wide faith that their tenets were true. The Chicago School subscribed to the premise that markets cleared with the same certainty that philosophers and theologians might proclaim 'all men are created equal'.

On the other hand, the premise of MIT subscribed to a scientific tenet rather than a matter of faith. To it, the scientific method should act as the basis for the engineering of everything. Those scholars drawn to MIT, like Samuelson and his colleagues Norbert Wiener and Franco Modigliani at that time, followed by other great minds in finance like Robert Merton, Myron Scholes, and Stephen Ross, were unified under a more rigorous mathematical approach and the collective rejection of hand-waving arguments that seem to do little more than preserve the faith and vaunted elitist positions. These scholars, too, were of Jewish descent, and MIT seemed to benefit from its focus on mathematics and science without regard for heredity or academic pedigree. The economics and finance disciplines were eagerly anticipating a new fervor based on the scientific method, and Samuelson's *Foundations of Economic Analysis* became the figurative bible for the new faith.

This sudden upsetting of conventional wisdom and the doctrines of the established schools must have been quite irksome to some. Those who found their way to MIT no doubt revelled in their upstart reputations, but were also determined to revolutionize economic and financial thought. However, the revolution was not without some not unexpected recalcitrance. It was believed that Samuelson's nemesis, the chair of the economics department at Harvard, tried to undermine Samuelson behind the scenes. And a raucous public debate emerged between the young upstart Samuelson and one of the grand professors of the day, Milton Friedman (1912–2006), the patriarch of the Chicago School.

Friedman, who was covered more fully in the first book of this series on great minds, was not quarrelling with an economic or financial theory of Samuelson's. Indeed, he was primarily a macroeconomist, with an interest in the role of the money supply on economic stability, despite his forays into probability with his colleague Leonard Jimmie Savage and his brief foray into the Life Cycle Model of finance through his concept of a household's permanent income. The hallmark of Friedman's expositions was rhetoric. Few scholars could match his academic flourish.

Friedman used mathematics only sparingly and without great sophistication. Instead, he was determined to produce testable conclusions rather than demonstrating the beauty and compactness of the model itself or its assumptions. If one could discover water with a divining rod and could consistently do so more quickly and accurately than another could with a more scientific approach, Friedman would accept the former. Indeed, after receiving criticism in the literature for his academic pragmatism, in a paper on risk, he responded by finessing his assumptions so that he could produce a more generally accepted conclusion. He did not bother to defend his analytic approach. Instead, he took the lead and recast his paper with Savage on probabilities in economics as a vigorous re-statement on positive economics. In this article, and a subsequent book, Friedman took on the new young and more mathematically sophisticated scholars in economics and finance by stating that it is the product, not the accuracy of the assumptions, that is most important.

Samuelson found such an intellectually bereft and pragmatic argument to be patently absurd and was more than willing to take on Friedman, and the University of Chicago and Harvard too, perhaps. He stated that no scientific model ought to be accepted by the scholarly community if the assumptions were absurd, regardless of the predictability of its conclusions. In fact, he would probably have been willing to reject any theory that made successful predictions if its assumptions did not make intuitive sense. In his view, a model must provide insights into the way systems work, given our understanding of our economic world and how decisions are, or ought to be, made.

Developments in stochastic processes

Over the same time period as Samuelson was building a new foundation for economics, Wiener, Andrey Kolmogorov, and others had completed the formalization of the Brownian motion model discovered by Louis Bachelier. Bachelier's thesis did not fully generalize the mathematics of his stochastic process, but others, most notably Wiener, did so by the 1930s.

Norbert Wiener was a brilliant mathematical prodigy who showed the hallmark of greatness. He applied his genius to many seemingly disparate fields in mathematics, physics, biology, computing, engineering, sociology, and philosophy. He was the first-born child, on November 26, 1894, of Leo Wiener and Bertha Kahn of Columbia, Missouri. His parents were of Polish and German Jewish descent. His father secured a position in Slavic languages at Harvard University and the young family moved from Leo's mother Bertha's birth state of Missouri to the rural town of Harvard, Massachusetts, which was a short commute to Harvard University in Cambridge.

Norbert's father valued scholarship and literature highly, and was determined to imbue young Norbert with a richer education than public schools could provide. The family home-schooled him until he was prepared for high school at the age of 9. He graduated subsequently from Ayer High School in nearby Ayer, Massachusetts, in the spring of 1906, at the age of 11. His family then moved to Medford, Massachusetts so that he could enter Tufts College. Three years later, he was awarded his undergraduate degree in mathematics, at the age of 14, and began graduate studies in zoology at Harvard University. However, he suffered from poor eyesight, which challenged the necessary lab work. After only a year at Harvard, he transferred to Cornell University in Ithaca, New York, to continue in philosophy. A year later, he resumed his studies at Harvard, in mathematics and logic, while he simultaneously studied at Cornell.

Wiener earned his PhD at Harvard in 1914, at the age of 19, and immediately departed to Europe to work on logic and philosophy with Bertrand Russell at Cambridge University and on the axiomatic approach to mathematics with David Hilbert at the University of Göttingen. He returned the next year to teach philosophy at Harvard and to assist the USA in its war effort. While he was determined to serve his country as a soldier, his poor eyesight denied him the chance to become a foot soldier. Instead, the Army had the good sense to employ his great mind to better understand the mathematics of ballistics.

At the end of the War, Wiener sought a permanent position at Harvard, but was denied it because of (he believed) an anti-Semitic bias, an accusation others subsequently leveled against the institution. Instead, he moved down Cambridge Avenue to MIT, where he spent the rest of his career.

Wiener's work in ballistics for the Army intrigued him. The physics of ballistics in a vacuum is a relatively trivial physics exercise. However, a projectile that must move through a fluid like the atmosphere and is buffeted constantly by random currents forges a less deterministic path. His insights culminated in his first very important work, entitled "Differential Space" and published in the prestigious *Journal of Mathematics and Physics*, in 1923.[33] The paper, at 44 pages, was very long for a journal article and constituted a treatise in stochastic calculus, within which the Wiener process was developed. Three years later, he began a particularly prolific year as a Guggenheim scholar in Europe, where he continued his work on Brownian motion. There, he also married Margaret Engemann, as arranged by his parents.

Wiener continues to be known for his Wiener process that traces the movement of particles that bear random shocks. While Bachelier had performed the same analysis using arguments of discrete mathematics in his 1900 thesis, Wiener generalized the results in continuous time.

A Wiener process is characterized by a uni-dimensional distance $W(t)$ over time as follows:

- $W_0 = 0$.
- The function $t \to W_t$ is almost everywhere continuous.
- W_t has independent increments with (for $0 \leq s < t$).
- $N(\mu, \sigma^2)$ denotes the normal distribution with expected value μ and variance σ^2.

The third condition, that the process has independent increments, implies that for times $0 \leq s_1 < t_1 \leq s_2 < t_2$, $W_{t1} - W_{s1}$ and $W_{t2} - W_{s2}$ are each independent random variables. This implies that any arbitrary increment is also an independent random variable.

The Wiener process is directly related to Bachelier's discrete results in that it represents a scaled limit of discrete-time random walk stochastic processes with stationary independent increments.

From these conditions, Wiener proved the following properties:

- The expectation $E(W_t) = 0$.
- The variance is t.
- The process can be scaled up or down such that the resulting process remains a Wiener process.

Let us look at this scaling result and show how a discrete-step random walk can be converted to the continuous-time calculus that Wiener, Bachelier, and Paul Lévy explored. Using the previous walking drunkard example, let P_{ij} be the probability that such a random variable which begins at position i will end up at position j.

If the movement space is one-dimensional, for example, a distance, then $P(X_{i+1} = x) = .5 * P(X_i = x+1) + .5 * P(X_i = x-1)$. This expression is equivalent to:

$$P(X_{i+1} = x) - P(X_i = x) = .5 * (P(X_i = x+1) - 2P(X_i = x) + P(X_i = x-1))$$

If the process is neutral to rescaling of the length of each step, then let the step size be reduced to h and the time step to τ. Then, if we denote by P(x,t) as the probability of the drunk arriving at position x at time t:

$$\frac{P(x,t+\tau) - P(x,t)}{\tau} = \frac{h^2}{2\tau} \frac{P(x+h,t) - 2P(x,t) + P(x-h,t)}{h^2}$$

Let the ratio $h^2/2\tau$ be labeled D. Then, in the limit as h and τ go to zero:

$$\frac{P(x,t+\tau) - P(x,t)}{\tau} \rightarrow \frac{\partial P(x,t)}{\partial t}$$

$$\frac{P(x+h,t) - 2P(x,t) + P(x-h,t)}{h^2} \rightarrow \frac{\partial^2 P(x,t)}{\partial x^2}$$

$$\text{and} \quad \frac{\partial P(x,t)}{\partial t} = D\frac{\partial^2 P(x,t)}{\partial x^2}$$

We arrive at the familiar diffusion equation relationship discovered by Bachelier, Einstein, and, much later, Fischer Black. The solution to this equation has been well known since the early nineteenth century as a Gaussian distribution:

$$P_0(x,t) = \frac{1}{2\sqrt{\pi Dt}} e^{\frac{-x^2}{4Dt}}$$

for t > 0. This relationship was also key to Einstein's conclusion – that heat diffusion occurs because of the random collision of molecules.

The pure mathematical continuous-time stochastic process and the Gaussian position distribution have been applied to problems of ballistics, quantum physics, biology, signaling theory, and finance ever since. While we described the process for linear distances above, as might be relevant in a price space, the extension to a higher dimension m is relatively straightforward, with the probability:

$$P_0(x,t) = \frac{1}{(4\pi Dt)^{m/2}}\, e^{\frac{-x^2}{4Dt}}$$

Even in higher dimensions, we see that the distribution remains proportional to the root of t.

Samuelson was aware of the mathematics of diffusion processes, as he was with Itô's new tool of stochastic calculus. In 1944, Kiyoshi Itô published his Itô stochastic integral first in the *Proceedings of the Imperial Academy of Tokyo* and then in an article entitled "On Stochastic Differential Equations" in the *Memoirs of the American Mathematical Society* in 1951.

Itô described a generalized differential equation form of Brownian motion with drift, in which movements are described as:

$$dX_t = \mu(X_t,t)dt + \sigma(X_t,t)dB_t,$$

where B follows the classic standard Brownian motion as defined by a Wiener process. A straightforward integration of this expression gives:

$$X_{t+s} - X_t = \int_t^{t+s} \mu(X_u,u)du + \int_t^{t+s} \sigma(X_u,u)dB_u.$$

This equation is not difficult to interpret. Over a small time interval of length d, the position X(t) changes based on the normally distributed mean drift term $\mu(X_t, t)\, \delta$ and the diffusion (or variance) term by an amount $\sigma(X_t, t)^2\, \delta$. If this is a Wiener process, each of these increments moves independently on past increments, so there is a simple path independence in the integral. Sometimes called the martingale property, this result shows that position is independent of the past behavior of the process, so long as there is no structural change in drift and diffusion.

Recall that, for a Wiener process:

1. The displacement X(t) is a random variable.
2. For any points in time s and t, X(s) – X(t) is a normally distributed random variable with a mean of zero and a variance equal to s – t. This creates the result that the standard deviation must then be proportional to the root of the time interval.
3. Finally, for any interval of time involving s < t < u, the normally distributed random variables X(u) – X(t) and X(t) – X(s) are independent, based on the Markov assumption.

By Itô's time, it was well known that the evolution of position in such a process could be described by a probability function f(x,t) of the evolving position x(t) as given by:

$$f(x,t) = \frac{1}{\beta\sqrt{2\pi t}} e^{-\frac{(x-x_0-at)^2}{2\beta^2 t}}$$

and followed the Fokker-Planck diffusion equation:

$$\frac{\delta f}{\delta t} = \frac{\beta^2}{2} \frac{\delta^2 f}{\delta x^2} - a\frac{\delta f}{\delta x}$$

To see how Itô derived his important stochastic calculus lemma, recall the ordinary chain rule from basic differential calculus for any function f of time t:

$$df = A dt$$

and let a function y = g(f,t) be a function of both f and t. Then the differential of g is:

$$dg = \left(A\frac{\delta g}{\delta f} + \frac{\delta g}{\delta t} \right) dt$$

When Itô applied this chain rule to the Wiener process, he observed that a function f of position W and time t becomes:

$$df = \beta\frac{\delta f}{\delta W} dX + \left(a\frac{\delta f}{\delta W} + \frac{\beta^2}{2} \frac{\delta^2 f}{\delta W^2} + \frac{\delta f}{\delta t} \right) dt$$

The extra terms, when compared with the simple chain rule, occur because of the effects of higher order terms arising from the variance, or second moments of the stochastic process. We see that these higher order terms will fall off quickly because they include $(dt)^2$, which goes to zero very quickly for infinitesimally small changes in t. Expanding the process and collecting terms, we see:

$$df = \frac{\delta f}{\delta W} dW + \frac{\delta f}{\delta t} dt + \frac{1}{2}\frac{\delta^2 f}{\delta W^2}(dW)^2 + \cdots$$

$$= \frac{\delta f}{\delta W}(a dt + \beta dX) + \frac{\delta f}{\delta t} dt + \frac{1}{2}\frac{\delta^2 f}{\delta W^2}(a dt + \beta dX)^2 + \cdots$$

However, we can simplify this by noting that:

$$(a\,dt + \beta dX)^2 = a^2(dt)^2 + 2a\beta(dt)(dX) + \beta^2(dX)^2$$

On the right-hand side of the expression, the first two terms involve this infinitesimal term $(dt)^2$, and another term will vanish in the limit as dt goes to zero, i.e. the product of $(dt)(dX)$. When we also impose that the mean square position $(dX)^2$ equals dt, we find:

$$(a\,dt + \beta dX)^2 = \beta^2(dX)^2 + \cdots = \beta^2 dt + \cdots$$

Finally, if we substitute this result back into our original expression, we find:

$$df = \frac{\delta f}{\delta W}(a\,dt + \beta dX) + \frac{\delta f}{\delta t}dt + \frac{1}{2}\frac{\delta^2 f}{\delta W^2}\beta^2 dt + \cdots$$

After collecting terms, we are left with Itô's lemma:

$$df = \beta\frac{\delta f}{\delta W}dX + \left(a\,\frac{\delta f}{\delta W} + \frac{\beta^2}{2}\frac{\delta^2 f}{\delta W^2} + \frac{\delta f}{\delta t}\right)dt$$

This lemma permits financial theorists to describe the evolution of stochastic processes based on the mean and variance of the underlying random variables.

The first discussions of the efficient market hypothesis

The martingale independence property of the Wiener process in one dimension was thoroughly integrated into the sciences and engineering by the 1950s. Meanwhile, the investment by Alfred Cowles III in the Cowles Commission and its databases and new econometric methods had substantiated the proposition that the expected value of an individual security tomorrow was equal to its value today. The finance discipline was set on a path that would merge the calculus of stochastic processes with the econometric tools flowing out of the Cowles Commission.

The stage had actually been set a few years earlier for such an innovation. During the 1940s, there had been an extensive discussion on the pricing of futures markets. John Maynard Keynes and John Hicks asserted that the future commodity price must be related to the present price by the cost to store the commodity in the interim and the fee an underwriter would need to attach to cover its risk of underwriting. These results suggest that financial markets ought to follow a random walk.

We discussed earlier that a physicist, Matthew Fontaine Maury Osborne, first brought the physics and mathematics concept to the finance discipline in 1959. In his paper, he quoted the 1900 thesis of Bachelier. Savage had also been intrigued by Bachelier's mention of true prices and the role of individual subjective probabilities, and had sent out his inquiring postcard to dozens of economists, including Samuelson. Finally, Paul Cootner published a book in 1964 that discussed randomness in prices. While his own work focused on futures markets in the vein of Keynes' conclusions, his book also included a translation of Bachelier's results. This tide of results begged for more formalism in the interplay between prices and information. Within the emerging void jumped Samuelson with an article entitled "Proof that Properly Anticipated Prices Fluctuate Randomly." On its publication, the random walk became associated with what would soon be known as the efficient market hypothesis, and Bachelier's work began to be more properly appreciated.

9
The Theory

Paul Samuelson, in a foreword to the full translation of Louis Bachelier's *Theory of Speculation: The Origins of Modern Finance*, stated:

> [The] discovery or rediscovery of Louis Bachelier's 1900 Sorbonne thesis, "Théorie de la spéculation," began only in the middle of the twentieth century, and initially involved a dozen or so postcards sent out from Yale by the late Jimmie Savage ... in paraphrase, the postcard's message said, approximately, "Do any of you economist guys know about a 1914 French book on the theory of speculation by some French professor named Bachelier?" ...
>
> [O]pportunistically, I suggested replacing Bachelier's absolute Gaussian distribution by "geometric" Brownian motion based on log-Gaussian distributions. Independently, the astronomer M.F.M. Osborne made the same suggestion.[34]

In an interview with Samuelson and his former prodigy, Robert Merton, Samuelson told the story of how he discovered the work of Louis Bachelier. Even before he received that fateful postcard from Leonard Jimmie Savage that elevated the discipline's awareness of Bachelier, Samuelson was aware of Bachelier's work. He also had an almost life-long interest in price dynamics and was familiar with the analyses of commodity futures prices by Holbrook Working and Maurice Kendall who concluded that such a time-series plot appeared much like a random walk.

At first, economists balked at the seeming random pattern of prices that Working and Kendall observed. After all, economists are almost bred to look for patterns in data and are especially receptive to the presumption that one could comprehend and model, and hence predict, markets. Samuelson had a different reaction. Perhaps the apparent randomness of markets was precisely because markets were incredibly insightful and efficient in gleaning all available information and incorporating it into the market price. Working and Kendall may have not been observing that markets were random and haphazard, but rather that after all the analysis and dynamics are complete, there remains nothing intelligent and discernible, much like the lack of information content in the white noise in between radio stations on the FM dial. Anything that one imagined could happen has already been factored into the market price.

Samuelson pondered this pattern for years, vacillating between his concern that he was merely stating the obvious and his belief that he was on to something fundamentally important. Matthew Fontaine Maury Osborne's provocative article in 1959 that it may be relative prices that are random piqued his interest. Then, he had a conversation with Stanislaw Ulam, a mathematician who had also worked out the process of Monte Carlo studies with John von Neumann, one of the originators of game theory, when both had been working on the Manhattan Project. Ulam asked Samuelson about Bachelier and his popular book (in French) on game theory, which could be found in the MIT library. Samuelson could not find the game theory book, but he did find Bachelier's thesis. He persuaded his friend Paul Cootner to translate the book.

Born in Logansport, Indiana, Cootner (1930–1978) was a financial economist who earned a PhD in industrial economics from MIT in 1953 and had joined the finance faculty of the MIT Sloan School of Management in 1959. His empirical work was on the random walk, which resulted in his seminal book called *The Random Character of Stock Market Prices*, which included the first English translation of Bachelier's work.[35]

Following his discovery of Bachelier's work, Samuelson immediately recognized the random walk paradigm as most significant. He noted that the square root result derived by Bachelier had been postulated by others for decades and had even been described in eighteenth-century books written by Spanish Jewish refugees writing on the financial markets in Amsterdam.

Let us derive this result. To see it, we apply this principle of a relative Wiener process as Osborne had postulated for financial markets. In that case, we take the proportional changes in a security price as following a Wiener process with diffusion σ and drift (or growth) μ:

$$\frac{dS}{S} = \sigma dX + \mu dt$$

Normally, in deterministic calculus, this left-hand side would simply be d(ln(S)). However, the relationship is more complicated in a stochastic world. To discover the relationship, we can apply Itô's lemma. Let us first postulate such an exponential function of a Wiener process as $F(W,t) = e^W$. Then, Itô's lemma tells us that:

$$dF = \beta e^W dX + (a e^W + \beta^2 e^W) dt$$
$$= \beta F dX + (a F + \beta^2 F) dt$$

This implies that:

$$\frac{dF}{F} = \left(a - \frac{\beta^2}{2} \right) dt - \beta dX$$

which is just like our equation for the relative drift of a security price only if we let $\sigma = \beta$ and $\mu = \alpha + \beta^2/2$. Then we can conclude that the growth or drift coefficient is $\mu - \sigma^2/2$ and the diffusion remains σ. The determination of how the relative securities price evolves can then be inserted into the parameters in the diffusion process to find the expected path of the security price, subject to the known value S_0 at the initial time $t = 0$. We are left with what is now known as the familiar probability distribution function for an asset $S(t)$:

$$S(t) = \frac{1}{\sigma S \sqrt{2\pi t}} e^{-\left(\log\left(\frac{S_t}{S_0}\right) - \left(\mu - \frac{\sigma^2}{2}\right)t \right)^2 \Big/ 2\sigma^2 t}$$

Samuelson held a keen interest both in the mechanics of such stochastic diffusion processes and in the implications of the Wiener process on the market's reaction to information.

The first inkling of an efficient market

In his "Proof that Properly Anticipated Prices Fluctuate Randomly,"[36] Samuelson put forth a simple proposition: in an informationally efficient market, prices must incorporate all information available to market participants. This implies that it must not be possible to forecast any additional price changes. Five years later, Eugene Fama more economically stated Samuelson's result by saying that "prices fully reflect all available information."

The mathematics of Samuelson's result, at least in this case, is not particularly sophisticated. More relevant is the intuition that Samuelson had formed over a lifetime of pondering securities prices. By 1965, when he argued that a market has the martingale property, he had turned 50 years of age. However, in the study of the dynamics of prices, he was just getting started.

Years later, Samuelson recalled his intellectual process with his prodigy Merton. He related how he would visit New York City and make a visit to a neighborhood of Manhattan where options traders were concentrated. He could not view options trading in his home town of Chicago because options trading was considered illegal gambling there. The trading of options in New York was pursued by a group of mostly European Jews who wondered why this young Jewish boy from Chicago would come by and ask so many questions.

Samuelson explained that he was trying to understand the science of options. He related how he started by trying to understand the simpler option that cannot be exercised until the settlement date, as opposed to the more customary option that could be exercised at any time. Herbert Filer, the subject of his inquiries, one day said that it required a European quality of mind to understand options. In response, Samuelson labeled simpler options as European options, and the more sophisticated options as American options, to credit his new homeland.

Through this exercise, Samuelson became convinced of something that economists were increasingly taking as a matter of faith. One could not systematically beat the market. So strong was his belief that when Edward Thorp and Sheen Kassouf published their popular book *Beat the Market*[37] in 1967, which argued that warrants could be used to consistently earn a profit on Wall Street, he wrote an indignant review with a recollection of memories of his family's loss of a small fortune in Florida real estate in the Roaring Twenties and his own nerve-wracking attempts to invest in options and warrants. From his life experiences, he concluded that there could be no perfect hedge.

The great discoveries

Ironically, it was Samuelson's unwillingness to consider a perfect hedge that could earn a safe interest rate that prevented him from discovering the Black-Scholes formula half a dozen years before Fischer Black, Myron Scholes, and Robert Merton formulated their great insights. He was teasingly close, though. In fact, two papers in one volume of a relatively obscure journal in 1965 changed everything, even if Samuelson is not generally credited with either the discovery of the options pricing formula or the efficient market hypothesis.

Samuelson amassed a lifetime of accolades and is still considered one of the top three market theorists of all time, if not at the very apex. However, he argued that a discovery is rarely an idea out of the mind of one unique individual. Sir Isaac Newton and Gottfried Leibniz arrived at calculus at the same time, and the biologists Charles Darwin (1809–1882) and Alfred Russel Wallace (1823–1913) both simultaneously arrived at the notion of the survival of the fittest. When Samuelson wrote in 1965 that a formula derived from the random walk and diffusion processes allowed the pricing of warrants, and, in a second article in the same issue of the journal, determined that markets are efficient, there were others on the verge of arriving at the same conclusions.

In fact, Samuelson never believed that prices follow a random walk in the same way that Einstein observed that a molecule colliding with other molecules from any direction displays a random walk. Rather, in "Proof that Properly Anticipated Prices Fluctuate Randomly," he nonetheless demonstrated that an efficient market would generate the same sort of martingale memoryless property that also described a random walk.

While the random walk was an enticingly simple way of looking at the problem of white noise in an efficient market, it is not for the reasons most people suggest. Instead, Samuelson asserted that self-interested investors individually take best advantage of every morsel of available information in their efforts to earn a profit. This process eliminates all profit opportunities and leaves only random and unknowable events to buffet prices. In the limit that perfectly arbitraged markets are frictionless and trading is costless, there is nothing that can be further anticipated in prices, and only randomness and unpredictability remain.

Samuelson's innovation that arbitrage is a condition of equilibrium was of course not completely novel in finance. However, his characterization of arbitrage as a force that defines equilibrium was perhaps more strident and fundamental in his thinking and, of course, among proponents of the Chicago School where he spent his formative years as an undergraduate student.

It is this condition that very nearly brought Samuelson to the Black-Scholes equation in 1965, well before Black and Scholes arrived at their conclusion. Actually, in his 1965 paper on warrant pricing, he noted that he had been thinking about such issues since at least 1953. His innovations over the Bachelier result were to treat geometric Brownian motion, which means that relative prices follow Brownian motion rather than Bachelier's absolute prices, to allow the returns on an underlying stock to grow at an exogenous rate α and to permit the warrant to earn an exogenous return β. While he chose to treat warrants, the right to purchase a new future issue of a stock, rather than options so that the model need not be complicated by such extraneous issues as the issuing of dividends, his results were tantalizingly similar to the discovery by Black and Scholes.

Samuelson's treatment paralleled that of these successors, and his predecessors Bachelier and Einstein for his geometric Brownian motion. Like his predecessors, he too realized that the formulation resulted in a second-order differential equation that was identical to the well-known diffusion process. However, he did not take his analysis that one final step. While he provided a general solution for various growth rates β and α for the warrant and underlying stock returns, respectively, he did not make these parameters endogenous by imposing the obvious arbitrage condition. Under arbitrage, if there could be a perfect hedge, then α and β would converge to the prevailing risk-free rate of return that Black and Scholes both reasoned. Had he done so, he would be known as the person who discovered the single most fundamental equation of modern finance.

Samuelson retained a nagging frustration over his inability to close his model. In the late 1960s, the brilliant young Robert Merton had arrived at MIT's graduate school with a California Institute of Technology applied mathematics Master's degree in hand and was assigned as a research assistant to Samuelson. Merton was given a copy of the warrants paper and set to work to close the model, together with Samuelson's additional intuition about the arbitrage condition. Merton succeeded in completing Samuelson's results and making them much more general, compact, and elegant. In fact, he did so more generally than his two other MIT faculty and associates, Black and Scholes. However, Black and Scholes did not have the pedigree of Samuelson or his prodigy – in fact, nobody did – and had trouble getting their results published. In deference, Merton delayed publication of his superior results until Black and Scholes could publish their work.

This act of gracious deference did not go entirely unrewarded or unrecognized, though. Merton shared the Nobel Prize with Scholes a few years after Black died at a prematurely young age. However, the famous equation is forever known as the Black-Scholes equation rather than its more accurate name, the Bachelier-Samuelson-Black-Scholes-Merton equation.

When asked about that timing in his interview with Merton years later, Samuelson commented that he did not believe that Black and Scholes completely understood the calculus or the differential equation and solution they ultimately stumbled upon. However, he did offer a somewhat patronizing but nonetheless accurate observation. When we see the final equation, in its brilliance and accuracy, it is natural to assume that it appeared in a moment of great clarity, intuition, insight, and wisdom. Yet rarely is the science of discovery so perfect. Sometimes, perhaps even often, it is simply sheer dumb luck. He noted "We are all sleep walkers when we are doing original work. Later, everything is cut and dried."[38] Perhaps. If so, though, Samuelson could walk in his sleep much better than just about any peer could walk fully awake.

10
Discussion and Applications

Paul Samuelson's result that prices follow a random walk buffeted only by random and unknowable forces once arbitrage has extracted value from every last bit of price disparity clearly created a school of its own, and perhaps even a faith, among financial theorists. Believers have constructed myriad reasons why it must be true as a matter of faith. Still others believe that markets are not as perfect as the arbitrage proponents insist. Both can cite many examples and scenarios to "prove" their case. However, their protestations seem to do little but preach to the converted and seem to have little effect on changing the minds of the skeptics.

For instance, in a pair of seminal papers, Nobel laureate Joseph Stiglitz with his colleague Sanford Grossman in 1980 had extended Grossman's 1976 result that argued that even the concept of market perfection is an impossibility.[39] We know by the billions of dollars spent on research each year that the gathering of information is costly. A rational agent will continue to invest in information to the point that the cost of a bit of additional information gathering merely equals the benefits that this bit of information will generate, perhaps by generating some arbitrage profits. However, as the price of an asset approaches its "true value," in Bachelier's words, the benefits of information accumulation decline rapidly, and so would the information research. In fact, if information is always costly to produce, disseminate, or absorb and process, prices generally do not converge fully to their true values. Alternately, if prices are correct, there is no return to the investment in determining whether prices have departed from their fundamental values.

While Louis Bachelier's notion of a true value remained a lone voice in the woods for more than six decades, other researchers began to state eloquently the notion of a true value in the reflective wake of the Wall

Street Crash of 1929. For instance, Benjamin Graham and David Dodd in their classic book *Security Analysis* (1934) wrote:

> [An analyst] is concerned with the intrinsic value of the security and, more particularly, with the discovery of discrepancies between the intrinsic value and the market value. We must recognize, however, that intrinsic value is an elusive concept. In general terms it is understood to be that value which is justified by the facts, e.g., the asset earnings, dividends, definite projects, as distinct, let us say, from market quotations established by artificial manipulation or distorted by psychological excesses.[40]

In fact, participants in financial markets may include the fundamentalists who believe their arbitrageur efforts make the market converge to equilibrium, and hedge fund managers who sometimes profess that they trade in ways to add noise, to create price inefficiencies, and then to try to profit from the inefficiencies they produce. Meanwhile, technical analysts, or chartists, and all other investors go along with the ride. Clearly, each group has a different sense of how markets work, while some wonder whether markets are, by their nature, a paradox.

We can look at this paradox in an alternative way. Only sufficiently large price gaps around a true value will create the incentive to carry out the market research to determine how to profit from the price gap. In other words, there must be a perceived price inefficiency to invest in the information to determine that there is a price inefficiency.

In fact, Fischer Black pondered this dilemma and concluded that inefficiencies and price gaps are sometimes manufactured to produce profit opportunities for what he called "noise traders," who trade on random noise and the gyrations of random walks rather than on true information. Presumably, such trades are bound to lose money, at least according to the arbitrage proponents. These losses are then transferred to the smart traders who make their investment decisions based on their superior, perhaps purchased, information as to the true price of a security.

One version of this theory might be in the differentiation of rational money and emotional money. Rational money flows to those trades that reveal to the smart investor price inefficiencies and profits to be had. On the other hand, emotional money is whimsical, prone to jump on the bandwagon of a popular stock, and aims to buy low and sell high, but, for one reason or another, seems to buy high and sell low. In this view of the market, the smart money always gets ahead and always at the expense of everyone else.

These less well-informed or less sophisticated traders may also suffer from imperfect or limited access to capital, may make trades based on tax consequences as much as for price disparities, and may even suffer from margin calls when they try to ride out some of the greater spikes in the random walk and instead find themselves involuntarily removed from the market. Milton Friedman viewed this culling of emotional investors from markets as an example of financial Darwinism that would inevitably improve market efficiency and rationality.

To the efficient market proponents, the smart money investors trade based on their analyses of market and security fundamentals, as first described eloquently by the Harvard Business School graduate John Burr Williams in the 1930s. These investors take advantage of the technical analysts who seek to discover patterns in price movements. The efficiency proponents see the residuals of price movements as mere white noise, while their technical analysis nemeses see pictures in the white noise. The two groups talk across each other, and each group remains completely baffled about the naivety of the other.

An alternative view believes that these residuals will not be mere white noise even if prices have reflected all available information. For instance, Nobel laureate Robert Lucas (1978)[41] and Stephen LeRoy (1973)[42] created plausible scenarios in which prices fully incorporate all information but still behave unlike a random walk.

Even the creation of more complete markets cannot eliminate all market imperfections. Let us postulate that there is a market that does not converge to its true value because sufficient random noise makes it impossible for all observers to come to an agreement on its true value. This difference in beliefs can then create a market in which individuals "bet" until they arrive at a common set of beliefs. Such markets abound. For instance, bookmakers will adjust a point spread in a sports game until there are equal amounts of bets for those on each side of the spread. Thus, we all, at least on the margin, arrive at a median consensus on the best information.

The extensive creation of costless side markets to capitalize on each bit of information or, in its logical conclusion, every possible state of nature would be expensive in itself, and many such markets would be thin indeed. Therefore, there are costs associated with too many markets, in transactions, lack of economies of scale in information, and in market thinness and hence monopolization. The number of markets necessarily remains finite. But then, each market must be incomplete because it is not defined over every possible state.

These damning critiques of Samuelson's arbitrageur are especially apparent in financial markets. The entire industry reveals that, on the one hand, it does not believe that markets are always efficient, otherwise it would not invest billions each year in financial research. On the other hand, the paradigm of the arbitrageur is almost universally invoked in financial theory. And one could view the vast sums spent on sophisticated modeling as redemption of the notion that potential arbitrage profits exist. These institutions are designed to wring arbitrage profits to zero and hence make markets more efficient by doing so. Moreover, the very high entry costs to compete in the club of smart money confer upon arbitrageurs some barriers to entry that likely reward them with profits unattainable by lesser investors.

Implications of a rejection of the random walk hypothesis

While it is very difficult to prove that the market is efficient, or perfectly arbitraged, it is at least a simpler task to show the converse. To disprove the hypothesis, it is only necessary to establish that the noise of price movements shows some sort of discernible pattern. Samuelson labeled the alternatives to white noise as either red or blue noise. He noted that such noise could appear to be serially correlated. For instance, a stock could rise and fall in streaks, just as does the economy or the batting average of a baseball player. Alternately, there could be an autoregressive tendency to bring deviations back toward the mean. Actually, we find that analyses designed to detect such time-dependent tendencies, in refutation of the efficient market hypothesis, are more or less successful. Tests have not yet been successful in refuting the principles that flow from Samuelson's arbitrageur paradigm.

In fact, even Samuelson implored the reader to avoid reading too much into his postulate that the price anticipates all information. First, in a tip of the hat to his friend and colleague Leonard Jimmie Savage, he allowed that, just as beauty is in the eye of the beholder, so is value. Just as bookmakers set point spreads or payouts to find a center of mass among the beliefs of gamers, a price merely mediates the beliefs (rational or not) of those who follow a given security. He even closes his paper postulating that prices fluctuate randomly by noting:

> One should not read too much into the established theorem. It does not prove that actual competitive markets work well. It does not say that speculation is a good thing or that randomness of price changes would be a good thing. It does not prove that anyone who makes

money in speculation is ipso facto deserving of the gains or even that he has accomplished something good for society or for anyone but himself. All or none of these may be true, but that would require a different investigation.[43]

Samuelson may have been an original high priest of the information content of prices, or the lack of information, once arbitrage has taken place. However, he remained a skeptic, perhaps, about what that meant more precisely. Indeed, in his companion piece on warrant pricing in the same journal issue, he seemed unwilling to take the arbitrage principle as far as his mentee Robert Merton was willing to go with it.

In the early 1960s, though, others were considering an expanded efficient market hypothesis with even greater faith and conviction. They were successful in adding to the discussion greater nuance to the meaning of market efficiency. We shall discuss this more nuanced approach later in these pages through the eyes and insights first of Eugene Fama and then of Stephen Ross.

11
The Nobel Prize, Life, and Legacy

Paul Samuelson is not the definitive economist known most broadly among laypeople. In the latter half of the twentieth century, the names of John Maynard Keynes or Milton Friedman were more familiar. At the start of the new millennium, we have perhaps heard of Ben Bernanke and Paul Krugman. In the first half of the twentieth century, Professor Irving Fisher was well known. Among finance theorists, William Sharpe, Fischer Black, Myron Scholes, Michael Jensen, and Eugene Fama might be more familiar, perhaps because each, except Fama, had their name immortalized in the names of famous equations or coefficients. However, among financial and economic scholars, Samuelson stands alone, much like Albert Einstein might among physicists, or Robert Goddard and Werner von Braun among rocketeers.

By 1992, Samuelson himself had begun to recognize the tremendous contributions of great minds to finance theory within the decision sciences by their increasing recognition by the Nobel Prize Committee.[44] Given his status in both economics and finance, and his seminal work that began in the 1930s with his PhD thesis and continued until his death, it would seem natural that Samuelson would be awarded with a Nobel Prize for the firm mathematical foundations he provided for both the twin disciplines of finance and economics.

Samuelson was awarded the Nobel Prize in only the second year of its existence of the Nobel Prize in Economics and Finance. While the Nobel Foundation has awarded a prize for achievements in physics, chemistry, physiology or medicine, literature, and for contributions to peace every year since 1901, the economics prize is relatively new. The Prize, funded by a foundation in memory of the Norwegian inventor of dynamite, Alfred Nobel, expanded on the 300th anniversary of Sweden's central bank to include an award, beginning in 1969, to recognize achievements in the economic sciences.

The first awards of Nobel Prizes in Economics were somewhat controversial. Not all have agreed that studies in economics and finance make the same contributions to our social welfare as do the other award categories. Some of the first few recipients of the economic sciences award also included Milton Friedman and Friedrich August Hayek (1899–1992), two controversial figures in economics who advocated for unfettered markets when free enterprise has been blamed in some circles for its excesses and displacements. In 1969, the first Sveriges Riksbank Prize in Economic Sciences in Memory of Alfred Nobel was selected in a most palatable way with regard to domestic politics. The Norwegian economist Ragnar Anton Kittil Frisch (1895–1973) and the Dutch economist Jan Tinbergen (1903–1994) were awarded for their work on econometrics and their definition of the dual fields of microeconomics and macroeconomics. These two scholars were hardly the best-known economists among laypeople, or the most widely read economists among their colleagues. However, the second awardee, Paul Samuelson in 1970, was highly prominent among economists.

Before the American academic ascendency beginning in the run-up to and the aftermath of the Second World War, most awardees in the traditional Nobel disciplines were European. After the American ascendency, and for the period since the creation of the economics award, the recipients are predominantly American or associated with American universities. This continental shift has created a peculiarity for the announcement of the Prize.

The prizes for the various disciplines are announced each fall over a three-week period on the day that each committee elects from the nominations its respective awardees. Those who have been considered by the nominating committees typically know that their name has been put forward. Indeed, groups typically campaign for the nomination and election of their favored scholars. This process is relatively public and widely known among scholars at the apex of their disciplines. However, awardees do not know that the Nobel Committees have chosen them until the announcement is made public and the Committee makes a courtesy call to the recipient. Recipients who live in the Eastern Time Zone of the USA usually receive the courtesy telephone call before 6:00 am local time. Prominent scholars know when the Committee meets, so they can reasonably assume that a call that early in the morning must be either very good news from the Committee or very grave news from a family member.

When Paul Samuelson received his call in the fall of 1970, his wife was worried that one of their children had had an accident. The Committee spokespeople usually immediately qualify their call to let the recipient know they have good or interesting news for the recipient. In this case, the caller asked Samuelson how it felt to win a Nobel Prize. He responded that he was grateful that his hard work was recognized. His wife later told him that she thought that answer sounded rather pretentious.[45]

The Nobel Committee made the following announcement:

> The Sveriges Riksbank Prize in Economic Sciences in Memory of Alfred Nobel 1970 was awarded to Paul A. Samuelson "for the scientific work through which he has developed static and dynamic economic theory and actively contributed to raising the level of analysis in economic science."[46]

His award was for a vast body of seemingly all-encompassing work. It spoke of foundational and fundamental contributions to the economic sciences, and it specifically spoke to the contributions that his thesis and early textbook made and his career added to our understanding of the scientific and mathematical method in the discipline.

Samuelson contributed across a wide swathe of economics and finance, but invariably maintained a rigor and mathematical sophistication that continually raised the analytic bar. In his seminal 1947 book, *Foundations of Economic Analysis*, he firmly established the scientific method within the decision sciences. He advocated for the use of the compact and universal language of mathematics for economics and finance, and, through his life's work, established the grammar and vocabulary for this language within the discipline.

He also introduced the notion of maximizing behavior and the dual problem of profit or utility maximization and cost minimization. He strived to treat systems and derive stable equilibria. From the characterization of equilibrium, he created the method of comparative statics in which one may explore the interrelationship between variables as the broader system remains in equilibrium. Moreover, he firmly established the paradigms of preference theory and of welfare economics that we continue to use today.

His work cannot be summarized quite so compactly. A five-volume set includes almost 400 of Samuelson's academic papers and omits some others. They cover almost every imaginable area of economics and many areas of finance, and they do so with a combination of rigor and style that is invariably unsurpassed.

Samuelson's contributions to finance alone are spectacular. He used and helped disseminate the "overlapping generations model" that Maurice Allais had developed and subsequently inspired the Life Cycle

Model used in finance by Franco Modigliani.[47] In a single issue of the *Society for Industrial and Applied Mathematics* (SIAM) journal described earlier, he published two remarkable papers that explored options pricing and the mathematical formality of arbitrage and the efficient market hypothesis. He also tipped his hat to Harry Markowitz's Modern Portfolio Theory and described financial diversification in his 1967 works "Efficient Portfolio Selection for Pareto-Lévy Investments"[48] and "General Proof that Diversification Pays."[49]

Samuelson remained at MIT for the remainder of his academic life. During his illustrious career, he was a recipient of numerous awards. He was a member of the American Academy of Arts and Sciences and he presided over the Econometric Society in 1951, the American Economic Association in 1961, and the International Economic Association from 1965 to 1968. He was also admitted to the American Philosophical Society, was a foreign member to the British Academy, and was given membership to the Harvard Society of Fellows.

Samuelson's civic duty included the US National Resources Planning Board from 1941 to 1943, consulting with the US Treasury Department from 1945 to 1952, and the US Council of Economic Advisers for both the Kennedy and Johnson administrations from 1961 to 1966.

He was also a member of the Phi Beta Kappa Society and was a recipient of the 1947 John Bates Clark Medal, and a Guggenheim Fellowship in 1948. He prided himself on his writing – he was a celebrated columnist for *Newsweek* magazine from 1966 to 1981 – and his inclusion on President Nixon's enemies list.

Samuelson's professional, spiritual, and familial partnership with Marion Crawford Samuelson ended when she died of cancer at the age of 62 in 1978. He subsequently remarried and was survived by Risha Clay Eckaus. When he died on December 13, 2009 at the age of 94, he left behind two daughters, Jane Raybould and Margaret Crawford-Samuelson, and four sons, William and the triplets John, Paul, and Robert. His brother Robert Summers is Professor Emeritus of Economics at the University of Pennsylvania, as is Robert's wife, Anita Summers, the sister of Nobel Laureate Kenneth Arrow. One of their children, and Paul Samuelson's nephew, is Larry Summers, who has served various cabinet and economic advising positions in the Clinton and Obama administrations and was the President of Harvard University. He was also survived by 15 grandchildren. There is little doubt that Samuelson and his progeny represented the first family of American economics and finance, a family dynasty not unlike the Bernoulli family of mathematics fame from the eighteenth century.

Section 3
Eugene Fama's Efficient Market Hypothesis

Paul Samuelson was the first to mathematically formalize the implications of arbitrage and the incorporation of all available information into the price of a security. He then deduced that any remaining variation in prices must follow some variation of a geometric random walk. At the same time, another great mind was formulating a notion that we call the efficient market hypothesis. This was Eugene Fama.

12
The Early Years

Malden, Massachusetts and nearby Melrose, Stoneham, and Medford are working-class towns north of Boston known early in the twentieth century for their population of immigrants to America and for the sports legends produced by neighborhood heroes. The streets and sand lots were where local boys played baseball, basketball, and street hockey. These towns had a tradition of hard work, of pride in their local boys and girls, and of healthy sporting competition between the high schools in the area.

It was near this area that the grandparents of Eugene (Gene) Francis Fama settled when they arrived from Sicily early in the late 1890s. Guy (Gaetano) Fama and his young bride Santa (née Rossard) made their way to the North End of Boston, still known today as Little Italy. Soon, the family settled down at 553 Main Street in Charlestown, across the Charles River from the North End, where Guy held down a job as a barber. They were a good Catholic family and had many children: Antony, Elizabeth, Leo, and Frances, with Francis Fama, born in 1910, in the middle, followed by Joseph, Morris, and Mary.

Guy and Santa Fama's fourth child, Francis, met his future wife Angelina Saraneco in the North End of Boston, where her father Vincent and mother Gaitna had started a family grocery and convenience store soon after they too arrived from Italy. Francis and Angelina decided to raise their family in Malden, Massachusetts, then as now an urban community of just under 60,000 people across the Mystic River about five miles north of the North End of Boston. There the young couple gave birth to Eugene, on Valentine's Day, February 14, 1939. By then, "Gene" was a second-generation American boy of Italian ancestry with the solid working-class values of Malden.

Figure 12.1   The family tree of Eugene Fama (1939–)

As was characteristic of boys in his neighborhood, young Eugene thrived on sports. While he was only 5'8" tall, he played basketball, came in second place in the high jump at a Massachusetts state track and field competition, and participated in a state championship football team and a baseball team that made the state semi-finals twice. His high school, Malden Catholic, had a strong tradition both of rigorous education and of sports.

One of Eugene's proudest accomplishments in a life of academic accomplishments was in his permanent place in the Malden Catholic High School's athletic hall of fame. In the summer 1956 season, as he prepared for university in the fall, his high school baseball team had a record of 14 wins and two losses, and was tied for second place in the Catholic league. He was a Catholic All-Star and shared the captainship with his classmate Joseph Mahoney as they made the state tournament. He fondly recalled this experience and looked up to his teachers and especially his high school baseball coach, Brother Firmin. At the age of 17, he entered university early, determined to teach high school French and Italian and to coach baseball himself someday.

While Malden bordered Cambridge, the home of two of the best universities in the world, aspiring local kids often set their sights on Tufts University in nearby Medford. Tufts, too, is a top university in the shadow of nearby Ivy League schools, and promised the young and academically advanced 17-year-old Eugene an excellent education toward his goal of high school teaching someday. His Malden Catholic High School's tradition of high-quality education and extracurricular sports had inspired Eugene to be a sports coach upon graduation.

However, not long after he entered Tufts in 1956, he had a change of heart. His original determination to teach romance languages waned and he decided after two years to take his first economics course. At about that time, he also decided to marry his high school sweetheart, Sally Ann Dimeco.

Certainly, Eugene was enthralled with Sally Ann. He was also inspired by his economics teachers at Tufts, and changed his major from the romance languages and Voltaire to the finance philosophies of Irving Fisher. He thrived in economics and received the superior grades necessary to attend the prestigious University of Chicago in the early 1960s to further his emerging fascination with the study of finance.

Despite having been trained mostly at Harvard, Fama's Tufts professors actually encouraged him to look to Chicago's business school if he was serious about economics and finance. Fama was sure he wanted to earn a PhD from a great school and actually viewed the diploma as a license to have the flexibility to pursue his sports interests that had to be temporarily placed aside when he married after his sophomore year at Tufts and had his first child. In his mind, his sports aspirations had been delayed but would not be denied. Later, he commented to Richard Roll in an American Finance Association History of Finance series that he had hoped and had found that graduate school was actually less difficult than he had experienced in his rigorous Tufts program.[50]

Fama became determined to attend Chicago even after he was accepted at other schools in the spring of 1960, yet he had not heard from the University of Chicago as late as April. In a fit of courage, he called up the Dean of Students at Chicago and discovered that they did not receive his application. His perseverance paid off. While on the telephone, Dean Metcalf told him that there was an unused scholarship at Chicago reserved for a qualified Tufts student. This scholarship paved the way for a relationship with the University of Chicago that, but for a two-year period of leave to teach and research in Belgium, has been maintained ever since.

Even during his graduation year at Tufts, Fama discovered a keen interest in financial markets. One of his economics professors, Harry Ernst, specialized in stock market forecasting and asked Fama to come up with ideas to better forecast the market. The various strategies Fama developed seemed to work very well in back testing on past data, but failed when subjected to out-of-sample tests. In his second year in Chicago's economics program, he recalled his Tufts experience with market strategies as he pondered some of the presentations at Chicago's econometrics workshop by Harry Roberts, Lester Tesler, and the new arrival in the program, Merton Miller, who would go on to win a Nobel Prize for his work with Franco Modigliani, another Chicago teaching alumnus.

In the late 1950s and early 1960s, Benoit Mandelbrot, the applied mathematician already well known not only for chaos theory but also for his novel work in financial securities pricing, was at that time exploring the observed distribution of securities prices. Mandelbrot was a frequent visitor to the Chicago campus and Fama, as a young PhD student, had the pleasure of long walks on campus with him, where they would discuss an emerging consensus that financial market data did not seem to fit the prescripts of the theory at the time. These discussions were reinforced by Fama's mentor, Miller, and by his colleagues Harry Roberts and Lester Telser. Roberts in particular was an excellent statistician and instilled upon Fama a fascination with empirical studies that he would maintain throughout his career.

There remained one limitation in that era in the early 1960s, though. Computing power remained insufficient to make the calculations necessary to implement the finance state-of-the-science, Harry Markowitz's Modern Portfolio Theory. In addition, William Sharpe, John Lintner, and others were yet to produce the simpler CAPM interpretation of the Modern Portfolio Theory that was capable of pricing a single security instead of an entire market portfolio and required much less computing power.

At that time, the Chicago Business School was beginning to embrace the digital age. Miller, in particular, was an early adopter, with the assistance of another young graduate student at the time with more computing experience named Myron Scholes. With leading-edge computer power at hand and with the development by IBM of its 300 series mainframes in the early 1960s, more tools were now available to budding financial econometricians. There were so many interesting questions that would benefit from this convolution of tools, and Fama was the right mind in the right place at the right time, with a most rigorous Tufts Bachelor's degree in hand and with a critical mass of assembled scholars at Chicago that may have only been equaled in terms of quality by the scholars at MIT at the time.

Toward the end of their second year, it was expected that PhD students should be honing in on a thesis topic. Fama recalled his market price analysis experiences while at Tufts and proposed to explore for himself whether Mandelbrot's belief that price distributions display fatter tails, or more extreme price departures, than predicted by the normal distribution was indeed well founded. Researchers had observed for decades that these price distributions seemed to violate the assumed Gaussian distribution that results when the unexplained residuals of prices follow a random walk. Fama began to explore whether these residuals are also serially correlated rather than random and uncorrelated over time. This exploration became the basis for his PhD thesis.

Actually, this topic was but one of five potential topics Fama had identified. He trusted the intuition of his supervisor, Miller, who subsequently rejected four of the topics. However, the last topic would be Fama's graduate school home run.

13
The Times

As Eugene Fama researched and prepared his PhD thesis at the University of Chicago under the supervision of Merton Miller, he sought to resolve an increasingly problematic empirical observation at odds with emerging theory. By the early 1960s, especially after the analysis by Matthew Fontaine Maury Osborne in 1959, it had become accepted that the logarithm of securities prices was the appropriate measure of analysis. However, the resulting distribution of unexplained price variations under this transformation remained a subject of debate, and the serial correlation of observations that follow this distribution was a topic of growing interest.

Forces of nature often follow a normal distribution. The normal distribution will occur if the forces that buffet a particle, for instance, are each drawn from a distribution that need not be itself normal but that maintains a constant uniform variance, or second moment. It would be academically comforting if relative price movements also followed such a pattern. However, Benoit Mandelbrot, among others, had argued otherwise.

Mandelbrot's observation

Mandelbrot was born in Warsaw, Poland on November 20, 1924 to a Jewish Lithuanian family of intellectuals and professionals. His mother was a dentist and one of his uncles was a mathematician living in Paris. With the threat of invasion by the Nazis in 1936, the family fled to France. There, Mandelbrot attended the Lycée Rolin preparatory high school (now called the Collège-lycée Jacques-Decour, after the French resistance fighter Jacques Decour). The War disrupted Mandelbrot's studies as the family moved to Tulle, about 500 kilometers south of Paris and twice as far away from the Western Front. In this interim, he was partially self-taught, under the guidance of a local rabbi, but was also able to continue his studies in Lyon and then at the Ecole Polytechnique under Bachelier's one-time nemesis Paul Lévy, upon his return to Paris once the War ended.

In 1947, Mandelbrot left Paris to earn a Master's degree in aeronautics at the California Institute of Technology. Two years later, he returned to Paris to complete a PhD in mathematics at the University of Paris. He defended his thesis in 1952.

In the years before and after his thesis defense, Mandelbrot also performed research at the Centre National de la Recherche Scientifique and spent time with the great mind John von Neumann at the Institute for Advanced Study at Princeton. In 1955, he married Aliette Kagan and in 1958 he moved to the IBM Thomas J. Watson Research Center in Yorktown Heights, New York, where he spent the bulk of his professional career.

His Princeton colleague John von Neumann was a strong influence on Mandelbrot. While Lévy was a pure mathematician, von Neumann was an analytically trained mathematician who turned his considerable ability and intuition to problems ranging from mathematics to physics, economics and finance, fluid dynamics, rocket science, the nuclear bomb, and information theory and early computing. Mandelbrot demonstrated this same mathematic athleticism.

In one of his early explorations, Mandelbrot demonstrated that cotton prices followed a more general, fat-tailed Lévy distribution rather than the traditionally assumed Gaussian distribution. This observed distribution remained stable, as in the Gaussian distribution, in that the sum of many random events still asymptotically generates a regular distribution.

Mandelbrot took this insight still further. He realized that his idea that a series of random events can converge to some sort of regular form could be applied to many different fields, from cosmology to chaos theory, through a methodology he called fractal geometry. He showed that discrete and discontinuous processes in humankind and nature, from the shaping of mountains and coastlines to the clustering of galaxies, the composition of music, the movement of commodity and stock prices, and even Brownian motion, could be considered applications of fractal geometry, of which the Gaussian distribution could be derived as a special case. In his world: "Clouds are not spheres, mountains are not cones, coastlines are not circles, and bark is not smooth, nor does lightning travel in a straight line."[51]

Mandelbrot spent much of his career explaining, applying, and popularizing his new set theory. Then, after 35 years, he left IBM for Yale University in 1993 when the IBM Research Center was disbanded. In 1999, at the age of 75, he became the oldest Yale professor to receive tenure. He retired six years later as the Sterling Professor of Mathematical Sciences. Over his lifetime, he earned many distinctions, including the Wolf Prize for Physics in 1993, the European Geophysical Society's Lewis Fry Richardson Prize in 2000, the Japan Prize in 2003, and the prestigious American Mathematical Society Einstein Lectureship in 2006. He died while under hospice care in Cambridge, Massachusetts on October 14, 2010, less than a month short of his eighty-sixth birthday.

Mandelbrot especially influenced one of his disciples, the young graduate student Eugene Fama at Chicago. Fama's thesis verified Mandelbrot's intuition that the distribution of stock returns had the fat tails Mandelbrot predicted. The significance of this result is that there are more extreme outliers in the residuals of financial market analyses than the Gaussian distribution predicted. Fama's result suggested that dramatic financial market upheavals are more likely than the then-prevailing theory suggested and that returns exhibit time-series properties that defied the prevailing theory.

Fama was researching this thesis for a 1965 publication at the same time as the renowned great mind Paul Samuelson was preparing his work that asserted that the remaining errors, once arbitrage had wrung all profits arising from available information out of securities prices, must follow a Gaussian distribution. In fact, Samuelson's title "Proof that Properly Anticipated Securities Prices Fluctuate Randomly" is strikingly similar to Fama's 1965 publication in the *Selected Papers of the Graduate School of Business at Chicago*, entitled "Random Walks in Stock Market Prices." Samuelson derived a less general property based on arbitrage. Fama produced a more general hypothesis that he called "market efficiency."

In fact, both Samuelson (1965) and Mandelbrot, in his 1966 paper "Forecasts of Future Prices, Unbiased Markets and 'Martingale' Models,"[52] were both arriving at the memoryless martingale conclusion for stock market prices, and for the same reasons. A decade earlier, in 1953, Maurice Kendall was commissioned to look at weekly returns from some London stock market indices and concluded that these returns were statistically independent, consistent with the martingale property. This research line had been most active since the pioneering work of Alfred Cowles III and his funding through the Cowles Commission on statistical and econometric work on securities pricing beginning in the 1930s.

Harry Roberts discovered the same result in 1959 based on the Dow Jones Industrial Average. By the late 1950s, the results were thought to be conclusive.

While Kendall and Roberts demonstrated what was occurring, financial theorists were pondering why. Even if securities prices properly reflect all available information, Samuelson and Mandelbrot postulated that the random walk analogy, in which all changes are identically and independently distributed, was too strong an assumption. Instead, an assertion that a security price reflects all available information may imply that the process is a sub-martingale in that the appropriate price deviations must only exhibit a zero expected value relative to all past information. The bounds of an intuitively appealing and financially appropriate process were beginning to take form. Before Fama, though, there was little discussion of a coherent underlying process that would unite theory and observation.

14
The Theory

In 1889, George Gibson wrote in *The Stock Exchanges of London, Paris and New York* that when "shares become publicly known in an open market, the value which they acquire may be regarded as the judgment of the best intelligence concerning them." More than a century later, the finance literature still grapples with the significance of that simple statement.

Before Eugene Fama's 1965 results, the prevailing literature strived to establish that stock returns were statistically independent over time. Fama pushed knowledge still further. He sought to show that the technique used by chartists, now often called technical analysis, could not be a consistently profitable strategy.

Fama's result was at the time viewed as in support of the martingale property approach as espoused in the random walk. However, his assertion was more general than but not inconsistent with the random walk, just as the random walk was neither as inconsistent nor as general as Lévy stable distributions.

At the time, the random walk model was misunderstood to mean that not only was there no rationale for technical analysis, but there was also no justification for fundamental analysis. Paul Samuelson's (1965) and Benoit Mandelbrot's (1966) analyses demonstrated that the random walk applies only once the analyses of fundamentals are fully incorporated into a security price.

These theorists were instead arguing that efficient financial markets exhibited the "fair game" property in that only with some informational advantage could a trader "beat" the market. Beyond the public information that is incorporated into the market, any additional changes in the price must be random and are equally likely to be positive or negative. This full information and full rationality approach in finance at the time was analogous to the rational expectations school of macroeconomics that was also developing in the 1960s. Its conceptual roots dated back to discussions by Sir John Hicks and Lord Milton Keynes on the rational determination of futures prices, which determined that the market should drift only to track the time value of money and the cost of commodity storage until delivery.

Fama had been pondering these issues during the years leading up to and immediately following his 1965 thesis. However, he did not fully articulate his emerging concept in his thesis, even if he may have alluded to a new concept of efficient capital markets. Then, in 1970, he produced a work that crystallized the by then murky academic discussion. In "Efficient Capital Markets: A Review of Theory and Empirical Work," he brought together the state of finance understanding and created a new sub-discipline that is both profound and has remained controversial ever since.[53]

Fama revolutionized our thinking by defining Samuelson's information properties not based on esoteric mathematics that are inaccessible to most readers but rather on some relatively simple concepts that can be more broadly understood. His resulting definitions now define part of the vocabulary of finance.

To arrive at his definitive definitions of market efficiency, Fama wrote a number of papers up to and including his thesis that nibbled around the edges by invoking a notion of efficiency without stating it outright. He had been exploring a problem implicit in Samuelson's and Mandelbrot's treatment of prices. He had been using econometric techniques to analyze securities prices ever since his Tufts days and was wrestling with a clear formulation of his econometric hypothesis. He realized that a statistical exploration of Samuelson's expected returns will be invalid unless the market is in equilibrium in the strongest sense that sufficient time and trading has allowed all available private and public information to be incorporated into the price. Only then will there be no autocorrelation of expected returns as all serial correlations of returns are exhausted once the price incorporates information and has fully converged to equilibrium.

Fama's realization of the implications of this process arose because of a distinct Chicago innovation. Two University of Chicago professors, James H. Lorie and Lawrence Fisher, received a grant from Merrill Lynch, Pierce, Fenner & Smith to create a database that could allow for the systematic analysis of stock prices. The database, originally stored on large computer tapes beginning in 1960, adjusted stock prices for dividends and splits so that a researcher could model the historical movement of a stock price over time. The Center for Research in Security Prices produced its first CRSP tape in 1963 that included monthly prices for stocks listed on the New York Stock Exchange from 1926 to 1962. Subsequently, the tapes were expanded to include daily prices, and other financial securities have also been included.

The CRSP tapes, and the Compustat database of similar scope, have since become an invaluable finance research. However, the Center founders were concerned early on that researchers would not adopt their tool. They encouraged Fama and some of his Chicago colleagues to use their new tool to analyze stock splits. This application of the CRSP tapes created a new methodology that finance has since called event studies. Such studies could also be used as a methodology that explores how a stock price adjusts to any new piece of information, such as stock splits, dividend payments, or the announcement of any pertinent information.

The methodology induced Fama to contemplate the dynamic process by which the stock price fully digests information. In a perfect market in equilibrium, this process would be infinitely fast. In fact, he realized that information could be incorporated in stages. It also created for him a realization relevant to all security price analyses. The testing of a hypothesis is actually a hypothesis of the process that is the subject of the analysis and the joint hypothesis that the market is in equilibrium. He described the implications of his realization in his seminal 1970 paper.

Efficient capital markets

During the 1960s, as Fama pondered the degree to which financial markets digest information, he was already progressing toward a working version of a definition of an efficient market, consistent with Samuelson's arbitrage market.[54] In 1965, he concluded:

> An "efficient" market is defined as a market where there are large numbers of rational, profit-maximizers actively competing, with each trying to predict future market values of individual securities, and where important current information is almost freely available to all participants. In an efficient market, competition among the many intelligent participants leads to a situation where, at any point in time, actual prices of individual securities already reflect the effects of information based both on events that have already occurred and on events which, as of now, the market expects to take place in the future. In other words, in an efficient market at any point in time the actual price of a security will be a good estimate of its intrinsic value.[55]

By the time his 1970 survey article was published, Fama had refined his analysis still further. He defined strong form efficiency as the most demanding information concept, in which all available public and private information has been incorporated and arbitraged into the price of a publicly traded security. This is the limiting case that requires even those corporate officers with inside knowledge of the strategies of their particular company to have capitalized on that information and purchased or sold the stock until the price has risen or fallen to the point where the stock price fully anticipates their insider knowledge.

Such a strong form of market efficiency is only a limiting case because there may be institutional constraints on insider trading or access to capital constraints that prevent all potential arbitrage from being realized. More common is semi-strong market efficiency, in which market prices reflect only all publicly known information about the overall economy and the fundamentals of a particular asset, perhaps based on financial analyses and corporate news releases.

In the final measure, weak form efficiency, the asset price incorporates all known information on market trading patterns, volume, and other technical measures. In this weak form efficiency, all technical analyses have been arbitraged into the market price. Any measure that points to a higher security price will result in greater excess demand for that security and a rise in price as marginal demanders bid the security away from the marginal suppliers.

Once such technical analyses are exhausted, those who trade on fundamental analysis and all publicly available information arbitrage the security price still higher or lower, again by trading stock between marginal suppliers and demanders, until the price reflects both technical and fundamental analysis.

Most often, strong form efficiency is invoked. If this condition is satisfied, all available information is incorporated into securities prices through technical and fundamental analysis. At that point, even insider traders can no longer profitably trade on their information, and all available information is incorporated into the security price, as assumed in Paul Samuelson's 1965 approach.

The arbitrage process

Long-run market efficiency, in which a security price incorporates all available information, requires a sufficient period of time for all information to be disseminated and incorporated, all necessary access to capital to be exercised, and all trades to be executed. However, the efficient market paradigm is also conceptually useful in the short run. It predicts the short-run direction of response to the release of new information, even if only time will permit the convergence to the new equilibrium.

It also serves an additional function. Because strong-form information efficiency is the limiting case for a perfect market, it acts as a theoretical measure of market imperfections. Rapid convergence toward a stable equilibrium price indicates that capital markets induce sufficient arbitrage trades, information is transparent, and rational trades overcome noisy or technically based trades. The efficient market benchmark is more likely to be realized in mature and widely traded markets with a large number of informed buyers and sellers. Less efficient price convergence in other *thin* markets acts as a measure of relative market inefficiencies.

The intellectual beauty of the efficient market hypothesis was in harmony with the Chicago School's faith in free and efficient markets. The model was paradigm-affirming, even if it was fundamentally unverifiable. It created a gulf between the approaches of the chartists, or technical analysts, and the fundamentalists. It also created a gulf between theorists who claimed that there can be no long-run benefits to investments designed to outsmart the market, and practitioners who made their living trying to do just that. The remainder of this volume is devoted to refinements and criticisms of the efficient market hypothesis. It will begin with discussion and applications of the model.

15
Discussion and Applications

By the late 1960s, a number of scholars began to research the new tools of the CRSP and Compustat tapes and the event study methodology, and implicitly began to explore the implications of the efficient market hypothesis. The resulting sequence of studies seemed to support the semi-strong version of market efficiency in which a security price incorporated all available public information.

Some of these studies suggested that there might be exceptions or anomalies to the efficient market hypothesis. Others appeared to cast doubt on the hypothesis, while still other apparent anomalies were attributed to improper model specification. Such apparent problems as "the January effect," the "alpha effect" for small capitalization stocks, and the under-reaction or over-reaction of a stock price to an information event gave some pause for concern and offered others an opportunity to improve model specifications.

The year before Fama's 1969 event study, Michael Jensen had already concluded that managed funds do not earn a sufficient premium over the market to justify their management fees. This result was consistent with the semi-strong efficient market hypothesis.

Jensen, a student of Fama's at Chicago, had worked in the late 1960s in the analysis of the returns of mutual funds. In one assembly of titans, Fischer Black consulted with Jensen and the great mind William Sharpe, father of the CAPM, to determine whether Yale University's managed investment fund performed consistently better than the market overall. Black brought to the group his unconventional intuition, and a fund-ranking methodology he had constructed with Jack Treynor. Sharpe brought with him the insights of the CAPM, while Jensen, by then a recent graduate from Chicago, brought with him the efficient market hypothesis that Fama had already been formulating.

Upon the completion of the consultative collaboration, the three concluded that Yale's fund did not earn a sufficient premium to pay for its management costs, something Yale was reluctant to hear, and that the efficient market hypothesis prevailed.

Before the Yale endowment study, Jensen had been working with this thesis under the mentorship of Fama. In 1968, he published "The Performance of Mutual Funds in the Period 1945–1964" in the *Journal of Finance*.[56] This study was consistent with the Yale consultancy. Most managed mutual funds fail to outperform the market, especially net of management fees. In the study, he adjusted mutual fund returns for risk, using Sharpe's beta measure from the CAPM and concluded that only a little more than 20 percent of mutual funds outperformed the market on a risk-adjusted basis. His research was highly influential and resulted in significant reflection in the mutual fund industry by placing into the public debate that even highly experienced managers cannot consistently outperform the market. This conclusion troubled professional financial managers and gave credence to the efficient market hypothesis.

In 1969, Fama combined with his former student Jensen, and his colleagues Richard Roll and Lawrence Fisher, to analyze the price adjustment process in financial markets.[57] Their work came in the interim between the pioneering study by Ray Ball and Phillip Brown in 1968[58] and Fama's most famous work on the definition of an efficient market in 1970.

These three papers created a flood of research. Fischer Black and Myron Scholes, and then Robert Merton produced their options pricing theory, based on the assumption of an efficient market, and Scholes produced his study that concluded that a market is efficient, but that there may be some adjustment lags following a relevant market announcement. Paul Samuelson then published a much more refined and extensive analysis, "Mathematics of Speculative Price," based on his 1965 paper, and the Princeton economist Burton G. Malkiel first published his popular and influential book *A Random Walk Down Wall Street*. The efficient market hypothesis floodgates were suddenly thrown open.

Malkiel's work did more to establish the efficient market hypothesis in the investing public's mind than perhaps any other work.[59] In his analysis, he critiqued why technical analysis, managed funds, fundamental analysis, and past performance studies will all fail in the long run to outperform the market. The book also slightly confused the issue in that some came to regard the random walk as synonymous with an efficient market.

By the mid-1970s, there was broad acceptance in the philosophy of the efficient market, at least if one took as an article of faith that money flows toward opportunity. By 1978, Jensen wrote that he believed "there is no other proposition in economics which has more solid empirical evidence supporting it."[60]

Fama observed that if one is to accept the commonly accepted price determination process, in which excess demand (supply) results in a rise (fall) in prices, then one must likewise accept the efficient market hypothesis, at least in its semi-strong form if insider trading is not possible, or its strong form if there is trading on private information. This duality is labeled the "joint hypothesis problem." If there is a gap between a predicted and an actual stock price, it is then impossible to know if the gap is due to an inaccuracy in the model or an imperfection in the market. It is then possible to make additional refinements to the model and include additional explanatory factors, but it remains impossible to know if all such factors have ultimately been incorporated into securities prices. This paradox highlights the tautology of Fama's efficient market hypothesis.

While the analysis of price convergence and market responses is intuitively meaningful, and while one can measure the various factors that help promote market efficiency, there can be no direct measure of market efficiency. The concept is useful in describing a process, and especially for describing factors that undermine efficiency. However, since strong form efficiency requires all insider information to be known, it is not possible to publicly know whether a stock is at its efficient price and whether remaining price movements are truly random or representative of unknowable insider information. The concept is most helpful as a limiting case goal rather than as a test of the correct pricing of a security.

Failure of a competitive equilibrium

However, a year earlier, in 1977, an economist at the University of California and New York University named Avraham Beja described a potential flaw in the efficient market hypothesis.[61] His influential paper, "The Limits of Price Information in Market Processes," and a subsequent paper in 1982 by Paul Milgrom and Nancy Stokey,[62] describe the following problem. In the competitive model for which we generally assume every participant is small, the agent with private information must have a negligible effect on prices if the agent is to remain small relative to the market. Alternately, if the agent has sufficient access to capital to conduct the trades that entirely capitalize on privately held information, the *small relative to the market* assumption is violated.

From an informational perspective, there are a couple of additional conceptual problems. If we assume that a market process is consistent with rational agents, each of whom can view who is trading, but not the private information they may have, and an auctioneer that orchestrates trades at equilibrium, any private information is almost immediately incorporated into the market price. As such, a stockholder who owns the stock will benefit from the private information, but so too will all others who hold the stock. From this perspective, a change in the market price very quickly signals any new privately held information with an efficiency that makes it impossible for the speculative arbitrage profits to be earned. The price fully incorporates any new information, but not necessarily through the mechanism of the arbitrageur.

Failure in the market for information

The late 1970s also saw a dramatic growth in what we now call the rational expectations approach. From this novel perspective, sophisticated market participants incorporate all available information into the market price. In 1976, Sanford Grossman was the first to point out an informational paradox when the collection and action on information is costly. He stated that "informationally efficient price systems aggregate diverse information perfectly, but in doing this the price system eliminates the private incentive for collecting the information."[63] Three years later, he teamed up with a future Nobel Laureate, Joseph Stiglitz, to clearly state the problem. In their paper "On the Impossibility of Informationally Efficient Markets,"[64] the authors noted that if the research of private information is costly and designed to extract profits from the Grossman and Stiglitz result, then the resulting competitive equilibrium confers the same returns on private and public information-holders alike. Those who seek information perform a positive externality by contributing to market discipline and efficiency, but are unable to fully profit from their information investment. This is a classic case of market failure in which investment in private information would then not occur, and full market efficiency is unattainable.

At about the same time, Robert Lucas, another future Nobel Prize winner for his work on the rational expectations model, demonstrated that in a model of rational but also risk-averse agents, the martingale memoryless property is violated. Also in 1978, J. Michael Harrison and David M. Kreps published their paper "Speculative Behavior in a Stock

Market with Heterogeneous Expectations" that posed the "no trade theorem."[65]

To understand the dilemma postulated by Harrison and Kreps, notice that the economic notion of gains of trade arises because individuals have different preferences and are endowed with different income, commodities, and resources. Typically, a traded good is more valuable to the demander than its price, while the supplier values the good at an amount lower than its price. In the exchange, each trader, except perhaps for the marginal trader, has a gain of trade, called the consumer's or producer's surplus, respectively.

However, financial markets are a little different. A financial asset or, basically, a form of money is being exchanged. However, neither party should value that asset any differently if complete capital markets exist. Moreover, in an informationally efficient market, there remain no information differentials in equilibrium. These observations imply that there should be no trades, at least unless one imposes differences upon the model, or heterogeneities among financial traders. Yet, we know that trade occurs because there are bulls and bears on opposite sides of every trade, even though all have access to the same information.

This model would also suggest that any heterogeneities should resolve themselves fairly quickly. Only a vastly and rapidly changing informational landscape could motivate the billions of shares traded each day, even on a single market. Every trader must also believe that the price determined by a market described as efficient is nonetheless wrong. This leaves us to consider further whether trades are better described as irrational or behavioral rather than driven by a rational expectations arbitrage process.

Empirical challenges

Fama's original assertion was based on many studies that demonstrated that managed funds do not offer better returns than the overall market. The state of the econometric art in the 1960s was only slowly gaining access to rich financial databases and new econometric techniques. However, by the late 1970s and through the 1980s and 1990s, many new econometric studies were published that showed the apparent inconsistency of observed market returns or market volatility with the predictions of the efficient market hypothesis.

One of the first studies was by Robert Shiller in 1979, which showed that long-term interest rates appear greater than the hypothesis predicted. His study two years later also demonstrated that stock prices tend to overshoot what would be justified by a rational response to a dividend announcement. While we describe more of Shiller's work in the last section of this volume, his observations were also gleaned by others. For instance, Werner F.M. De Bondt and Richard Thaler also discovered, in 1985, that stock prices over-react, which cast doubt even on the assertion of weak form efficiency.[66] The work of Shiller, De Bondt, and Thaler thrust these researchers and many others into the new realm of behavioral finance.

The mid-1980s became an era in which different camps in the finance discipline began to form along the efficient market hypothesis fissure. One camp tried to repair the cracks in the efficient market hypothesis edifice, while others sought to replace the hypothesis with new methodologies not based on the arbitrage principle or even full rationality. Methodologies were created and refined, and finance advanced in sophistication, even if greater insights seemed to produce yet more questions.

For instance, in 1988, Andrew Lo and Archie MacKinlay developed a new tool called the variance ratio test based on the premise that if the random walk approach is accurate, the logarithm of price changes for weekly or monthly intervals should maintain the ratio predicted by the random walk methodology.[67] This ratio test allowed the researcher to cancel out the technical violations of time-series econometric assumptions known as heteroscedasticity and non-normality. Using this new methodology, Lo and MacKinlay produced compelling evidence that the market does not follow a random walk.

The previous year, James Poterba and Larry Summers, the nephew of the great mind Paul Samuelson and later Secretary of the Treasury under US President Bill Clinton, demonstrated that stock returns tend to overshoot in shorter periods but revert to the mean over longer periods.[68] This result challenged short-run market efficiency, but it may not undermine long-run strong form information efficiency. Consistent with their observation of overshooting, they demonstrated that stock market returns seem to respond to more than market news or cyclical economic conditions. Instead, they concluded that prices stray from those determined based on market fundamentals. Their conclusion stoked Shiller's claim that there is simply more volatility in financial markets than would be predicted by the efficient market hypothesis.

Meanwhile, researchers were beginning to further explore and better understand the implications of the random walk and recognized that it was an unnecessarily restrictive formulation of the process that generates stock market returns. In fact, Samuelson had recognized this in 1965.

Instead, he asserted that the correct specification for the process ought to be a martingale, in which the expected change in a price over an interval should have a zero mean and follow a fair game. It is these deviations that follow a fair game, not the price itself. The broader specification actually allows the variance of a security to change over different intervals, in violation of the random walk specification. If this provision of the martingale property is combined with risk neutrality, changing variance patterns would not impinge on the market return, and the fundamentalist's approach to asset pricing becomes the focal price for the martingale process.

This greater understanding of the martingale process forced a reformulation of the various tests designed to confirm market efficiency. Under the Fama definition, a financial market is efficient if stock price changes are not autocorrelated, or the unexplained components of price movements are random and unrelated, over time. However, increasingly, scholars began to draw different conclusions from the same set of facts. If a study demonstrated that deviations in asset prices show discernible patterns over time, skeptics argued that markets are not efficient while proponents created explanations for the correlation of deviations.

For instance, Myung Kim, Charles Nelson, and Richard Startz observed in 1991 that historical data seemed to demonstrate a predictable mean reversion pattern in the data up to the Second World War.[14] Others viewed their discovery as vindication of the claim that markets were efficient after the Second World War. Then, in 1999, Lo and MacKinlay published their *A Non-Random Walk Down Wall Street*[70] as a refutation of the claims in the similarly titled popular investment book written a generation earlier by Makiel.[71] The following year, Shiller published another challenge to the efficient market hypothesis in his popular book *Irrational Exuberance*. Then, in 1997, Andrei Shleifer and Robert Vishny noted that institutional or other market imperfections introduce the trading restrictions that make trading strategies difficult and an efficient market elusive.[72]

This growing movement based on a repeal of the law of the rational agent had a number of dimensions. The traditional efficient market story required agents to arbitrage away any temporary market pricing imperfections. Arbitrageurs may be confounded by noisy nanotraders or hedge fund-induced momentum swings. Such a financial market might suffer from the forcing to the sidelines of rational traders in times when irrational traders rule the market, not unlike how Gresham's law forces good money out of a market containing bad, or how Akerlof's

"Market for Lemons" theory implies that only cars that are proven to be undependable remain in the used car market. Under this theory, market efficiency returns only once the forces of inefficiency have run their course.

Defenders of the faith

Likewise, defenders of the efficient market hypothesis continue to turn the arguments of their detractors on their heads in attempts to salvage it. For instance, Fama and Kenneth French (1988) argued that the observed changing degree of capital availability over the business cycle could cause the observed nature of the variance of stock returns.[73] They also argued that the lemons, or the irrational traders, in the market may add some noise and volatility, but are dispatched away from the market through the equivalent of economic Darwinism as they practice an irrational strategy that should not succeed over the long term. As Fischer Black himself noted in 1986, an irrational element that adds noisy trading is a necessary device to explain the number of trades each day in violation of the "no trade theory."

In fact, some even argued that the very criticism of the efficient market hypothesis only made the model even more robust. G. William Schwert claimed that each anomaly to the efficient market hypothesis uncovered by a researcher gave sophisticated traders yet another insight into an imperfect market upon which they could capitalize and arbitrage, and hence make the market more efficient and the autocorrelation disappear.

Most began to accept, though, that the efficient market hypothesis was an exercise rich in intuition but perhaps poor in testability. Scholars began to create more sophisticated tests for short- and long-run autocorrelations. In a pair of sequels to his 1970 review article, beginning in 1994, Fama did not revisit his previous definitions of an efficient market, but rather reviewed the empirical strategies designed to confirm his hypothesis. He followed this rebuttal up in 1998 with his third review article where he proclaimed that the hypothesis had survived all challenges to long-run deviations in the expected pattern of returns.

A final set of challenges

The efficient market hypothesis came under increasing criticism following the 1987 stock market crash, the deflation of the dot-com bubble of the late 1990s and the dramatic global financial meltdown in the fall of 2008. Proponents claim that these dramatic market corrections merely prove the long-run appropriateness of the hypothesis, or that the dramatic market declines are caused by institutional factors such as margin calls and frozen capital markets. Some even argue that regulatory reforms may help to prevent irrational run-ups and declines in the future. However, the majority of commentators assert that such market gyrations are evidence of systematic divergences from market fundamentals and the efficient market hypothesis.

16
Life and Legacy

Eugene Fama formulated the most compact and profound statement in modern finance. Many academics have adopted his notion of the efficient market as an act of faith that has defined entire scholarly careers. Still others created careers around its refutation. Regardless of this controversy, Fama is considered an elder statesman of modern finance and is the name most strongly associated with finance's most powerful and controversial paradigm.

Fama's confidence in the efficient market hypothesis seems stronger with each passing year. Even the recessionary declines leading up to the crash of 2008 gave him confidence in the ultimate foresight of a market characterized by his hypothesis. However, even he has recognized that it would be difficult to tell whether the paradigm so closely associated with his name can be proven conclusively.[74]

Following his contributions during the 1960s and 1970s to the development of the efficient market hypothesis paradigm, Fama also became increasingly interested in macroeconomic issues and international finance. By the 1970s, the great mind Fischer Black had taken up residency at Chicago, and Fama and Black became famous colleagues who would debate the issues from their unique perspectives that usually diverged from conventional economic theory. Neither had a strong background in macroeconomics, so neither was constrained by the conventional wisdom of macroeconomists. Some of these discussions culminated in a paper Fama co-wrote with André Farber in 1979 on money, portfolio choice, and trade as transactions costs are dissolved away between nations.[75] They used the model to predict that the purchasing power parity paradigm would negate exchange rate risk and facilitate international capital movements.

Fama also studied the role of banks over the first half of the 1980s and maintained a lifelong interest in corporate finance, which he had arrived at quite naturally, given his tutelage under the Merton Miller half of the Modigliani-Miller duo that developed the important corporate finance principle that shares their name.

More recently, Fama, with the principal collaborator for much of his career, Kenneth French, has worked to expand the CAPM. Considered revolutionary in the mid-1960s, the CAPM has not demonstrated superior predictive performance. As a predictor of returns, the CAPM uses only two predicting variables – relative risk and a risk-free return. Fama has worked to add additional factors to the model and with French has produced a three-factor version of the CAPM. These additional measures, capitalization and value, lend themselves to practical application, even if the approach is relatively free of theoretical motivation.

Fama has also co-authored the textbook *The Theory of Finance* with his mentor and Nobel Prize winner, the late Merton Miller. Currently, he chairs the CRSP at the University of Chicago, the same group that inspired him to use their newly developed CRSP tapes to perform some of finance's first event studies in the mid- to late 1960s. Beyond academia, he has participated as the director of research for the Dimensional Fund Advisors, Inc., an investment fund valued at more than $200 billion. Other directors of the fund include Kenneth French, Roger G. Ibbotson, and the great minds Robert Merton and Nobel Prize winner Myron Scholes.

Awards and recognitions

Fama has earned some of finance's most prized awards. In 2001, he was the first elected fellow of the American Finance Association and is a fellow of the Econometric Society and of the American Academy of Arts and Sciences. He is also an advisory editor of the *Journal of Financial Economics*. In 2005, he was the first recipient of the Deutsche Bank Prize in Financial Economics and received the 2007 Fred Arditti Innovation Award by the Chicago Mercantile Exchange Center for Innovation for his:

> pathbreaking insights into the functioning of markets, asset pricing theory, and corporate finance that have benefited market participants worldwide. He has written extensively on the efficiency of markets, setting the backdrop for the transfer of risks through futures contracts such as those traded on the CME. His innovative research has resulted in his participation in the development of many new

finance products and in the development of new futures contracts for hedging risks.[76]

He has also been awarded the 1982 Chaire Francqui (Belgian National Science Prize), the Nicholas Molodovsky Award from the CFA Institute for his contributions to portfolio theory and asset pricing in 2006, the Morgan Stanley American Finance Association Award for Excellence in 2007, and the Onassis Prize in Finance in 2009. He has received honorary doctoral degrees from the University of Rochester, DePaul University, and the Catholic University of Leuven, Belgium, and his alma mater, Tufts University, awarded him a Doctor of Science Honoris Causa in 2002.

He has published well over 100 journal articles, most of which have been published in the top journals in economics and finance. A number of his papers have won major association awards, including the Smith Breedan Prize from the *Journal of Finance* for his 1992 paper with Kenneth French, "The Cross-Section of Expected Stock Returns,"[77] and "Market Efficiency Long-Term Returns and Behavioral Finance,"[78] which secured the top prize in 1998 for publications in the *Journal of Financial Economics* on the topic of capital markets and asset pricing. He is also the longest-serving professor at the University of Chicago's Booth School, where he will celebrate 50 years at that institution in 2013.

Fama is a father of two sons and two daughters, and a proud grandfather of ten.

Section 4
Stephen Ross and Arbitrage Pricing Theory

The principle of arbitrage that underpins the efficient market hypothesis was also employed by such great minds as Paul Samuelson, Robert Merton, and Myron Scholes to "close" their respective models of financial security pricing. In the early 1970s, the arbitrage concept was used to marry the models of two other great minds in finance – the CAPM model of William Sharpe and the competitive equilibrium of Kenneth Arrow. Stephen Ross then used arbitrage to define a new model in finance – arbitrage pricing theory (APT).

17
The Early Years

Like so many of the great minds in finance before him, Stephen Alan Ross' ancestors were from Eastern Europe. His grandfather, Benjamin Ross, was born in Courland, Russia in March 1880 and made his way to the USA as a very young man of 17 in 1897. Soon after he arrived, he met his future bride, Katherine Cohen, who, while also born in Russia, had come over with her parents and older sister Elizabeth in 1885 when she was only two years old.

One may legitimately observe that Ross does not sound like a Russian name. In his American Finance Association History of Finance series interview, Stephen Ross explained that one of his Russian ancestors was the Scottish equivalent of a Singer door-to-door sewing machine salesman who ended a bit off his regular route when he found himself in Minsk and married to a local Russian Jewish woman. The Scottish name Ross had planted its Russian roots.[79]

Ross met his future wife Katherine soon after he landed in the USA in the late nineteenth century. They married, and the newlyweds settled down in the first decade of the new century in an apartment at 55 Spruce Street in the working-class area of Boston called Chelsea, about a mile away from the Boston Bunker Hill landmark. There, Benjamin worked as a laster, one who operates a lasting machine that joins the sole of a shoe to its upper. By the 1920s, he had transitioned to the burgeoning new profession of automobile mechanic.

The young Ross couple had two sons, Herbert, born in 1903, and Arthur Isadore, born on March 20, 1905, and a daughter Myrtle, born in 1911. Arthur, Stephen Alan Ross' father, was destined to be the first in the family to attend college when he put himself through night school to eventually become an engineer. This younger Ross boy graduated from Chelsea High School in 1922 and from Northeastern University's engineering school in 1926. He was described in his yearbook as a "quiet lad" who, at university, gave up wrestling as a sport to wrestle with rubber as a chemical engineer.

A few years after graduation, Arthur met and married Betty Grechesky and they established their home in the more affluent side of the Boston in Brookline, Massachusetts. Betty, too, had a Russian heritage. Her father, Louis Grechewsky, and mother, Fannie Chidnoff, had also arrived from Russia, in 1905 and 1906 respectively, when each was 18 years old. They had four children, Arthur in 1908, Bessie (Betty) in 1910, Samuel in 1915, and Lillian in 1919. While Arthur's father made shoes, Betty's parents, Louis and Fannie, were tailors and fitters and lived at 310 Washington Street in the town of Haverhill, Massachusetts.

Arthur and Betty Ross had two children; Linda in 1937 and Stephen Alan, born on February 3, 1944 in Boston, Massachusetts. Both children attended Brookline High School and both were excellent students. It was Stephen's task to overachieve so that he might find his way out of his older sister's academic shadow. This was in a school chock full of the overachieving children of professors in this affluent community just across the Charles River from Harvard and MIT. While in school, Stephen liked sports as well. However, he did not have the athletic successes Eugene Fama was having a few years earlier and a few miles up the road in Malden, and so he gave up this extracurricular activity to concentrate instead on physics.

There are two places in the USA to which any physics major will universally aspire. Conveniently enough for Stephen, one was just a stone's throw across the Charles River at MIT. The other was on the other side of the continent and, from a Massachusetts perspective, was in a different world. By the time Stephen graduated from high school, California was a land of endless sun, the Beach Boys, and the beatniks of the 1960s that would soon spawn the hippie movement. A college recruiter from the California Institute of Technology had been visiting some of the top schools in the Northeast with the hope of attracting some bright young physics majors right from MIT's backyard. The recruiter had mostly convinced Stephen to attend Caltech, but, when Stephen told the MIT application officer that he was also invited to apply to Caltech, the MIT officer said "if you get in there, you should go." Stephen was concerned that the application officer was politely suggesting he would not get into MIT, so he asked if that was the case. The officer retorted that yes, he would get into MIT, but "Caltech's the best place in the world." He heeded the counselor's advice.

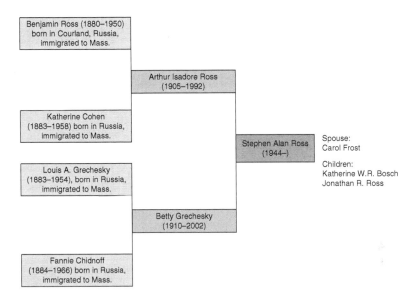

Figure 17.1   The family tree of Stephen Ross (1944–)

In fact, Stephen was bound to be accepted by any university to which he applied. He had earned the highest score in New England on a national mathematics test, but he was on his way to a school that attracted only the very best students. In freshman orientation at Caltech, the instructor tried to impress upon Stephen and his new classmates just how hard they must work to succeed there. Just as in Marines boot camp, he told the students to look to their left and to their right because two of the three would not succeed to graduation. Stephen figured it might be good to get to know these two poor lads, so he asked them how they did on their national mathematics exam. One had earned the top score in the entire nation and the other had scored very highly too. He got his first inkling of how hard he would have to work to succeed there in physics. Unfortunately, his two new friends did not. They were both flushed out of their programs.

Ross was studying physics at a time before computers were widespread. It would take another decade after he graduated from Caltech before it would be possible to buy the world's first personal computer, the Altair 8800, from an electronics magazine. The revolutionary IBM 360 mainframe computer was yet to be produced. Before broadly accessible computing power became available, the students at Caltech would have to numerically solve complicated differential equations through tedious calculation and computing. The mathematics was difficult, but the experience was priceless.

At Caltech, Ross was fortunate to be able to take physics each year of his attendance from the master, Richard Feynman (1918–1988), including an advanced theoretical physics class in his senior year. He related the story of how the smartest kids in the country sat down for their first college course with a true genius, and how every person in that room, in experiencing Feynman, quickly understood the meaning of a truly great mind.

Ross graduated in physics from Caltech in 1965 and made his way back to Cambridge and Harvard for graduate school just as one of his future colleagues, Robert Merton, began to attend graduate school in applied mathematics at Caltech. However, while Merton had decided to study more mathematics and delay his eventual foray into finance, Ross had been exposed, in his senior year, to game theory and linear programming, and decided that he liked the type of mathematics performed in economics and finance more than the more prescribed mathematics employed in physics at that time.

Ross came to Harvard at a time that he later regretted. Harvard had a reputation as an institution that was a loose collection of independent consultants united around a mutual concern over a lack of parking spaces. It attracted some of the best students in the world, and these students were bright and determined enough to teach themselves, regardless of the level of attention afforded them by their assigned mentor.

Ross had been assigned to work with the German economist Gottfried Haberler, but did not manage to work long with him because the German shepherd dog Haberler kept in his office was mean enough to scare away young PhD students. Instead, Ross sought out a more receptive supervisor and came across the field of decision theory and statistics and the business school professor Howard Raffia. He also had the opportunity to work with the great mind and subsequent Nobel Prize laureate Kenneth Arrow while at Harvard and managed to eke out a thesis and a diploma from there. He graduated in 1970 at the age of 26.

While at Harvard, Ross met and married Carol Frost on August 12, 1967. In contrast to Ross' heritage that was only a couple of generations removed from ancestors in Russia, Frost had roots as far back as the first European settlers in America. Her ancestors had arrived from England and settled in Maine in the early 1630s. Her family remained in Maine until her great-grandfather John Mason Frost (1834–1893) moved and started a family in Waltham, Massachusetts. Her grandfather, Harry Gardner Frost (1876–1950), subsequently moved his family, including

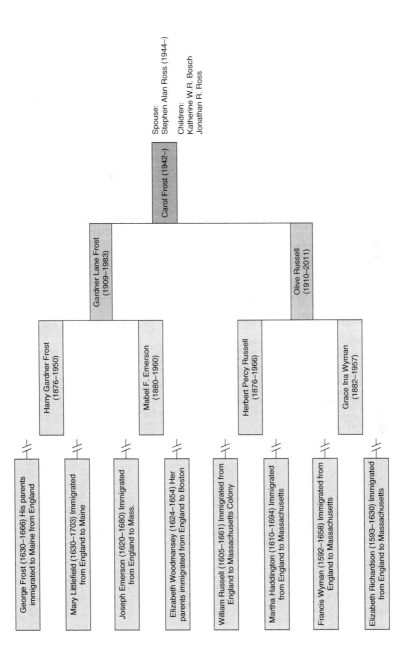

Figure 17.2 The family tree of Carol Frost (1944–)

Carol's father, Gardner Lane Frost, to Lexington, Massachusetts. Carol has grown up in Lexington and graduated from Lexington High School in 1960, a couple of years before Ross made his way to Caltech.

Following his graduation from Harvard, Ross and Carol moved to Philadelphia, Pennsylvania so that he could take up a position in the economics department at the Wharton Business School. He had harbored hopes of remaining at Harvard upon graduation, but suffered from a distinctively Harvard principle at that time to not hire its own graduates, but instead to hire those who had established their careers at other institutions. Later, he lamented that Harvard maintained a model of poaching of talent developed elsewhere rather than of nurturing of its own talent. This Harvard philosophy saved him from becoming a mathematical general equilibrium theorist, which he later described as a "fate worse than death."[80] It also allowed him to develop an independent research agenda, instead of depending on the numerous research opportunities afforded him simply by working on the issues for which Kenneth Arrow did not have time. In 1970, though, the young couple had to leave their home territory and took the difficult journey to Philadelphia. Soon after they arrived, they had two children, Katherine and Jonathan, both born while Ross prepared his epic work on the APT at Wharton.

While at Wharton, Ross continued to work on the general equilibrium theory and the principal-agent problems for which Arrow was world-renowned. Ross' teaching schedule in those early Wharton years was very difficult. He was required to teach four different courses taught each semester. He later joked that he eventually taught every course on the curriculum except Soviet economics, despite his Russian heritage. He feared that if his ancestry had been discovered, the administration might have required him to take a Berlitz course in Russian and teach Soviet economics too.

The Wharton Business School is unusual among business schools in that it is actually housed in a school that contains many social science disciplines. While Ross went to Wharton as an economist, he had the opportunity to attend finance seminars. Two of his earliest presenters were Fischer Black and Richard Roll. Almost immediately, Ross was hooked on finance, despite the discouragement from some of his economics colleagues who were concerned that the pragmatic and practical bent of finance would only dull the sharp theoretical edge required for good economics.

At that time, in the early 1970s, Fischer Black and Myron Scholes were yet to publish their Black-Scholes options pricing approach. The prevailing technique in finance was the CAPM. When Ross asked probing questions about the workings of the CAPM and whether the appropriate cost of capital in the Model ought to be the average cost of capital or the incremental cost, or what economists call the marginal cost of capital, he was met with blank stares from his finance colleagues.

In fact, the originator of the CAPM would have understood what this budding finance theoretician was talking about. A decade earlier, William Sharpe asked a similar question of his mentor, Harry Markowitz. What would happen if one small asset were added to an already optimal portfolio? This is an exploration of an optimal portfolio on the margin that gave rise to the familiar CAPM formula. It also inspired Ross to develop his own theory of arbitrage based on marginal perturbations of a competitive equilibrium.

Ross' first impression of finance in general and the CAPM in particular was that the rhetoric was rousing and the intuition compelling but the mathematics was unconvincing. He was forced to first understand, and then improve upon the mathematics of optimal portfolio and arbitrage that existed at the time. The result would be a new theory of his design that we now call *arbitrage pricing theory*.

18
The Times

The two-decade period from 1952 to 1972 created a revolution in finance theory. However, the modern era in finance started slowly. Harry Markowitz had developed the Modern Portfolio Theory, which, while intuitively appealing, was nearly impossible to apply because of limitations in computing power. Indeed, Modern Portfolio Theory was not even taught at the business school of its creation until the great mind Eugene Fama began teaching there. Nor was its intuition immediately obvious until James Tobin, the great mind described in the next part of this book, created a new interpretation based on a risk-free asset.

Over the decade following its creation, the father of Modern Portfolio Theory worked to develop and refine the algorithms that would allow practitioners and scholars to calculate the necessary covariance matrix for the portfolio of securities. His work was timed perfectly. After a decade a development of software, the IBM 300 series mainframe had become the mainstay of university computing resources.

However, another innovation at least partially obviated the need for the Modern Portfolio Theory. When Markowitz's student, William Sharpe, took Markowitz's advice and explored the effects of adding a single security to an optimal market portfolio, a very simple methodology to price this marginal security resulted. The CAPM was born. Its advantage lay in its elegance, intuition, and great simplicity. Its weakness was also its greatest strength.

Many careers have subsequently been devoted to improving the realism of the CAPM without significantly sacrificing its simplicity. For instance, it is apparent that pricing depends on the relative risk of the marginal security and the larger market portfolio. This portfolio should, ideally, include all stores of value, including those that are often regarded as falling outside of one's financial portfolio but that may be in the category of consumer durables or housing investment. In addition, the portfolio of other stores of value has become necessarily global. In reality, the CAPM has some very complex underpinnings in the extensiveness of the benchmark market portfolio. The intertemporal version of the CAPM, developed by the great mind Robert Merton, also necessarily introduces a dynamic rebalancing of the simple model over time.

The other interesting quality is that the CAPM model did not directly require the arbitrage condition that had been articulated by the great mind Paul Samuelson in his 1965 theory of prices and employed by the great minds Merton as well as Fischer Black and Myron Scholes in their simultaneous development of the Black-Scholes options pricing theory. In other words, the CAPM was not making a statement about market efficiency, even if efficiency may have been implicitly included in the measurement of the benchmark risk-free and market returns.

Finally, as Fama signaled in his work on a three-factor version of the CAPM, there are some obvious factors that should influence a security's pricing rather than its relative volatility vis-à-vis the market. In fact, most multi-factor models of securities pricing must almost necessarily include the CAPM, explicitly or implicitly, even if many do not also invoke an arbitrage condition.

The CAPM provided hundreds of researchers and hundreds of thousands of practitioners with a new tool. Meanwhile, those who studied derivatives sought to master the Black-Scholes formula. A few scholars began to think more about some of the unexplored insights of the security market line from the by-then underappreciated and underapplied Modern Portfolio Theory.

The goal was to create a model that invoked an arbitrage condition rather than the condition that all investors behave alike, as did the CAPM, the Modern Portfolio Theory and, in its elementary version, the efficient market hypothesis. Ross set out with multiple goals of determining a simpler approach to the determination and application of the Modern Portfolio Theory's security market line, the relaxing of the homogeneity of investors assumption, and the explicit consideration of the systematic risk element of a given security. The new theory turned out to be quite elegant, remarkably inclusive of factors that our intuition tells us ought to be important in security pricing, and reasonably simple to apply, given the emerging tools of computing and market databases.

19
The Theory

The primary goal of Stephen Ross' APT was to relax the implication that every investor chooses the same portfolio. Instead, Ross sought to show that different investors balance a spectrum of possible risks. This relaxation allowed an investor to ameliorate those risks based on his or her individual risk preferences.

As such, it is an elegant combination of the microeconomics of individual finance decisions and the macroeconomics of managing the systemic risks that affect all markets. Since some of these broad risks pervade the entire market, they can be mitigated but not avoided. The return that a security must offer is then proportional to the degree to which these risks impinge upon the asset, not unlike the role played by the beta factor in filling in the more simplistic and restrictive CAPM.

Because the model departs from the then-standard approach of the representative investor and the market equilibrium that arguably should apply to all, the distinct microeconomic nature of APT has resulted in the erroneous label that the model is behavioral. However, this model is distinctly rational. Well-informed investors will manage and diversify their risk based on their own risk profile by choosing a portfolio with the loadings of the risk factors that best address their individual preferences. For each of these risk factors, investors can determine their individual factor loading, and their resulting portfolio will have the correct beta and return to match their preferences. While the model will be developed as a static equilibrium, an extension of the model can be considered dynamic as the investor must re-optimize each period.

The model also anticipates an entire industry of investors, risk managers, information solicitors, and market arbitrageurs, just as we observe in practice. In other words, this model will not obviate the need for fundamental analysis and the seeking of private information, as the Grossman-Stiglitz model of efficient markets paradoxically predicts.

The APT model

Let us develop Ross' APT using notation familiar to us from the CAPM. We shall generalize the CAPM specifications in that we will not need to maintain its two most restrictive assumptions that investors have preferences only over the mean and variance of an asset and that they hold only traded assets.

Let there be a jth risky asset offering a return r_j as a linear function of a constant asset a_j and n systematic factors F_k, each with a postulated sensitivity b_{jk}. We allow the risky asset to also have a random idiosyncratic (non-systematic) error e_j, such that:

$$r_j = a_j + b_{j1}F_1 + \cdots + b_{jn}F_n + e_j$$

We further assume that the error term is a random variable with zero expected mean that is uncorrelated with the factors and across assets. Then, continuing in an analogous manner with the CAPM, we can calculate the expected return of the asset:

$$E(r_f) = r_f + b_{j1}RP_1 + \cdots + b_{jn}RP_n$$

where RP_k is the risk premium arising from the kth factor and r_f is the risk-free return.

Implicit in this formulation are a number of assumptions. First, there must be more assets than factors to ensure that the beta matrix will be non-singular and hence invertible. Second, we will see that perfect competition is required. In fact, if these factors span all possible states, the APT satisfies the condition for equilibrium in an Arrow-Debreu economy, described more fully in the second volume of this series. The perfect competition requirement allows us to appeal to the arbitrage equilibrium and the Arrow-Debreu existence property.

An Arrow-Debreu economy allows for both long purchases and short sales. In this case, an arbitrage opportunity would allow an investor to earn a positive profit by offsetting long purchases of an undervalued asset with short sales of an overpriced asset, without risk. The resulting inequality-generating profit opportunity would occur if any assets were mispriced according to the model. We shall use the property that there is no arbitrage in a competitive equilibrium to generate results in the APT model.

Let us assume there is a mispriced asset that is a function of the same factors that span the market. To create an arbitrage portfolio, the arbitrageur will assemble a bundle of n+1 properly priced assets with weightings such that the weighting for the bundle has the same sensitivity, or beta, for each factor as does the mispriced asset. Then, by selling the portfolio short and using the proceeds to buy an underpriced asset, or buying the portfolio long funded by shorting the overpriced asset, it is possible to earn a certain profit with no risk once the mispriced asset reaches its equilibrium value. Assuming that each asset, including the mispriced asset, represents only on a small part of the overall market, this arbitrage has a negligible effect on other asset prices, and the mispriced asset is brought into alignment through arbitrage.

Much like the assumption of the CAPM pricing that past covariances are used to generate the expectation of today's security pricing, the APT assumes that a linear regression of past asset returns on the span of factors generates the factor loadings for the expectation of present security prices. However, these factor loadings are not the constant and easily interpreted risk premiums relating one asset to another, as occurs in the CAPM model. Instead, these "betas" are not static, and differ over time across portfolios and across different economies. The factors are discovered empirically to provide the most reliable *fit* and are chosen based on a researcher's intuition of the variable's reasonably expected effect on unexpected movements in an asset's price. As such, they may represent macroeconomic influences that would otherwise be undiversifiable and included in the systematic market risk.

Such factors could include changes in inflation or gross domestic product (GDP), or shifts in consumer confidence or in the yield curve. However, since many relevant macroeconomic data are reported monthly, quarterly, or less frequently, spot prices for assets that provide expectations for various economic variables can act as a proxy for these factors. For instance, the gap between a forward treasury bond rate and the forward rate for a comparable inflation protected treasury (TIP) can be used as a proxy for expected inflation. Similarly, commodity futures can be used as a proxy for GDP growth, while exchange futures can measure investor expectations.

The strength of the APT, based on an arbitrage argument for the accuracy of the factor loadings, is that these loadings, while not as easily interpreted as the betas of the CAPM, provide an explanation of the effect of factors on asset returns rather than simply a statistical correspondence as provided by the CAPM. The model also allows all investors to "price" their own portfolios, while the CAPM is a market-wide or a representative investor approach. In fact, the CAPM can be considered a special case of the APT for a single factor chosen to represent the value of the fully diversified market. Then, the APT solution to the linear regression is identical to the security market line in the CAPM and the Modern Portfolio Theory. However, while the CAPM is a relatively primitive model of convergence in the demand price of a security, the APT is interpreted as the effect of supply factors on the pricing and hence the portfolio of diverse investors.

Despite the intuitive appeal that securities prices should be a function of the underlying factors that influence the overall economy and the relevant industry sector in particular, the APT was the first fully specified multi-factor model in finance. It came not long after the necessary econometric and computational tools became widely available. However, its success was that it was not simply a *kitchen-sink* econometric model that attempts to explain a dependent variable by throwing in every conceivable independent variable but the kitchen sink. Instead, its roots were in the Arrow-Debreu state-space economy, with the arbitrage condition cleverly formulated along the lines of the Arrow-Debreu budget constraint, and the linear relationship then imposed as a linear regression on a market assumed to be in equilibrium.

The APT also has the appealing quality of relying on the same arbitrage principle espoused by Samuelson in his 1965 tour-de-force on financial market pricing and on the condition used effectively by Nobel Laureates Merton and Scholes in their Black-Scholes option pricing model and the laureates Franco Modigliani and Merton Miller in their Modigliani-Miller theorem that is the cornerstone of modern corporate finance.

20
Discussion and Applications

Finance is an analytically challenging discipline. Often, simplifying assumptions or conditions, such as risk neutrality, a representative investor, arbitrage, or market efficiency, are imposed to allow formal models to be tractable. However, the overly simplifying assumptions run the risk of creating theories that create an analytic power that is out of proportion with the various assumptions, such as the premise of the efficient market hypothesis. Other models adopt assumptions of such strong generality that it becomes difficult to draw strong conclusions from them. This is the criticism that at times has been leveled against the APT.

The APT was formulated with a number of goals in mind. First, the model offered an opportunity to further motivate the CAPM and remove some of its most troubling assumptions. Second, it was designed to be a relatively simple tool for practitioners to apply so that they might better manage market risk. The model offered to manage both systematic risk and the idiosyncratic risk of a particular industry. Third, the model can be predictive rather than simply reflective of today's securities based on their history of variation relative to the overall market.

The APT has been shown to perform relatively well. For instance, Nai-Fu Chen, Richard Roll, and Stephen Ross tested the theory against various US macroeconomic variables.[81] In their 1986 paper "Economic Forces and the Stock Market," they discovered that stock returns are priced based on their correlation with systematic macroeconomic news and various idiosyncratic measures, such as commodity prices and consumption. The model was simple to apply and performed better than the CAPM. It also has the advantage that broad systematic news will not affect all returns equally, as each asset will have associated with it a unique factor loading for a given systematic variable.

Testability of the APT

The Chen, Roll, and Ross results should not be surprising. We can reasonably deduce that the APT should be able to perform at least as well as the CAPM because it can be designed with a risk-free asset and a single mean-variance efficient market portfolio as two of the independent variables, just as had defined the CAPM. As such, the APT can be regarded as a superset of the simple mean-variance efficient pricing model. However, in the more general case, it is impossible to test whether the pricing relationships are predictive or whether the factor choices are accurate.

Given the impossibility of validating the model based on its theoretical justifications, its arbitrage assumption, and its validation of the Arrow-Debreu competitive equilibrium, an acceptance of the model lies in the usual acceptance of its practical econometric properties.

At the econometric level, the model depends crucially on the choice of macroeconomic and idiosyncratic variables. The appropriateness of these variables is measured in two ways. First, the overall explanatory power of the model can be verified by the usual model statistics such as the R-squared. Then, each explanatory variable can be independently measured on the strength of its t-statistics and other measures.

One problem that presents itself is in the APT's practical departure from the Arrow-Debreu foundation. In the Arrow-Debreu specification, a security provides returns based on various future contingencies. These different future states are orthogonal, or independent because each represents its own unique state. As a practical matter, these states or their proxies would be impossible to represent, especially given that the very nature of uncertainty means that even the possibility of some states cannot be known in advance. Instead, it is necessary to construct reasonably representative proxies that likely span the appropriate future states. However, while there is a plethora of potential future states, there are only a handful of regularly published proxies for future states.

Many reasonable proxies, such as the projected GDP, perhaps as measured by market futures, the projected commodity prices, anticipated inflation, and expected interest rates are indeed correlated with each other. When these correlations occur, while the overall model performance may remain strong, the mean and the variation of the factor loadings may be biased as the model struggles to determine how to attribute variations to each cross-correlated variable.

Ultimately, because one cannot know what one does not know, the impossibility of creating factors uniquely correlated with all possible future states leaves the researcher or practitioner with the task of choosing factors as a matter of judgment. Of course, the resulting factor loadings and pricing properties of one specification will differ from even a relatively similar specification based on only a mildly different judgment on the appropriate factors.

Not to be overly hindered by such technical problems, the scholarly discussion glosses over the challenge of the determination of orthogonal variables that are unrelated to each other but contribute to the explanation of a security's price. The conversation instead focuses on the appropriate factors that capture properties that researchers find intuitively appealing. These discussions cannot be tested against any standard or model, except by appeal to the great mind Milton Friedman's assertion that the proof should be in the pudding. If the factor arguably makes some theoretical sense and if its inclusion seems to improve the APT fit, then a case can be made for that factor.

Using this approach, Gur Huberman and Shmuel Kandel used the APT model to differentiate the factors that influence firms of various sizes. They argued in their 1985 paper that indexes of small, medium and large firms should use separate factors based on their supposition that the institutional and market factors that affect these cohorts are specific to their respective classes of securities.[82] Fama and French simplified this approach in 1993 by instead using the gap between returns in small and large firms as a factor.[83] Others, including Fama and French in 1992,[84] suggest a factor which measures the ratio of book (or accounting) value to market value, while Fama and French in 1993 recommended using the gap between returns of value stock and growth stock as a factor to explain the pricing of an individual security.

Still others confine their factor intuitions to more traditional macroeconomic factors, as described previously in the discussion of the Chen, Roll, and Ross explorations. These studies almost universally choose the CAPM as the comparison point and demonstrate that the APT performs better than the CAPM. However, there is a *survivor bias* in such publications. Obviously, the papers would not be published in justification of the APT had it performed worse than the CAPM, and the addition of variables cannot make the model perform less well. If the variables are irrelevant, the model's predictive capacity is unchanged. If, by chance or design, additional variables are relevant, the model will predict better. Consequently, it remains difficult to discern appropriate theory except for the effect it has on predictability. The literature awaits a more rigorous and justifiable methodology that can discern between the APT and any competing hypothesis in a more objective and less ad hoc way.

Applications of the APT

Ross' APT provides a very simple and straightforward framework for securities pricing. It is computationally feasible, is consistent with theory and intuition, and applies tools of econometrics that are relatively well understood. The APT is often applied to evaluate managed funds and to assist in asset allocation decisions.

The asset allocation application naturally arises because k well-chosen factors can be represented and modeled by k assets in a portfolio. The APT can then be used to construct a portfolio that satisfies the goal of a practitioner to manage such predefined risks. However, it is difficult to determine whether these managed risks truly span the spectrum of market risks and hence may not result in the creation and optimal allocation of a mean-variance efficient portfolio.

The use of the APT to evaluate fund performance is a bit more problematic. The APT is a static model, much like the CAPM. A given relationship between factor loadings and an asset price will change over time. Even the calculated implicit discount factor is calculated consistent with such a one-period model.

However, the APT has not been recast in a dynamic perspective as Merton had done for the CAPM and for the Black-Scholes models. Also problematic is the very foundation upon which the APT is based. It is an arbitrage model, so it implicitly assumes that securities prices accurately reflect all available information and that the market is efficient. To use a tool of market efficiency to benchmark supernormal profits of a fund manager is paradoxical.

Theoretically, the model should also lend itself to a determination of the cost of capital, as the CAPM, the other common asset pricing model, has been employed commonly to do. A number of researchers have used the APT to predict the effect on the cost of capital from changes in unanticipated inflation, interest rates and the yield curve, foreign exchange rates, and GDP growth. For instance, such a methodology would be helpful for the determination of the cost of capital in industries subject to rate of return regulation relative to the cost of capital. Utilities commissions have typically relied on the CAPM for such measures and have not adopted the APT approach because there is no universal agreement on the appropriate factors. Hence, different specifications do not produce mutually consistent results.

Despite these shortcomings and constraints, the APT remains an intuitive model based on sound economic and financial theory. It also lends itself well to the application of tools familiar to researchers and practitioners. Its greatest utility is likely to lie in the application of a consistent specification within one financial analysis unit rather than in the scholarly debate over the appropriateness of different specifications. The spectrum of factor loadings is simply so broad that such comparisons ultimately compare apples to oranges. While the CAPM shares many characteristics and tools with the APT, it has the advantage that it is less vulnerable to modification and differing interpretation.

21
Life and Legacy

Stephen Ross provided to the finance discipline the APT that was intuitively appealing, consistent with well-understood methodologies, that invoked the equilibrium concept of arbitrage and the efficient market hypothesis, and was rooted in the sound theory of the Arrow-Debreu competitive equilibrium. He was able to do so because he brought to the theoretical problem an excellent foundation in mathematics, from his attendance at Caltech, a firm foundation in economics from his PhD, and his experience from an immersion in leading-edge finance at the finance workshops upon his initial appointment at Wharton.

While his APT contribution to finance came very early in his career, Ross continued to innovate in other areas. His name is also associated with his joint work with John Carrington Cox.

Cox was a student at Wharton who left for the University of Wisconsin with an only partially completed thesis. When he returned to Wharton to defend his thesis in 1975, Ross was asked to work on his defense committee because he was the faculty member most familiar with partial differential equations. Ross was impressed with his innovative work on the then very new and mathematically sophisticated Black-Scholes-Merton options pricing theory.

There were a number of issues that had to be worked out regarding Black and Scholes' development of a new options pricing theory. Merton had already demonstrated that the theory could be derived based on the concept of arbitrage, and Black had the insight that options measure and price the variance of an underlying security. Cox and Ross added another insight. An option is a hedge. In fact, Myron Scholes had rationalized one interpretation of the Black-Scholes equation as a perfect hedge that involved both the security and its option. If such a hedge is perfect, in that, through arbitrage, it should offer no risk and the risk-free return, then one's risk profile should not matter. Thus, if one is willing to accept arbitrage and efficient markets, further analysis can proceed based on an assumption of risk neutrality.

Up to then, as to now, the nature of risk aversion had been an essential and continuously debated issue in finance. However, given myriad measures and profiles of risk, there could not be a universally acceptable inclusion into the academic finance models. Meanwhile, practitioners proceeded essentially in a risk-neutral manner, for the pragmatic reason that an imperfectly specified tool was arguably better than no tool at all. In addition, the model is based on the rationale that corporations and funds have access to complete capital markets and a diversified portfolio of projects or assets and have a profit maximization objective without regard for the second moment of returns.

Cox and Ross, along with their later collaborator Mark Edward Rubinstein, who was teaching at the University of California in the late 1970s (and still is to this day), parlayed the notion that the options pricing models could be constructed based on the premise of risk neutrality into a new approach to options pricing.

With Cox and Ross's risk-neutrality premise at hand, they began to explore an early version of what is now known at the binomial options pricing model (BOPM). In their model, to which Rubinstein contributed his insights into the mathematics, Cox and Ross explored how an option's price might evolve over time toward expiration. They constructed a discrete-time lattice, or tree, for dates between initial valuation and expiration, with every possible price at any date represented by a discrete branch or node. The process is then an iterative one. By starting at the expiration date, when the exercise price and hence the value of the option is known, and working backward through the branch to the original node at the valuation date, it is possible to theoretically calculate the evolution of the option price based on the fully specified tree, which calculates each option value at the terminal date and sequentially calculates the option price at each preceding date.

The BOPM is attractive because it is relatively easy to solve. It is now typically incorporated as an algorithm in modern financial calculators. Of course, in the limit as the number of time intervals grows asymptotically, it necessarily converges on a continuous-time solution like the Black-Scholes equation. It also lends itself more intuitively to changes in variance structures or the risk-free rate at discrete times in the options pricing process, so it can readily incorporate information at various points in time. Finally, the discrete model is more familiar to financial practitioners accustomed to working with spreadsheets and accounts all defined in discrete time. For these reasons, the Cox-Ross-Rubenstein options pricing formula is a common methodology employed by practitioners, especially for longer-term options with a richer set of factors that could influence the price beyond what the Black-Scholes formula can successfully accommodate.

Ross also contributed extensively to the empirical side of finance. However, his personal contributions typically rested in the theoretical econometric side, while his collaborators would then subsequently explore the data side. This separation between equations and econometrics is a common one for scholars who usually accumulate the tools of theory or data analysis, but only very rarely both.

One empirical study that Ross had been working on was at the cusp between classical finance and behavioral finance. Classical finance is based on the premise that markets are efficient and securities prices are based on the underlying fundamentals. Behavioral finance tries to understand why financial markets at times depart from what most would argue are their fundamental values. For instance, in financial bubbles, firms will often trade well above either their book value of assets or their discounted expected future net profits. During dramatic stock market declines, and especially when unaccompanied by a previous bubble, stocks may trade at values well below the book value, or even the liquidation or scrap value, of a firm. Market movements beyond these bounds do not appear rational.

One commonly observed example of such a phenomenon is in the pricing of closed-end mutual funds. These funds allow their subscribers to share the ownership of a portfolio that is managed for a fee. Such funds often trade below the cash and asset value of the firm. Ross showed that this apparent discrepancy could be explained by the management costs of the fund. As such, he discounted an argument that there is a behavioral explanation. In fact, Ross was exploring a hypothesis that the great mind Milton Friedman once asserted – that financial markets redistribute assets from the ignorant to the informed, and hence these markets weed out irrationality and increase market efficiency through a process of financial evolutionary theory.

Ross was also well known as an advocate of the Tobin's q measure in finance. In the most common finance application, the concept, named after its originator and the great mind James Tobin (who will be discussed in the next part of this book), is the ratio of the market value of a firm relative to its replacement cost. The market value is simple to calculate, based on its market capitalization. However, replacement cost is more difficult to calculate, especially in the determination of goodwill and the asset value of patents and innovations. The simple accounting measure of replacement costs is the book value of assets. Ross and his colleague Eric Lindenberg showed how, based on the assumption of rationality and market efficiency, the market capitalization and Tobin's q or book value could be used to develop measures of the value of a firm's intangible assets.[85]

It was not surprising that Ross was exposed to and adapted the Tobin's q methodology. He shared an intellectual background with Tobin. He also had an opportunity to work with Tobin when he was offered a position at Yale in 1976 that would afford both him and Carol an opportunity to be nearer to their families and their grandparents in the Boston area of their childhood. Ross and Tobin had an immediate affinity. Both were mathematically proficient economists and both successfully transitioned into finance theory. Tobin subsequently won a Nobel Prize for his contributions to finance. Both studied for their PhD at Harvard and both taught at Yale at the same time. Tobin's academic elegance, mathematical compactness, and intuition inspired the generation of economists that Ross represented. When he once asked Tobin who they should root for when they attended Harvard-Yale football games together, Tobin responded: "What kind of economist are you? You root for the guy who pays you."[86]

Ross commented in 2010 in his Foundation for the Advancement of Research in Financial Economics address that Yale benefited from an approach unique among finance programs at the time. While Wharton had followed the mainstream of the CAPM, options pricing, and the Modigliani-Miller theorem of corporate finance that had flowed out of MIT, Yale's approach, as shepherded by its philosophical anchor Tobin, was more along the lines of the economics of information and of market failure.

Ross left Yale in 1997 to come full circle. He took up a position at MIT, the school he had foregone to study at Caltech three decades earlier. Over his career, his experience was not separated from practice. He served on corporate boards that gave him a grounding in corporate strategy and practical concerns. He served on the board of General Reinsurance beginning in 1993 and on the board of directors of Freddie Mac, the Federal Home Loan Mortgage Corporation, from 1998 to 2008. Freddie Mac is a government-sponsored enterprise that was formed in 1970 to provide for additional securitization of mortgages into instruments that could be traded in financial markets. It was created by the US Congress to provide competition for the Federal National Mortgage Association (Fannie Mae), which had operated to securitize mortgages as a government-sponsored enterprise for 30 years beginning as a New Deal program in 1938. When the association went private in 1968, the fear that Fannie Mae would monopolize the mortgage market for the vast majority of US homes precipitated the creation of Freddie Mac, first under the supervision of the Federal Home Loan Bank Board, and more recently under the supervision of the US Department of Housing and Urban Development. Following the subprime mortgage meltdown of 2007 and the international credit crisis of 2008, Freddie Mac was placed under the conservatorship of the US Federal Government, on September 7, 2008, four weeks before the stock market crash that plunged the world into the Great Recession.

Ross later lamented that his days at Freddie Mac were challenging. He arrived at Freddie Mac at the apex of a President Clinton-motivated effort to move the national rate of home ownership beyond its traditional range of about 60 percent of households. The way to do this was to lower the cost of home ownership and thus approve for housing purchase households with lower incomes who would otherwise not be financeable. Freddie Mac succumbed to the political pressure to fund such home affordability programs and paid these subsidies by engaging in increasingly risky profit-making activities in the derivatives financial markets. This resulted in a series of accounting scandals at Freddie Mac and Fannie Mae and the subsequent action to place the organizations under conservatorship.

Ross is also Principal, Director, and Chairman of the Investment Advisory Board at IV Capital Limited., and had previously served as Chairman and Chief Executive Officer of Compensation Valuation, Inc., where, since 2003, he has consulted in the valuation of complex derivatives contracts. He has also served as a member of the advisory council for the hedge fund Taconic Capital Partners. He also partnered with his past collaborator Richard Roll to form Roll and Ross Asset Management Corporation from 1986 to 2004.

Ross is a fellow of the Econometrics Society, was the President of the American Finance Association in 1988, and is a trustee of his alma mater, Caltech, and of the Teachers Insurance and Annuity Association/ College Retirement Equities Fund (TIAA-CREF). He continues to reside as the Franco Modigliani Professor of Finance and Economics at MIT. He and Carol are grandparents now and still assemble their family on occasion at a second home in Old Lyme, on the Connecticut River near New London.

Section 5
James Tobin and a New Policy

The dramatic advances in intuition and methodology that arose from the pads of paper and pencils of Louis Bachelier, Paul Samuelson, Eugene Fama, and Stephen Ross revolutionized securities modeling. Necessary in the creation of order from chaos were some strong but not unreasonable assumptions and some leaps of intellectual faith. With the simplifications come efforts to make the assumptions less restrictive, the context more relevant, and the conclusions more helpful. It is into this foray that the great mind James Tobin leapt.

22
The Early Years

At one time, economics and finance did not include the many specialties they embrace today. Some of the giants of finance laid the foundations we all know nowadays, even if few current scholars have actually read their original expositions. Rather, their works have been incorporated into our standard theories, while we vaguely recall from whom the original ideas flowed.

There is another group that may not have been the very pioneers of finance and economics, but that have added insight into so many disparate specialties that their names become familiar. They, too, often made very deep contributions into an area or two, while they provided broad contributions to many other fields. These are the theorists who allowed the finance orchard to thrive by ensuring the cross-pollination of ideas that allow one tree to be fertilized by another.

James Tobin was this type of scholar. He produced insights of great depth, but he also discerned the strengths and weaknesses of our various approaches, with an eye on making our models perform better. He was an example of that rare scholar who combined great depth of understanding with just the right level of mathematical sophistication. He was not solidly in the traditional European camp that espoused model beauty over testable results. Nor did he want his models to be Rube Goldberg devices that generated results consistent with the data but without much intuition that would be especially valuable were the model to fail to predict well. In what has become an important value in finance, Tobin combined theory with practice and methodology with policy, all the while with a great deal of intellectual integrity.

Tobin credited his intellectual balance to his parents. His mother, Margaret Edgerton, was from a rich traditionally American heritage that traced its roots right back to the very first ships that arrived from Europe in

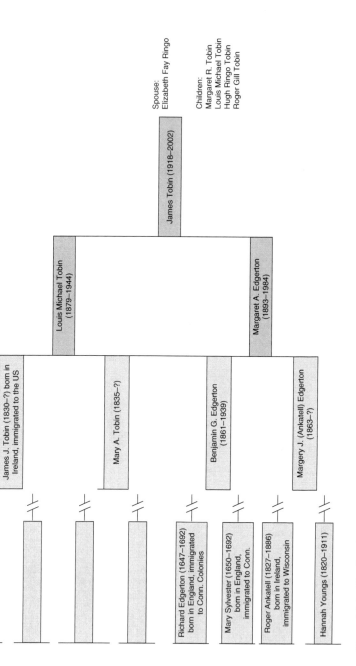

Figure 22.1 The family tree of James Tobin (1928–2002)

the early seventeenth century to settle in a new Massachusetts colony. Her ancestors included her great-grandfather, Elisha Edgerton (1783–1861), who was the grandson of Captain Elisha Edgerton (1719–1783). Their family had lived in and plied the waters of New London, Connecticut ever since the Captain's grandfather Richard Edgerton (1647–1692) and his wife Mary Sylvester (1650–1692) had arrived from Kent, England in the earliest wave of Connecticut seafarer settlement. With few exceptions, the 16 great-great-grandparents of Elisha Edgerton were born or raised in the towns surrounding New London.

Other ancestors of Margaret married into the Connecticut roots from the Massachusetts colonies of the mid-1600s. There could be no family with deeper colonial Connecticut roots than that of Margaret.

Elisha's son and Margaret's grandfather, Henry Kirk Edgerton (1820–1908) migrated from the seaboard of Connecticut to the farmland of Wisconsin in the mid-nineteenth century. There, he met Margaret's grandmother, Sarah Ann Loomis (1827–1915), the daughter of the local physician and surgeon. They raised Margaret's father Benjamin Grant Edgerton in Oconomowoc, Wisconsin. The Edgerton family ran a bank and lived a comfortable life in the early Gilded Age, with servants and a large and well-educated household.

Margaret grew up in the banking family in Oconomowoc. There, both the Edgerton family and bank were most prominent. Yet despite the affluence within which she was raised, she retained a gentle touch. Beyond the time she devoted to raising her family, she dedicated her life to advocating for human services. While her family was comfortable, many of those around her were not, especially during the Great Depression that began in 1930 and accelerated dramatically by 1932. Margaret proved a tireless defender of the poor throughout her life.

The Tobin name was not as deep in the Americas as was the Edgerton name. James Tobin's grandfather was born in 1830 in Ireland and immigrated to the state of Illinois in the mid-nineteenth century. En route to his adopted state of Illinois, he met his bride-to-be Mary, who was five years younger than him and who was born in Rhode Island. They married, and their son Louis Michael (1879–1944) was born in Danville, Illinois.

Margaret Auketell Edgerton and Louis Michael Tobin were married in the summer of 1916 during the First World War. By then, the family was living in Champaign-Urbana, the home of the University of Illinois, where Louis Michael was a journalist and a public relations specialist on behalf of the University athletic department.

James was the first-born child, on March 5, 1918, and his brother Roger arrived eight years later. They grew up in a family that was comfortable and valued education, university life, intellect, and human compassion. They were also politically astute and involved, and even young James was unafraid to air his more liberal views in a quite conservative area. This was a town of Herbert Hoover supporters, even during the depths of the Great Depression, and yet young James, even as a 14 year old, had the courage to support presidential candidate Franklin D. Roosevelt.

James graduated through the local elementary and junior high school, but attended the University High School that was run by the University of Illinois Champaign-Urbana department of education as a model and experimental school. He later reflected that he received an excellent education that produced at least three Nobel laureates and numerous national scholars.

At the University High School, James had the opportunity to play varsity sports, not necessarily as a celebration of any great athletic prowess, but rather because the relatively small graduating class size of the lab school created more demand for students to also be athletes. He thoroughly enjoyed this educational cocoon and fully intended to continue on at the local university, which was and remains an excellent public university, rather than attend the elite institution of Harvard 1,000 miles away.

However, his father had different ideas. James did very well at high school and had the grades and competitive test scores to attend the school of his choice. His father had by chance discovered that the then Harvard President, James B. Conant, was instituting a new program to diversify its student population through scholarships to students who were both intellectually promising but also geographically diverse, beginning with the Midwestern states. His father's best efforts prevailed and, in 1935, at the age of 17, James took the train to Boston on his way to Harvard.

Tobin remained at Harvard for six years. While he had intended to travel after he graduated with his Bachelor's degree in 1939, the outbreak of war in Europe convinced him to instead continue his graduate studies at Harvard. While at Harvard, he studied economics. He knew he had strong reasoning and analytic skills, and he shared with his mother a commitment to improving the human condition. He saw economics as an avenue for these energies. He also had the opportunity to pursue these interests when Harvard may have been at an economic zenith. Albert North Whitehead, Joseph Schumpeter, Edward Chamberlin, Wassily Leontief, and Gottfried Haberler, Stephen Ross' nemesis, were all teaching there at that time. His fellow students included Paul Samuelson, Richard Musgrave, Paul Sweezy, and John Kenneth Galbraith.

The philosophical bent of Harvard at that time were also resonant with Tobin's upbringing. The failure of the government to solve the miseries of the Great Depression had led to a school of economic thought that sought to understand the reasons why free markets could fail to keep an economy on an even and progressive keel. Halfway through Tobin's undergraduate studies, a new treatise, the great mind John Maynard Keynes' *The General Theory of Employment, Interest and Money,* was published.[87] Following this indoctrination, Tobin embarked on a lifelong study of market failure and market improvement.

Those who graduate from the University of Oxford often find themselves as civil servants in service to the government. Harvard had a similar tradition, which was especially pronounced when Tobin graduated in 1941 as the nation prepared to enter the Second World War. He was thrown into the middle of public policy at the highest level, and he enjoyed the challenge and excitement. However, when war actually broke out, he enlisted in the Naval Reserve and found himself preparing for an officer assignment on the USS *Kearny* destroyer and anti-submarine patrols in the Atlantic Ocean and the Mediterranean Sea.

After his four years of service, Tobin returned to his studies among a wave of service members who took up the educational opportunities of the GI Bill. He returned to Harvard, completed his PhD in 1947, and was offered a three-year membership in Harvard's Society of Fellows to pursue any subject matter of his choice without any teaching obligations, just as the great mind Paul Samuelson had enjoyed a few years earlier.

Tobin's thesis topic and initial research interest was in the theory and data analysis of the consumption function. He used the fellowship to hone his skills in the newly emerging study of econometrics, especially from the work of the Cowles Commission, then housed at the University of Chicago. When his fellowship ended in 1950, he joined Yale University. A few years after that, the Cowles Foundation moved to Yale as well, and the relatively young Tobin became its new director. Under his influence, Cowles began to include macroeconomics and monetary theory in its focus, in addition to its traditional work in econometrics, finance, and general equilibrium.

Tobin used his scholarly opportunity to keep one foot in Yale, near the heritage homeland of his mother, and the other foot in Cambridge and especially MIT, where Paul Samuelson, Robert Solow, and Franco Modigliani had settled. His affinity for Cambridge was dear to his heart for another reason. In the spring of 1946, the year after he returned from his service in the war, he met his future wife, Elizabeth Fay Ringo. Just as Samuelson had met his future wife, the economist Marion Crawford, who was also studying under Harvard professors, and the great mind Milton Friedman had met Rose Director in his PhD classes at Chicago, Tobin too married an economist.

Elizabeth had been studying under Samuelson at the nearby MIT, and had, coincidentally, grown up near his mother's childhood summer home in Wisconsin. She was already teaching economics at Wellesley College when they met. She also had that combination of compassion and pragmatism, and a commitment to education, children, and the less fortunate that was the hallmark of his mother's life. They were married three months later. She would become a true lifelong partner, anchor, and sounding board for Tobin, and had the background in economics that allowed him to bounce around some of his theories at home, including his comments on the efficient market hypothesis.

23
The Times

By the 1970s, the efficient market hypothesis was beginning to divide the field of finance into camps of supporters and detractors. Supporters subscribed to the Chicago School, which is premised on their faith in the ability of the free market to process and price information and maintain efficiency and competitiveness. This support was primarily from the academic side, even though there were some in the finance academy who were suspicious of its far-reaching implications.

Meanwhile, finance practitioners, most of whom earned a living trying to beat the market, recognized that the efficient market hypothesis had largely marginalized their role in financial markets. In fact, the most extreme interpretation of the efficient market hypothesis concludes that the profits that financial managers earn cannot exist. There are fundamental reasons why, from a theoretical perspective, it is almost impossible to determine who is correct. However, it is helpful to see if there is a pattern upon which the various sides of the battle are aligned.

In the beginning

The earliest definitions of market efficiency came from a scholar taught in the Austrian School of economics, who transitioned through the New School of New York, a bastion of liberal economic thought, and then moved on to Chicago and Yale. This great mind, Jacob Marschak (1898–1977), was chronicled in greater deal in the third volume of this series. Marschak argued that if individuals could all be characterized with a utility function based on the first moment, or mean, of wealth, and the second moment, its variance, we could price the value of a security based on its average expectation but also on its variance as a measure of risk. This notion was developed still further by his student, Harry Markowitz, when both great minds were at Chicago, and then by the great mind William Sharpe and the others who developed the CAPM.

Following Markowitz's esoteric framing of his Modern Portfolio Theory, but before Sharpe derived the much more accessible CAPM for securities pricing, James Tobin reformulated Markowitz's approach in his groundbreaking 1958 paper on portfolio theory entitled "Liquidity Preference as Behavior Towards Risk."[88] With the development of his "separation theorem," Tobin placed Markowitz's Modern Portfolio Theory in the now familiar framework of a combination of a risk-free asset and an efficient combination of risk and return, as determined by the financial market. In doing so, he implicitly accepted both the notion of an efficient market and, for model simplification, the tool of the *representative agent*. He later came to regret both of these paradigms.

Alternatives to market efficiency

By the 1970s, Tobin was growing concerned about the ability of a market to efficiently glean from all available information the appropriate price and then subsequently navigate to that price. These seeds of doubt had already been in place, well before Paul Samuelson's Harvard PhD thesis and subsequent textbook positioned economics and finance squarely within the school of rational thought so embraced at Chicago. Only a few years before Samuelson developed his methodology, the most well-known and celebrated economist and financier of his day, John Maynard Keynes, had postulated an entirely different paradigm for the workings of a modern financial market. In his *beauty contest analogy*, Keynes noted:

> It is not a case of choosing those [faces] that, to the best of one's judgment, are really the prettiest, nor even those that average opinion genuinely thinks the prettiest. We have reached the third degree where we devote our intelligences to anticipating what average opinion expects the average opinion to be. And there are some, I believe, who practice the fourth, fifth and higher degrees.[89]

Keynes viewed financial markets as primarily strategic and subjective rather than scientific and objective. This approach was in stark contrast to the emerging scientific methodology in the American schools of finance and economics at the time, except perhaps when compared to the emerging game theory of John von Neumann in the late 1930s and at Princeton University's Institute for Advanced Study. The Cambridge, England school of thought had few advocates on the American side of the Atlantic by the early 1950s.

Frank Knight in the 1920s and 1930s at the University of Chicago, the famous price theorists at Chicago who trained a whole generation of market thinkers, including Milton Friedman, Chicago's native son Samuelson, and the Cowles Commission at Chicago all contributed to the market-oriented scientific approach that defined the Chicago School at that time and to this day. While the Cowles Commission had moved to Yale University by the mid-1950s, certainly the body of work produced by Marschak, Markowitz, Kenneth Arrow, and others at that time at the Commission all reinforced the intellectual beauty and coherence of the perfectly competitive market paradigm. Fully consistent with the efficient market hypothesis that would be formulated at Chicago by Fama a decade later, the empirical work by the Cowles Commission was originally motivated by Alfred Cowles' early explorations that had concluded that financial markets are efficient. This effort laid the empirical foundation for the assumption of independent and randomly distributed residuals that is consistent with a random walk model. Without this foundation, modern econometrics could not develop.

The MIT School

While the Chicago School contained brilliant theorists who could support the conclusion of market efficiency, and emphasized strong empirical skills that could wring profound conclusions out of data, the mathematical and engineering-oriented MIT, under the leadership of Samuelson, Franco Modigliani, and others in the 1960s, was developing calculus and differential equation-based models of finance and economics, and, with it, began taking the lion's share of Nobel Prizes in economics. Its approach was one that did not employ the assumption of market efficiency as a matter of faith. Nor did it develop models that necessarily concluded that markets were efficient. At times, the MIT researchers adopted market efficiency as a way to close their models, as a matter of pragmatic academic convenience and mathematical elegance rather than faith. They could perhaps be persuaded otherwise if a more attractive paradigm came along.

In fact, others, too, were somewhat skeptical of an assumption that stated that the market is efficient and that equilibrium could be determined by a representative and fully rational investor. Indeed, this criticism was what had originally delayed Sharpe's publication of his 1962 submission on the CAPM until the editorship of the *Journal of Finance* was assumed by someone who was more receptive to such a leap of faith.

When Tobin first began to work with Markowitz's approach in the 1950s while directing the newly arrived and renamed Cowles Foundation at Yale, he too thought little about the far-reaching concept of a fully rational representative agent whose preferences dictated equilibrium in a financial market. He later noted that, had he anticipated that his foray into Modern Portfolio theory would become as seminal as we now know it to be, he would have been more qualified in his simplifying assumption of the representative agent. After all, he was most associated with the Yale School, which embodied an approach that assumptions should be made with caution rather than zeal and that markets fail sometimes.

For every Chicago precept, there seemed to be a Yale response. When the Chicago icon Arnold Harberger (1924–), a strident supporter of the competitive market paradigm, concluded in a 1954 piece that the inefficiencies arising from what many economists believe is the most inefficient market form, the modern monopoly, was perhaps only a tenth of one percent of GDP,[90] Yale's equally eminent icon Arthur Okun (1928–1980) noted that the economy may not produce at its theoretically efficient and sustainable level as predicted by the competitive paradigm. When balancing microeconomic inefficiencies to macroeconomic failures, Tobin articulated the Yale predilection when he stated: "It takes a heap of Harberger triangles to fill an Okun gap."[91]

Tobin was increasingly concerned about the acceptance of the efficient market hypothesis as a matter of financial faith. The Yale School believed that financial markets and the economy were rife with inefficiencies. His representative agent oversimplification was helpful in the mid-1950s because it permitted him to focus on one single financial market in his derivation of the separation theorem. However, he later realized that the representative agent is more difficult to defend when microeconomics is extended into the macrofinance of modern global financial markets. Today, dizzying volumes of trades from myriad market participants, even for a single security, do not seem to easily lend themselves to an assumption of a representative agent. Each of these traders apparently acts to optimize very different objectives, with one who believes that buying is optimal alongside another who believes that selling is necessary at any given moment. Moreover, when markets become more volatile, some are faced with capital constraints and margin calls that defy the assumptions of the perfectly competitive Arrow-Debreu equilibrium. Indeed, Tobin believed that such market volatility defies the very conclusions one would draw from the efficient market hypothesis.

We look next at Tobin's explorations on this dilemma. First, he developed a methodology, Tobin's q, that could potentially measure what he saw was a potential inefficiency. Then, he prescribed new practices for global financial markets.

24
Tobin's Efficient Market Paradigm

An ancient proverb attributed to an anonymous Arabic poet says:

> He who knows not and knows not he knows not: he is
> a fool – shun him.
> He who knows not and knows he knows not: he is
> simple – teach him.
> He who knows and knows not he knows: he is asleep –
> wake him.
> He who knows and knows he knows: he is wise –
> follow him.

It is this inability to know what we cannot know that stymies a proof of the efficient market hypothesis. One cannot tell in advance the degree to which pricing in the market is accurate. Nor can one back-test for efficiency of a given security because the subsequent profits that are presumably discounted and incorporated into a security arrive based on decisions predicated on such information not available when the security was priced. In this sense, the price of a security can only be considered efficient if it is an accurate reflection of what we collectively believe is the value of the asset, given what we know at the time and, inevitably, what we collectively imagine for the future. Yet, "there are things we don't know we don't know."

This realization inevitably places us at the foot of the concern Paul Samuelson expressed in the closing lines of his 1965 paper that provided the theoretical apparatus for the efficient market hypothesis. We cannot avoid the constructs of Leonard Jimmie Savage's personal probabilities theory, which was discussed more fully in volume two of this series. We can, however, attempt to construct the degree to which market valuations are either aligned or misaligned with alternative valuations. The most logical valuation methodology is the book value of the firm that an accountant would keep to tally the value of its assets. This was the tool Stephen Ross employed in capturing the goodwill of a firm as a measure of the discrepancy of value between the market value and the book value. Ross and others after him have relied on a theory now known as Tobin's q.

Tobin's q

In an effort to better understand how the price of a security reflects its ownership of physical assets and the degree to which it also reflects more subjective values of goodwill, Tobin developed a quotient (q) that expresses the security's market value, net of liabilities, in the numerator over the replacement value, net of liabilities, in the denominator. A measure of 1.0 implies that the firm is valued based on the sum of its measurable assets at replacement cost. A measure greater than 1.0 implies that there is a component of goodwill and expectations of supernormal profits above the expected return on the tangible assets. A measure of q less than 1.0 suggests the security may be undervalued or the company is worth more broken up than as an ongoing concern.

The finance literature usually treats a variation of Tobin's q that does not depend on the determination of the true replacement value of a corporation's assets, but rather measures its book value.

The quotient can also be gauged over the entire market as the ratio of total market capitalization over the sum of the market's book assets. This quotient provides a measure of excessive or undervaluation in the market as a whole. A market with a high q can also indicate that there are larger than ordinary profits being earned, relative to the value of assets invested, which Tobin argued would act as a signal for greater private investment.

Tobin's q remains one of the relatively common measures of market and individual security pricing. If a market is efficient, capital should flow toward those securities that provide returns above the risk-adjusted rate. These higher returns and higher prices should then yield a q at or near 1.0 once market equilibrium is established.

Four measures of market efficiency

Tobin also waded directly into the discussion of market efficiency by augmenting Eugene Fama's definition in his efficient market hypothesis.

In his Fred Hirsch Memorial Lecture "On the Efficiency of the Financial System," originally published in the *Lloyds Bank Review* in 1984, he considered four distinct conceptions of financial market efficiency:

1. Information arbitrage efficiency – asset prices fully incorporate all information that is available at no cost, for returns of no risk. This measure corresponds to Fama's weak efficiency.
2. Fundamental valuation efficiency – securities prices accurately reflect the historical flow of profits to the corporate assets. These profits are capitalized by investors demanding a share of the profits. This measure corresponds to Fama's semi-strong efficiency.
3. Full insurance efficiency – the prices of securities reflect all various contingencies in the provision of the goods and services of the firm. These prices would then be consistent with Arrow prices.
4. Functional/operational efficiency – securities are priced based on the ownership of the flow of goods and services that the corporations provide and as valued by those investing in the securities. This measure can be regarded as the price the market would be willing to pay for the product of firms as if the firms were run as a cooperative for the benefit of their owners.[92]

Tobin's measures are based on the view of financial assets for their products or flow of profits. These measures are based on financial or economic theory, and hence depart philosophically from Fama's more observational measures. Of course, a rationally priced security should also incorporate various components of Tobin's four measures as appropriate.

The Tobin tax

Tobin took a more functional and substantive view of securities markets and shared Keynes' concern that markets are sometimes characterized by speculation over substance. He took his cue from Keynes' lament that financial investment may become decoupled from the market's fundamental role as the owner and investor in the means of production. In Chapter 12 of *The General Theory of Employment, Interest and Money*, Keynes proposed a tax on financial transactions that were excessively speculative. He had argued that such a tax would reduce the rampant speculation and volatility that increases risk and drives down the risk-adjusted returns to those legitimately investing for more fundamental and substantive reasons.

Keynes wrote:

> Speculators may do no harm as bubbles on a steady stream of enterprise. But the situation is serious when enterprise becomes the bubble on a whirlpool of speculation … The introduction of a substantial government transfer tax on all transactions might prove the most serviceable reform available, with a view to mitigating the predominance of speculation over enterprise in the United States.[93]

Thirty-five years after Keynes recommended a tax to overcome what he saw as a peculiarly American speculative fever in the Roaring Twenties, Tobin proposed a modern version of Keynes' tax, since labeled the Tobin tax, to reduce the volatility of foreign exchange transactions. His proposal was meant to address an emerging global monetary problem. In the early 1970s, President Richard Nixon announced that the USA would move off the gold standard. His gesture meant the end to the Bretton Woods agreement among the post-Second World War allies to ensure that the response to a more unified post-war global economy would not become mired in rampant exchange rate speculation as investors judge and bet for and against the perceived winners and losers in increased globalization. To ensure that international transactions did not fall into vicious speculative cycles, the gold standard was imposed. With the effective end of the Bretton-Woods system, Tobin proposed his tax in an attempt to mitigate speculative volatility in foreign exchange markets.

Speculative bubbles and market gyrations in 1987, 1999, and 2008, and the credit crisis in 2007 and 2008 have caused many commentators to return to this idea. The concept was to impose a very small tax, in the order of 0.1 percent, or one part in a thousand, to reduce the speculative churning of the same shares multiple times per day not because of any change in the fundamental value of the public corporation, but rather because of the flow of money motivated by the chartists, or technical traders, who detect, or perhaps create, small trading opportunities.

By the early 1980s, Tobin had emerged as the leading skeptic of the efficient market hypothesis. He had augmented the definitions of market efficiency measures that included two of Fama's measures, weak and semi-strong form, as two of his four cases. He added two more definitions of market efficiency that were consistent with the Arrow securities and with the view that shareholders purchase stock to command the resulting flow of production. He also derived Tobin's q so that it would be possible to discern how the market value of a security relates to the replacement cost of its underlying assets. Finally, he observed that actual financial markets have greater variance than that warranted by all asserted theoretical paradigms used to price securities. To reduce such excessive financial market volatility, he proposed that markets revisit the approach recommended by Keynes in 1936 – the Tobin tax.

25
Discussion and Applications

James Tobin offered the finance literature a paradigm, a measurement tool, and a solution. He expanded Eugene Fama's efficient market hypothesis to explore further not only the arbitrage process arising out of information, but also the very definition of fundamentals pricing. He then offered one measure, Tobin's q, to benchmark a financial market's capitalization of a corporate security relative to the value of its underlying physical assets that create the means to produce and generate profits. He observed that the volatility of measures of Tobin's q or of market prices for securities seems to defy the current state of theoretical understanding of securities pricing. From this conclusion, his idea of a Tobin tax to stem excessive market volatility has been discussed extensively.

We have observed earlier that there can be no direct measure of the accuracy of the efficient market hypothesis. To test the hypothesis, we must also postulate a process by which we could arrive at the appropriate rational price for a security. The empiricist Fama offered no insights into such a methodology, while the theoretician Tobin proposed four different approaches to determining such a measure. However, any test of the efficient market hypothesis ultimately becomes a joint test of the hypothesis of what constitutes a rational security price.

The Tobin tax

Interest in Tobin's advocacy of John Maynard Keynes' small tax on financial speculation piques each time the market is beset by excessive volatility. Not all volatility is viewed as troubling, though. When the market is rising in a speculative bubble, few complain. However, when the market falls precipitously, the short selling and the dramatic increase in trading volume often results in greater calls for processes that can slow down a market freefall. Following the crash of 1987, such circuit breakers were proposed. These temporary trading curbs, invoked when the market fell by a large amount that exceeded a pre-specified level, were subsequently removed from the New York Stock Exchange in 2007 because they were deemed to be ineffective at preventing market volatility. However, exchanges began to reconsider and redesign trading curbs following the *flash crash* of 2010. This dramatic drop of almost 1,000 points for the Dow Jones Industrial Average at one point in the day on May 6, 2010 has been attributed to a number of different factors. While the precipitating factor remains debatable, most practitioners and scholars agree that a new style of trading, called *nanotrading*, exacerbated the decline. Before the creation of stock trading executed primarily through the Internet and computer software, nearly all trades were routed through specialists who managed the book of trades of a given security. Such specialists and market makers controlled the flow of trades to match supply and demand and to ensure that trades were conducted in an orderly manner. This human judgment could also act as a level of protection against accidental trades, the so-called "fat finger" trades that could result if one inadvertently added a zero or two to the number of shares proffered for sale or purchase.

By the 1990s, computers were replacing humans as the arbiter of trades. In addition, large trading houses were using computer algorithms to automatically generate buy or sell orders for the securities in their portfolio based on price movements and market conditions. These computerized trades were not designed to mimic the orderly order processing of specialists and market makers; rather, the computerized trading desks were designed to execute trades quickly to allow brokerage houses and sophisticated investment divisions to make profits on upswings and unwind or sell short positions on downswings.

At the same time, a new cohort of day traders began specializing in their favorite stocks. These traders would buy and sell the same security multiple times each day, but would close out their positions each afternoon before the market closed so that they did not expose themselves to any overnight risk or news they could not manage through immediate purchases or sales.

It has been argued that such trading adds liquidity to the marketplace. Under this theory, a large number of traders simply allow the market to adjust more quickly and hence, in the Fama semi-strong efficiency sense, new information is incorporated into the price more rapidly. Such an interpretation is valid if these traders were adjusting to shifting market fundamentals. However, most day traders or computer algorithms have little facility to measure market news as it impinges on the fundamentals of the securities they track. Instead, these traders to whom Keynes and Tobin showed such concern are the *chartists* of the *technical analysis* school of financial security pricing. They are responding solely to movements in a security price without regard to their feedback effect on other traders.

Four economists, including the chief economist of the Commodity Futures Trading Commission, explained the flash crash of 2010 as the result of the technical analysis and high-frequency trading gone awry:

> Based on our analysis, we believe that High Frequency Traders exhibit trading patterns inconsistent with the traditional definition of market making. Specifically, High Frequency Traders aggressively trade in the direction of price changes. This activity comprises a large percentage of total trading volume, but does not result in a significant accumulation of inventory. As a result, whether under normal market conditions or during periods of high volatility, High Frequency Traders are not willing to accumulate large positions or absorb large losses. Moreover, their contribution to higher trading volumes may be mistaken for liquidity by Fundamental Traders. Finally, when rebalancing their positions, High Frequency Traders may compete for liquidity and amplify price volatility.

> Consequently, we believe that irrespective of technology, markets can become fragile when imbalances arise as a result of large traders seeking to buy or sell quantities larger than intermediaries are willing to temporarily hold, and simultaneously long-term suppliers of liquidity are not forthcoming even if significant price concessions are offered.[94]

Physicists speak of two types of feedback. One is positive feedback and the other is negative feedback. The nature of this feedback from a technical sense is different from the way it is used in common parlance. While people often speak of negative feedback as criticism or a bad thing, and positive feedback as helpful and constructive, in the mathematical sense the implications are often the reverse.

Technically, negative feedback means the injection of a force to counteract another destabilizing force. The counteracting force then brings the system back into equilibrium. If the negative feedback brings the system back into equilibrium smoothly and without overshoot, the system is called *critically damped*. Such a system is resistant to forces that would otherwise divert it from a long-run and stable equilibrium. However, too much negative feedback can produce oscillations that cause the system to gyrate only slowly toward its long-run equilibrium.

On the other hand, positive feedback is almost always destabilizing. Such feedback occurs if a force that causes a system to deviate from its equilibrium induces another force that compounds its effect. The feedback one hears when a microphone is brought too near a speaker is of this destabilizing type. Without safeguard mechanisms, the screeching volume becomes louder and can cause the amplifier or the speaker to fail.

Technical trading can mimic this dangerous positive feedback. Without a market fundamental to act as the anchor toward which short-term trading should converge, a series of rapid sell orders can solicit a response from day traders and algorithmic trading desks that generates more sell orders until a stock can drop multiple percentage points with no change in its fundamentals. Hedge fund managers have learned to profit from such bandwagon effects and have even admitted to occasionally generating these effects in order to create profit opportunities.

With improvements in computer information technology, such algorithmic trading has recently reached new levels of sophistication. These so-called *nanotraders*, also called *high-frequency traders*, monitor certain securities in search of imbalances between the number of buy and sell orders, at various prices, for a given security. Because nanotraders receive their information directly from listing exchanges, and either co-locate at the exchange or as close as physically possible to it, their computers can sense imbalances just a few *nanoseconds* before other algorithmic traders, day traders, or market makers can respond. The nanotraders get to the trade first and get to ride the leading edge of the resulting shift in a stock price. Sometimes it may be on the leading edge in the wrong direction. There too, it can also get out before anyone else. Such an algorithm that trades tens of millions of shares in a given day and may make only a penny or two per transaction can nonetheless *earn* hundreds of thousands or millions of dollars a day.

These trades make the market more efficient on a *technical basis* or on Fama's weak-form basis. However, designers of nanotrading platforms readily admit that their trades have nothing to do with market fundamentals. As such, they have the destabilizing *positive feedback* effect and increase both trading volume and volatility in ways that defy the principles of semi-strong or strong form efficiency.

Such high-frequency traders constitute an increasing volume of trades on modern computerized exchanges. However, they do not hold significant inventories of stock over time and, indeed, avoid maintaining large positions for long. Thus, they cannot and will not absorb book losses that arbitrageurs engage in under the belief that their holdings prices will return to the fundamental values following a brief departure from equilibrium.

These volumes may mistakenly be interpreted as creating more liquidity in financial markets. This liquidity is defined as buying power to act as a buffer on each side of market supply and demand. However, greater liquidity is typically embraced as a dampening and moderating influence, while high-frequency trading actually increases volatility, especially as nanotraders must rebalance their holdings following any departure from which they profit.

Increased trading can then contribute either to semi-strong efficiency if designed to bring the market toward market fundamentals, or weak efficiency, at the expense of semi-strong efficiency, if it is in the form of technical trading. In the interests of rational security pricing, the former should be encouraged and the latter discouraged. The former efficiency should be volatility reducing, while the latter will increase volatility.

Tobin believed that financial markets were becoming increasingly volatile and hence departing from his first definition of efficiency, his semi-strong second, and perhaps also his third and fourth form definitions of efficiency. Economists generally agree that taxes can be employed to reduce activities that are undesirable and that produce problematic negative externalities. In the case of an increase in speculation-driven volatility, the negative externality Tobin feared was that increased speculative trading could create a cascading bandwagon effect.

Tobin was originally concerned about volatility in foreign exchange markets and the resulting destabilizing effect this volatility would have on the macroeconomy. However, many others have also applied his proposed Tobin tax to traditional financial markets.

The test of appropriateness then comes down to an empirical judgment as to whether such a tax decreases or increases volatility. On the one hand, such a tax will have the effect of discouraging *noise traders* such as the nanotraders that rely on the speed, or the first derivative, of price movements. Similarly, Paolo Pellizzari and Frank Westerhoff in 2009 showed that such a tax might also reduce the number of speculative traders by imposing a tax that rises in proportion to the frequency of trades rather than the total inventory of holdings.[95] On the other hand, Markku Lanne and Timo Vesala argued in 2010 that a transactions tax could amplify volatility, especially in foreign exchange markets, if it penalizes more informed traders who may correspondingly trade more often otherwise, rather than uninformed and hence less discerning traders.[96]

So far, empiricists have been unable to demonstrate that there is a statistically significant link between taxes or other transactions costs and market volatility. In fact, the announcement of higher trading costs may increase volatility in the short run as long-run traders may attempt to book their hedge trades before the tax is imposed.

Tobin's concerns can be interpreted in one additional light, the degree to which remains an open research question. His final definition of market efficiency, derived from a fundamental view that financial markets have the sole function of channeling actual production resources effectively between those who supply and those who need them, is one that makes economic sense, using the benchmark of Arrow's fundamental theorem of welfare economics.

Just as Adam Smith shifted the then-prevailing role of economic power from those who controlled markets to those who controlled actual production, Tobin advocated for a renewed emphasis on the needs of modern production markets rather than on modern financial markets. Yet, in 2006 in the USA, one out of every three dollars of profit was earned in financial markets. This observation implies that the proverbial tail was wagging the dog. A Tobin tax designed to discourage speculation by removing profits from the financial sector is designed to tilt the playing field from the paper economy to the production economy.

Rather than the imposition of a Tobin tax, Willem Buiter recommended that this reorientation can be done instead by reimposing risk in financial markets, in light of the financial bailouts of 2009 that indemnified downside risk. He expressed the concern that derivatives markets are increasingly devoting excessive effort to seek rents at the expense of others:

> [Since] derivatives trading is not costless, scarce skilled resources are diverted to what are not even games of pure redistribution. Instead these resources are diverted towards games involving the redistribution of a social pie that shrinks as more players enter the game.[97]

In fact, such rent grabbing, rather than value creation, can create a smaller economic pie. If bank and financial defaults are absorbed by the system as a whole, there is, in effect, a redistribution of property rights from those who produce to those who pursue paper profits.

Tobin was admittedly a theorist. He provided a theoretical basis for the description of markets gone astray under the purported pursuit of financial profits separate from production profits. In doing so, he was ultimately demonstrating that financial markets might not perform as predicted by the Arrow-Debreu competitive ideal. He gave a theoretical motivation for further explorations. He left the finance literature with two challenges. First, as an empirical question, is it the case that markets operate and are more efficient than the traditional efficient market hypothesis would predict? This is a challenge that our next great mind, Robert Shiller, would accept. Then, either modifications or replacements of the traditional efficiency paradigm will be necessary. We leave to a subsequent volume of this series a description by financial behavioral theorists of a paradigm that better captures the influence of the way in which humans make financial decisions as a replacement for the efficient market hypothesis.

26
The Nobel Prize, Life, and Legacy

James Tobin was the last of the pioneering breed who provided the foundations of modern financial theory. He specialized in the micro-economic foundations of macroeconomics, but he found himself inevitably exploring the important role of finance markets. He provided the first significant insight to Modern Portfolio Theory just as finance began to emerge as a distinct field in the study of decision-making. In developing his *separation theorem* that generalized Markowitz's theory, he brought Modern Portfolio Theory into the economic mainstream and initiated a wave of innovation in financial theory beginning with the CAPM model of the early 1960s.

Over the first 30 years of the Nobel Prize, seven scholars won the award for their work in finance. Tobin was the first. He was primarily a theorist who helped motivate thinking in finance that has always main-tained a strong tradition of empiricism. He was probably the last great mind in finance to have trained exclusively in economic thought and to reside in a department of economics. And his theoretical and intui-tive concerns about the efficient market hypothesis helped forge a new school of finance, the behaviorists, that has divided finance ever since.

When the Cowles Commission, with its motto "Theory and Measurement" moved to Yale University in 1955, Tobin, who had arrived at Yale after graduating from Harvard in 1950, became its director. He remained associated with what later became the Cowles Foundation and with Yale to the end of his career.

A tradition of public service

Almost exclusively, the great minds of finance since the development of Modern Portfolio Theory had a foot planted at least as firmly in the corporate and financial practice worlds as they had in scholarship. Some, most notably the great minds and Nobel laureates associated with *Long Term Capital Management*, suffered some public notoriety for their personal gain in the private markets of finance.

Tobin served government and public life instead. He was a frequent commentator on economic and financial issues as they impinged upon society. He was frequently drawn upon to comment and consult on public policy issues. He served on President John F. Kennedy's Council of Economic Advisors (CEA) from 1961 to 1962 and consulted with the CEA until 1968. He worked with the Nobel laureate Robert Solow and the laureate and great mind Kenneth Arrow to forge Kennedy's twist on Keynesian economic policy for the first half of the 1960s. He also consulted with the Federal Reserve Board of Governors and the US Treasury.

Tobin earned numerous awards throughout his life. In addition to the Harvard Junior Fellowship he enjoyed from 1947 to 1950, he received the John Bates Clark Medal in 1955, as had his colleague Paul Samuelson a few years earlier. Named after the American economist who pioneered the neo-classical theory of the firm, the medal is given by the American Economic Association to the American economist under the age of 40 considered to have made the most significant contribution to economics. It is not necessarily awarded every year, and two-thirds of the first 17 recipients went on to win a Nobel Prize, beginning with Samuelson in 1970. Indeed, 26 years later, in 1981, Tobin won the Nobel Prize for work he had published primarily in the late 1950s. The Sveriges Riksbank Prize in Economic Sciences in Memory of Alfred Nobel was awarded "for his analysis of financial markets and their relations to expenditure decisions, employment, production and prices."[98]

Tobin presided over the Econometric Society in 1958 and the American Economic Association for the year 1971, and was a trustee for the *Economists for Peace and Security* organization later in his career. He was also a fellow of the American Academy of Arts and Sciences and a member of the National Academy of Sciences. He retired from his position as the Sterling Professor of Economics at Yale in 1988 when he reached his mandatory retirement age at the University, but maintained an active involvement at Yale and in academia in his position as a Yale professor emeritus.

Beyond his Nobel Prize-winning contribution to Modern Portfolio Theory and his development of the Separation Theorem that shows that an optimal portfolio must only combine a risk-free asset and an efficient market basket, Tobin was also known for a number of other scholarly innovations. His Tobin's q remains an important measure among financial practitioners. His Tobit model is a statistical technique that makes it possible to regress the effect of an independent variable on a dependent variable only over those intervals when the dependent variable remains positive. He also produced a large body of important work on the role of money in a modern economy and the relationship between financial and physical assets in our financial and economic decision-making.

Over his life, Tobin wrote over 400 articles and more than a dozen books. He was also granted honorary degrees from many universities, including Harvard, Hofstra, Beloit, Gustavus Adolphus College, Swathmore, Syracuse, Marshall, Northeastern, Bard College, and the University of Wisconsin. He chaired the Department of Economics at Yale for a number of years and had a chair in economics at Yale created for him by an anonymous donor.

Family life and legacy

Tobin and his wife and life partner Elizabeth Fay raised four children. Their eldest, a daughter Margaret Ringo, named for Tobin's mother and for his wife's maiden name, became a writer and fashion designer. Their middle two sons, Louis Michael, named for his father, and Hugh Ringo, both became lawyers. Their youngest son, Roger Gill Tobin, named after his brother, graduated with a PhD in physics from the University of California and now chairs the Department of Physics at Tufts University, the alma mater of the great mind Eugene Fama.

Tobin and his wife lived in the same home in New Haven for their entire life together. He died on March 11, 2002, in New Haven of a stroke just six days after his eighty-fourth birthday. His wife died seven years later, on June 18, 2009, also in New Haven.

Upon his death, the great mind Paul Samuelson lamented the loss of "the leading macroeconomist of our generation." Tobin was remembered as a modest and self-deprecating economist who forever maintained a gentle and compassionate touch and attachment to humanity that his mother instilled upon him. He also well remembered the hardships of the Great Depression and harbored a lifelong concern that markets were not the efficient and self-correcting mechanisms that the Chicago School maintained. Consistent with his major innovation in broadening portfolio theory and establishing it as the foundation for the CAPM model, he maintained that characteristic prevalent of those who lived through the Great Depression: he commended that people diversify their assets, not just among financial assets, but also real and tangible assets that could provide investors with a flow of services regardless of the gyrations of financial markets. When he was asked about his work and philosophy during an interview following the announcement of his receipt of the 1981 Nobel Prize, he offered up the usual technical explanation. A reporter then asked just what that meant. He responded: "Don't put all your eggs in one basket." This well-grounded touch allows his research to continue to be intuitive and practical.

Beyond Tobin's profound contributions to finance and economics, he is also remembered for his intuition and advice when markets may fail to operate efficiently. He became an eloquent advocate for a new Yale school of economics and finance and helped motivate the need to measure whether markets were inefficient and offer behavioral finance and economics alternatives to the efficient market paradigm.

Section 6
Robert Shiller and Irrational Exuberance

Through the late 1970s, the market plunge of 1987, and the bubble and gyrations of the 1990s and beyond, the field of finance became increasingly divided. Classical financial theorists and empiricists, still the majority of academicians, remained wedded to the efficient market hypothesis. However, models of market failure, especially from James Tobin and from Sanford Grossman and Joseph Stiglitz, began to question the appropriateness, much less the logical testability, of the efficient market hypothesis. There began a series of explorations as to the degree that financial markets departed from the prediction of the efficient market hypothesis. However, neither a workable alternative nor an articulate spokesperson for an alternative theory of financial markets had emerged – until Robert Shiller damned financial markets for their irrational exuberance.

27
The Early Years

In the last decade of the nineteenth century and the first decade of the twentieth century, there was an exodus of immigrants from Eastern Europe and Russia who sought refuge in the USA from the increasingly volatile politics of their homeland.

Robert Shiller's grandfather, George Ignas Schiller (or Jurgis Szileris on his immigration papers), was born on December 10, 1885 on a farm near Raseiniai, Lithuania. His father, George Schiller, Sr., was also a farmer in their community near the border with Prussia.

This was a time during which Lithuania was torn between competing powers. The regions now known as Poland and Lithuania were on the front between the expansionary territories of Prussia and the Austro-Hungarian Empire. The Russian Tsar Alexander II had asserted Russian prerogative in Lithuania and had even forced the local population to use the Cyrillic alphabet for all writings. The Tsar's impositions fomented a nationalist movement, which was even further aggravated when the draft into the Russian Army was imposed.

The possibility of being drafted into the Russian Army induced young George to leave his homeland at the age of 20. He traveled to America as part of an immigration wave with others who wanted to escape the strife caused by nations fighting to expand their empires.

George arrived in the USA in 1908. He settled in Gardner, Massachusetts, where he found work in a stove shop for a wage of about $0.16 per hour for a 12-hour day. In his spare time, he participated in a Lithuanian music band that toured around Massachusetts. This opportunity allowed him to meet many girls his age. Two years later, Amelia Mary Miller also arrived from Lithuania, and they married following a year-long courtship. They almost immediately had a son, Benjamin Peter (1911–1979), and then a daughter, Anna, eight years later.

By the birth of Anna, the Schiller family had moved to Lenox Township, Michigan so that George could take up a job in the burgeoning automobile industry as a press operator. In 1914, Henry Ford announced that he would pay twice the going wage for assembly workers. As a result, George immediately applied and subsequently moved his family to Detroit.

Henry Ford's policy that brought together the next iteration of the Shiller family was a prime example of enlightened capitalism. The lesson had a profound influence on a future Shiller son. One might see the wisdom of offering a higher wage to reduce turnover and worker training costs. However, Ford had a grander vision. He realized that if industry did not pay a wage that would allow workers to buy their products, the business model was one only for the elite and was not viable, sustainable, or expandable.

George worked an eight-hour day at Ford for more than $0.60 an hour, or five times what he was earning in Massachusetts. He and Amelia also took in as many as four roomers so that they could save money to buy a farm and continue the livelihood they had forged in their home country. He would work the farm and hold down his job at Ford for the ensuing years, except for a brief period when Henry Ford found out that George kept roomers and promptly fired him. However, after a brief respite from the Ford Motor Company, he was hired back, with a 40 percent raise.

Despite the higher wages, the Shiller family was of modest means, and even took in an elderly widower as a boarder to help make ends meet a decade later on the cusp of the Great Depression. The family scrimped and saved their money so they could realize a dream to buy a 94-acre farm outside of Detroit where George could work with his brother Mike, who emigrated from Lithuania to join him, and employ his son to work the land.

While George's heart was in farming, he continued to also work for Ford until he was almost 60, in the last year of the Second World War. Meanwhile, the family faced fortune and heartache on the farm, including the loss of the farm to fire in 1928 and the rebuilding of their dream while the family lived temporarily in their chicken coop. George died of cancer in 1974.

George and Amelia's son Ben experienced their formative years in hard work on the farm. The disruption of the Great Depression made it difficult for him to realize his dream of being the first member of his family to attend college. He was bright, industrious, and hard-working, but the realities of the Great Depression challenged him and his family.

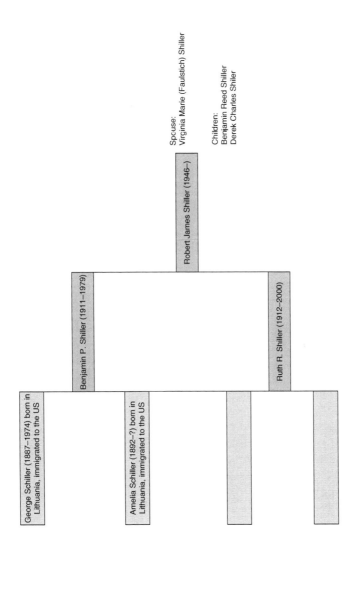

Figure 27.1 The family tree of Robert Shiller (1946–)

His mother had saved $100 and had borrowed another $100 so that he could attend university. However, as the Depression deepened, the family could not afford to keep him in school. Instead, he found out about a new engineering college, the Lawrence Institute of Technology, that had just opened. The college offered students admission if they pledged to pay what they could, and pay once they subsequently received a job. With perseverance, night-shift work, and study during the day, Ben finally graduated in 1936 at the age of 24 from Lawrence Tech in nearby Southfield, Michigan with a degree in mechanical engineering. In 1941, he petitioned the court to drop the "c" from his father's name of Schiller.

Meanwhile, another family of a tailor in Chicago also responded to Henry Ford's call and moved his family to Detroit. The son of one family, Ben, and daughter of the other, Ruth, would not have met but for the policy of Ford and the decision of the families to apply for jobs at Ford's River Rouge assembly plant. Ben's by then extended Lithuanian-American family threw him a party for his graduation. Invited to the party was a pretty young woman who was the stepdaughter of George's friend from the Ford factory. Two years later, and after a bout of ill-health from his overwork during which Ruth nursed him back to health, Ben and Ruth were married.

As a young engineer, Ben and Ruth created opportunities when they could. He obtained work in an industrial oven company whose products were employed in the automobile industry. Ben was a free spirited entrepreneur by nature, and was industrious. In 1970, he obtained a patent in 1970 for an industrial oven that was a precursor to the modern catalytic converter found in our automobiles.[99] In recognition of his entrepreneurship and innovation, his college conferred a distinguished alumni award on him for his professional accomplishments in 1952.[100]

The firstborn child of Ben and Ruth was John W., born on September 12, 1941 at the Women's Hospital in Detroit, just before the USA entered the Second World War. Once the country and the economy stabilized, the family had a second boy, Robert James, on March 29, 1946, in the first wave of the baby boom following the War.

Ben was able to provide more comfort for his family than he had known himself. He moved his family out to the nearby Detroit suburb of Southfield when Robert was 13 years old. Robert attended school near his new home just north of the city of Detroit at Redford High. Now slated for demolition and the creation of a site for a shopping mall in Great Recession-ravaged Detroit,[101] Redford High was a high school a mile south of Detroit's 8 Mile Road, and catered to the children of hard-working families in the automobile industry of Detroit.

Robert and John were both bright children and were very adept at mathematics. John graduated from high school at the age of 16 and matriculated into a small local college for two years before he transferred to study physics at the University of Michigan in Ann Arbor. Following his Bachelor of Science degree in physics, he attended Wayne State University for his Master's in physics, and later obtained a Master of Business Administration at Michigan.

Meanwhile, Robert was taking long walks contemplating whether he should be a physicist or a doctor, a scientist or a social scientist. His interest in economics was piqued when he was 11 years old and read John Kenneth Galbraith's *The Affluent Society*. He subsequently became hooked on exploring the role of finance and economics in the modern economy. He had graduated from high school at the age of 16 as well, in the top five percent of his class. He had won a National Science Foundation Scholarship that would somewhat offset the costs of going to a top college like Harvard University. However, the family could not afford their share, and he instead began at the local Kalamazoo College for a few years before he too transferred and graduated from the University of Michigan.

At his new university, Robert also felt a calling to share what he discovered with others, a value he had learned from his father. For instance, soon after arriving at the University of Michigan, he began writing for the student newspaper, the *Michigan Daily*. He also pursued his passion for the study of economics and graduated at the top of his class. This time around, the National Science Foundation scholarship was more lucrative. Upon graduating from the University of Michigan with a BA in economics in 1967, he was accepted onto the PhD program in economics at MIT, where he graduated in 1972.

Three years after Shiller graduated from MIT, his future bride, Virginia Marie Faulstich, graduated from nearby Brandeis University in Boston. Virginia had grown up in the Boston bedroom community of Waltham and attended Waltham High School before she went on to college at Brandeis. Her father, too, had attended college to become an engineer. Following their marriage, they had two sons together, Benjamin, named after his paternal grandfather and born in 1983, and Derek, born two years later. Virginia earned her PhD in clinical psychology from the University of Delaware in 1985 and maintains a psychology practice in New Haven.

It was his wife's study of psychology that influenced Shiller to view financial markets in psychological terms. While she studied for her psychology PhD in the 1970s, the family would entertain fellow graduate students at their home in Delaware. Shiller concluded that the analysis

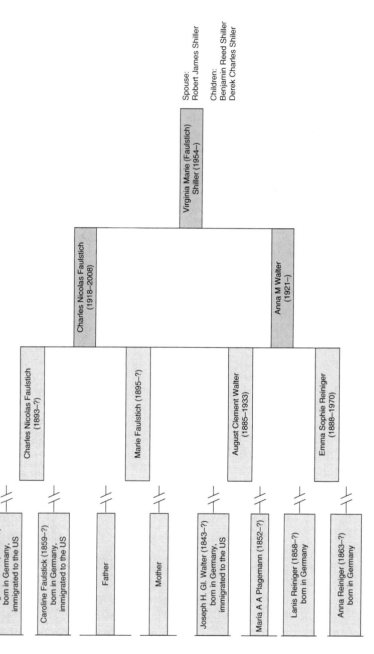

Figure 27.2 The family tree of Virginia Marie (Faulstich) Shiller

Spouse:
Robert James Shiller

Children:
Benjamin Reed Shiller
Derek Charles Shiller

Virginia Marie (Faulstich) Shiller (1954–)

Charles Nicolas Faulstich (1918–2008)

Anna M Walter (1921–)

Charles Nicolas Faulstich (1893–?)

Marie Faulstich (1895–?)

August Clement Walter (1885–1933)

Emma Sophie Reiniger (1888–1970)

Guding Faulstick (1857–?) born in Germany, immigrated to the US

Caroline Faulstick (1859–?) born in Germany, immigrated to the US

Father

Mother

Joseph H. Gl. Walter (1843–?) born in Germany, immigrated to the US

Maria A A Plagemann (1852–?)

Lanis Reiniger (1858–?) born in Germany

Anna Reiniger (1863–?) born in Germany

of a financial market is "very much like studying a disease epidemic. It's a contagion ... When it goes in an up direction, it's very impressive. But it can also work in the down direction."[102] This provocative prognosis spurred him in the 1990s to discuss the dot-com market bubble with the then Federal Reserve Chairman Alan Greenspan. Near the end of the decade, Greenspan recalled this discussion in a speech in Japan where he used the term "irrational exuberance" to describe what he saw as a troubling bubble in financial markets. The market corrected itself violently later that trading day, and Shiller's prognoses became notorious. Despite his insistence that he did not give Greenspan the new vocabulary of "irrational exuberance," the term remains attributed to him.

Years later, Shiller related another important life lesson, one that he attributes to his father.[103] The world is a random place. It is not enough to have a great idea and even to implement it effectively. There is an element of serendipity or misfortune that can beset any great idea. If it succeeds, one is a genius and, if it fails, one can lose everything. This is the perspective of a child from a working-class family who had to open doors for himself and had some doors slam shut. These same doors may have been left wide open for others with a more charmed pedigree.

Clearly, Shiller believes that the divine providence and faith in the efficient market hypothesis and arbitrage does not dictate the movement of markets, just as merit does not always ensure opportunities in life. Rather, it behooves us to also consider behavioral and psychological perspectives in our understanding of market dynamics. Much of his work is in incorporating behavioral aspects into finance using many of the same statistical tools and rigor upon which the discipline is built.

28
The Times

There is an almost irreverent and compelling regard for the power of nature that can likewise be applied to human-made creations. We use analogies such as a perfect storm and natural chaos theory to describe financial chaos, and John Maynard Keynes used the concept of animal spirits to describe investing behavior. The random walk was most helpful in explaining Brownian motion and the movement of molecules, and was successfully applied to the movement of securities prices as early as 1900 by Louis Bachelier.

The obvious attraction of the analogy from nature and the buffeting of stock prices by unforeseeable forces was compelling. This analogy was extended still further by Paul Samuelson's seminal 1965 work "Proof that Properly Anticipated Prices Fluctuate Randomly." The mathematical rigor one can bring from physics to finance is almost impossible to resist, even if one must also stretch the assumptions and paradigms we accept in finance as the price of this convenience.

The leap of faith that Samuelson required in the closing page of his seminal article was that an informationally efficient market incorporates into securities prices all but unforecastable information. He did not assert that this efficiency actually existed; he merely defined its properties if informational efficiency existed. He also noted that this informational efficiency does not imply allocative or competitive efficiency in the sense of the Arrow-Debreu competitive equilibrium or the stronger definitions of market efficiency created by James Tobin. Nonetheless, with the publication of Eugene Fama's 1970 review article, a mantra in finance emerged – "prices fully reflect all available information." In a manner analogous to Adam Smith's 1776 notion of an invisible hand that guides market prices to their natural and appropriate level through the collective outcome of individual self-interest,

Fama's conclusion was argued to be the result of a compelling vision of financial markets in which myriad interested analysts scour all available information for personal profit and collective efficiency.

If such information and effort is costless and widely available, and if analysts and investors with perfect access to capital at the risk-free interest rate behave not strategically but only on their desire to capitalize instantaneously on any security price mismatch relative to its fundamental value, then Samuelson's and Fama's idealized view of a strong-form efficient market can exist.

The implications of such an idealized model are profound. Prices would adjust almost instantaneously to any news that affects the value of a security. The only remaining component of price movements must be those random events that cannot be anticipated. As such, the random walk model and the efficient market hypothesis are closely linked. Unfortunately, these implications are also impossible to test because any test must first establish the appropriate fundamental security price. This test then becomes one of market efficiency and pricing model accuracy.

However, there are other implications of the efficient market hypothesis that can be tested. First, we can determine the reasonability of the assumption of frictionless markets with costless information. Second, we can explore whether markets respond to information in the consistent way that the efficient market hypothesis predicts.

The matter of faith

Such an exploration into the underpinnings of the efficient market hypothesis is not without its academic risk, though. Albert Einstein encountered resistance when he developed his theory that showed that Newtonian mechanics was accurate only as a special case of his more general theory. Physicists found the prospect of revising their understanding of the world around them and their theoretical place in it unnerving, even if Einstein's departures are necessary only once objects approach the speed of light or are extremely massive. In fact, the world entered a state of high physics drama as one group of scholars and experimenters set out to prove that Einstein was wrong, while another sought to affirm his predictions.

Even Einstein became unnerved when his theory of the large and the fast was replaced by quantum theory for very small particles. In this world of myriad small interacting particles, statistics and probabilities replaced Einstein's deterministic equations. In response, he proclaimed in exasperation that: "I, at any rate, am convinced that He [God] does not throw dice."[104] Later, he appealed directly to Max Bohr (1882–1970) in a letter:

> I find the idea quite intolerable that an electron exposed to radiation should choose its own free will, not only its moment to jump off, but also its direction. In any case I would rather be a cobbler, or even an employee of a gaming-house, than a physicist.[105]

In fact, Einstein resisted the new quantum mechanics for almost four decades. He saw the world of physics in compellingly classical terms, as do the efficient market hypothesists and many economists in the world of markets, and he was unwilling to discard his faith for something that described reality better but failed to satisfy his world view. Other physicists accepted that the statistical approach of quantum mechanics was an appropriate characterization of the interaction of millions of particles on a nano-scale, as uncomfortable as such an approach may be. In a perfect world, though, all would prefer a methodology along classical lines that models and aggregates each of these myriad interactions.

The academic community in finance and economics remains equally divided about theory based solely on statistics, just as physics was conflicted over statistical rather than theoretical models in its day. When empirical studies began in the 1970s and 1980s to highlight chinks in the armor of the efficient market hypothesis, the academic community reacted as if a heresy had been committed. Initial criticisms of the efficient market hypothesis were typically met with explanations that there must have been mistakes in the empirical techniques used to identify perceived flaws in the predictions of the hypothesis. However, a wave of studies of problems with these predictions began to at least generate a willingness to explore the issue, if not completely vindicate the first few scholars bold enough to buck conventional wisdom.

The first contribution to the scholarly debate came about in an analysis of whether the random walk indeed implies the efficient market hypothesis. The most compelling argument was from the 1995 Nobel Prize winner Robert Lucas in his 1978 paper entitled "Asset Prices in an Exchange Economy"[106] and published in the prestigious journal *Econometrica* by the University of Chicago. In his paper, Lucas, who is widely regarded as the father of the rational expectations theory, first argued that the rationality hypothesis underlying the efficient market hypothesis should be regarded not as a description of human behavior, which, in this case, determines how people process information and act in a rational manner to earn profits; rather, rationality should be considered as a property that characterizes equilibrium. Lucas pointed out that a hypothesis which assumes that agents have accurate expectations of future prices does not imply that these agents also behave rationally with regard to that information. In other words, there can exist full information and yet investors can still behave as Keynes postulated in his *beauty contest* example. Lucas went on to demonstrate within a theoretical model that rational and well-informed agents can potentially cause prices to follow a path that have the martingale property, or not. Proof of a random walk does not imply information efficiency.

This conclusion does not imply that Samuelson's original analysis was wrong. His model was a simple one that did not take into account either risk or strategic behavior. In fact, strategic investors may be willing to demand a security that is on an upward price trend, almost regardless of fundamentals. This notion is built into the algorithms that successfully drive nanotrading. Moreover, risk-averse investors may be reluctant to invest in a declining market, even if most commentators agree that the market is undervalued. Financial practitioners often argue that it is perilous to stand beneath a dangling sword, even if the sword "should" be pointing in the other direction.

Of course, as we have discussed earlier, by 1980 Sanford Grossman and Joseph Stiglitz had already also firmly established that the assumption of perfect and costless information was suspect. Perfect information requires an investment in its gathering. Yet, if perfect information was efficiently incorporated into a security's price, there is no reward to investing in its gathering. In addition, any such investment capitalized into the price will reward both holders of the security and investors in the information. There is then an externality in information gathering and hence a market failure in its gathering.

We can still hedge our bets and take refuge in a softer version of the efficient market hypothesis based on the appealing intuition that it should not be possible to consistently earn profits in a financial market unless one has superior abilities, information, technologies, or access to capital. This approach acknowledges that the efficient market hypothesis says nothing about market dynamics and the path of price convergence over time. It should perhaps only be interpreted as the end point. Perhaps it is the very groping of investors toward this end point that seems to confer profits on some, and hence losses on others. The efficient market hypothesis should not imply that there cannot be a pattern of profits for some, but rather zero risk-adjusted profits on average. The game is overall a zero-sum game at best, or a negative-sum game if investments are made to capture others' pieces of the financial pie.

If, by the 1980s, there began to emerge a healthy skepticism of the efficient market hypothesis, there remained few convincing alternatives. The chief advocate for the popularization of a reconsideration of the efficient market hypothesis was Robert Shiller. He helped motivate a movement to construct a new behavioral paradigm to the pricing of financial instruments. This paradigm will be the subject of a future volume in the great minds series.

29
The Theory

We spoke earlier about the contribution of the novel 1969 event study of Eugene Fama, Michael Jensen, and Richard Roll, and the earlier pioneering event studies by Ray Ball and Phillip Brown and by Jensen in the previous year. These were the first scholars to explore and affirm the efficient market hypothesis. Each of these event studies seemed to support the semi-strong version of market efficiency in which, upon the release of new public information, a security price is revised accordingly. Two decades later, Robert Shiller used an almost identical methodology to refute the efficient market hypothesis.

In "Do Stock Prices Move Too Much to be Justified by Subsequent Changes in Dividends?," Shiller responded to the growing clamor that stock prices seem too volatile in the sense that their gyrations appear to overreact to market news. He had previously produced evidence that the bond market may overreact to macroeconomic variables, and he built upon the work by Stephen LeRoy and Richard Porter that explored whether the variation of securities prices was uncoupled with the present value of future net income.[107]

The challenge before Shiller and those that followed him was to separate anecdote from the aggregate. Overshooting in one security at one time is difficult to claim empirically because the single sample yields no statistics. Instead, he took a longer view of almost a century of security price responses to dividend announcements. He found statistically excessive volatility based on a null hypothesis that the stock price should equal the expected sum of discounted dividends. Under such a formulation, the *ex post* rational price for a security $p_t{}^*$ should equal the discounted value of the price in the next period plus the next period dividend:

$$p^*_t = \beta(p^*_{t+1} + d_{t+1})$$

189

where d is the dividend paid and β is the discount factor. Shiller was able to use a backward iterative process to show that actual prices are actually much more volatile than rational prices. In fact, a second moment measure of variance was 5 to 13 times higher than predicted by an efficient market hypothesis-based model.

Shiller went on to produce additional studies that consistently revealed excess volatility. A new empirical body of research was ultimately spawned. For instance, in 1985, Werner De Bondt and Richard Thaler showed that stocks which seemed to perform unexplainably well for periods of up to five years tended to revert back to their mean fundamental values in the next five-year interval. Consequently, excessive positive returns in the medium run resulted in excessive negative returns. This phenomenon was reinforced by Narasimhan Jegadeesh and Sheridan Titman in 1993 and has since become known as the mean reversion phenomenon. Their results flew in the face of the efficient market hypothesis that offers reasons why such a phenomenon should not occur over prolonged time intervals.

The debate over this empirical evidence spawned by Shiller took on proportions in finance that were reminiscent of the schism created between the Chicago School of classical economists and the Cambridge, England and Cambridge, Massachusetts Schools of Keynesians. That macroeconomic debate also fell along similar lines, between those classicists who had faith that Adam Smith's invisible hand operated quickly and efficiently and those Keynesians who wondered if it worked only slowly, or at all. The dividing line was once again between the classical efficient market hypothesists at Chicago and a growing group at Yale who were more likely to support Keynes' damning beauty contest parable.

A number of possible explanations were offered to account for the irrational exuberance of securities markets. Inefficiencies arising from cognitive errors or cognitive dissonance, the anchoring of expectations based on observed market momentum, and the dichotomy between rational development of short-term and long-term planning horizons drew increasingly from the field of psychology rather than finance. Without a behavioral foundation grounded in rationality, the emerging collective theoretical skepticism, spearheaded especially by Shiller and Richard Thaler, was variously labeled *behavioral finance*, not for what unified the new branch, but rather in opposition to what the academic orthodoxy challenged.

What ensued was an unusual era in which classical scholars who advocated the efficient market hypothesis and postulated that consistent profits could not be made in financial markets were isolated from the practitioners whose very livelihood was based on earning such profits consistently. In an attempt to better understand real financial markets and decision-making, this new and upstart behavioral school was actually given an airing among practitioners. Then, in October 1987, stocks plunged dramatically worldwide, only to recover almost entirely within a month. The behavioral approach, that markets are not necessarily rational, at least for certain intervals of time, was increasingly appreciated, not because of a hypothesis it postulated, but rather because of the hypothesis it rejected.

Shiller, as one of the leading scholars to first cast doubt on the efficient market hypothesis, increasingly engaged in surveys and writings designed to better gauge and describe a new behavioral and emotionally or psychologically based financial market paradigm. The data generated since 1989 now resides at Yale's Investor Behavior Project within Shiller's Workshop in Behavioral Finance. To illustrate that the unifying concept of behavioral finance theorists is not a unified behavior theory but unified opposition to the efficient market hypothesis, the main web page for the Workshop on Behavioral Finance quotes not what they have necessarily discovered, but rather a graph which shows that the use of the term "efficient markets" in the literature and popular press from 1985 to 2006 has been waning, while reference to the term "behavioral finance" has been waxing and is poised to overtake its rival paradigm.

This new, if yet ununified, theory of finance rings true to practitioners and business leaders driven more by intuition and instinct than the equations and paradigms necessary to publish scholarly work. These practitioners, hedge fund managers, and chief financial officers do not need the affirmation of journal referees to have confidence in what works – for them. They observe and profit from speculative bubbles and meltdowns for which classical efficient market hypothesis proponents deny the existence. In addition, they contemplate the difference between dividends and capital gains strategies and policies that both the efficient market hypothesis and the Modigliani-Miller theorem proponents argue should not matter.

Shiller continued a prodigious research agenda and scholarly publication record in support of his fundamental observation that financial markets are not consistently efficient. However, his genius may not be in these observations. Instead, he captured the mood of a nation. His warning in 2000 of a speculative bubble in his book *Irrational Exuberance* was written both for his fellow scholars and for the popular press. His book was listed as a *New York Times* bestseller just as the speculative bubble began to deflate. Three years later, he wrote a paper for the Brookings Institute entitled "Is There a Bubble in the Housing Market?" just a few years before the most dramatic unwinding of US and global housing prices in the post-Second World War era.[108] He accurately warned of a world of bankruptcies and foreclosures that ran the risk of plunging financial markets into the meltdown that slowly began in 2006 and reached an apex in 2009–10.

After his book on speculative financial and housing bubbles, Shiller became an oracle for millions of people who were deeply worried about the mass destruction of financial security. His star had risen seemingly permanently. Others appear brilliant by calling ten of the previous five financial meltdowns, sometimes after the fact. He had the uncanny ability to identify troubling trends and make prophecies in advance by making observations that others unwilling to abandon their assumptions of the efficient market hypothesis could not see.

In a *FiveBooks* Interview with Sophie Roell, published on January 23, 2011, Shiller explained the root of his psychological view of the world of finance and markets.[109] He qualified that animal spirit of selfishness that has become misconstrued from the writings of Adam Smith in his *The Theory of Moral Sentiments* and *An Inquiry into the Nature and Causes of the Wealth of Nations*. These eighteenth-century explorations of capitalism emphasized the role of self-interest, but also noted that humans are community-minded creatures who have an enlightened natural perspective of self-interest that does not preclude the effect of their myriad independent decisions on others. Shiller took from Smith's writings that people's worth also depends on the good work they do. He noted that Smith's work on such moral sentiments was the foundation for Smith's subsequent great work on markets and the wealth of nations in 1776.

Certainly, in a tip of his hat to his PhD psychologist wife, Shiller exhibits a fascination with the psychology of the individual and the aggregate sociology of an entire economy. Virginia persuaded him that psychology, not esoteric and highly rational mathematical models of human behavior, is the only explanation for seemingly irrational exuberance and buying at the peak of bubbles. He credits her for his transformation from a classical to a behavioral economist[110] and he acknowledged that self-interested individuals live in an "engineered environment" designed to advance an aggregated and collective will. For this juxtaposition to function, our personal integrity cannot depart from a greater set of principles. He sees finance as focusing too much on the former and not enough on the latter.

It is from this observation that irrational exuberance flows. He views speculative bubbles as economy-wide social epidemics and he laments that financial theorists have an insufficient understanding and appreciation of the sociology of the masses that ebb and flow according to dynamics not at all described by a dismal science too often wedded to the motivations of the individual and the assumption of rationality.

30
Discussion and Applications

Robert Shiller is, admittedly, an empiricist, a prognosticator, and an advocate. His advocacy is in the rejection of the efficient market hypothesis, even if he does not necessarily assert a better paradigm. While his approach has not been without controversy, few can deny that he has become one of the most influential economists of his generation.

Shiller has helped to spawn new research in behavioral finance and has helped to create the public awareness for which research funding has followed. Once considered on the very periphery of economics and finance, scholars in behavioral finance and economics are now considered worthy of Nobel Prizes in Economics. In addition, the research has contributed to a better understanding of modern portfolio decisions, even if it is yet to redefine a new post-modern portfolio theory.

Critics may conclude that Shiller's clarion calls had simply been sung at the right place at the troublingly right time. Our markets had been lulled into an overconfidence of the scientific method following the triumphs of computing and of databases in the early 1960s, and of the efficient market hypothesis, the CAPM, and the Black-Scholes equation of the late 1960s and early 1970s. It was easy for Michael Jensen to say in 1978 that "there is no other proposition in economics which has more solid empirical evidence supporting it than the efficient-markets hypothesis." The Chicago Board Options Exchange, Internet-based computerized trading, hedge funds, and high-frequency trading were further triumphs of a new science of finance. Then, financial crises, first in 1987 and then most spectacularly in 2008, cast all this science into doubt. Financial engineering was demoted to alchemy and free markets went from a pinnacle to a pariah. The emerging lack of faith in classical finance has, unfairly, cast financial theorists as part of the problem rather than part of the solution, with the exception of the cohort to which Shiller belongs.

Still, there remains a question of where to go from here. Financial theorists such as Andrei Shleifer have successfully verified that capital markets are simply not deep enough to allow smart investors to overwhelm noise traders any longer. The financial world has seemingly shifted from the fundamentalists to the technicians. This new paradigm, with its dangerous cycles of positive feedback, rather than the mean reverting negative feedback driven by fundamentals, suggest that booms, busts, and increasing volatility may be the new norm. The new theories of behavioral finance seem to support this observation. Irrationally overconfident traders with high testosterone levels and with privatized gains but, in the worst of times, socialized losses seem better able to explain recent circumstances than the classical theories they replace.

Others advocate much more active regulation to overcome what is perceived as increasingly glaring failures of markets unable to self-correct without those outside of financial markets suffering collateral damage. It behooves such regulators to tap into the collective wisdom of some of the very financial theorists they would otherwise prefer to discredit. Much is known about risk management, the role of capital reserves, and the need to police the worst without punishing the rest. Finance and economics well understand incentives, and global financial market failures do not repeal this wisdom. Models of moral hazard and the market for lemons, of regulation and of the principal–agent problem are perfectly sound, even if paradigms like the efficient market hypothesis may be accurate only in a subset of circumstances. Shiller understands the valuable contribution that forensic finance can perform in providing a better understanding what has occurred, with an eye to ensuring that financial folly occurs less frequently in the future.

31
Life and Legacy

Following his MIT PhD in 1972 and his residencies at the University of Minnesota and the Wharton Business School over the next decade, Robert Shiller has remained at Yale University since 1982 as its Arthur Okun Professor of Economics.

While at Yale, he has created the Workshop on Behavioral Finance and is an organizer for the National Bureau of Economic Research (NBER), has written a dozen books, more than 150 journal articles, and hundreds of columns and articles for the popular press. His topics range from behavioral finance to real estate finance, economics, and the global macroeconomy. His 1993 book *Macro Markets: Creating Institutions for Managing Society's Largest Economic Risks* won the first annual Paul A. Samuelson award given by the TIAA-CREF.

In 1991, Shiller teamed with Karl Case, of Wellesley College in Massachusetts, to create the Case-Shiller index to measure national trends in housing prices. This index has emerged as the leading quality-adjusted housing price index and is considered to be an indicator of financial markets that rivals the prestigious Consumer Confidence Index in the USA.

Shiller had maintained a strong interest in housing issues. He recognized that the majority of households own their own home and he acknowledged Tobin's realization that financial assets are augmented by housing assets in a household's asset portfolio. Inevitably, housing markets affect traditional financial markets and vice versa. His concerns over an overheated and overly speculative housing market, and its implications on the health of the US economy, caused him to proclaim in 2005 that the nation was on the verge of the deflation of a dangerous housing bubble. Just as he timed the unwinding of the stock market bubble with his publication of *Irrational Exuberance*, he once again called the failure of the US subprime housing market, which was followed by the credit crisis and then the global financial meltdown. He had his great detractors following those comments, but global financial misfortune vindicated him a year later.

Shiller has served as the Vice President of the American Economic Association in 2005 and as the President of the Eastern Economic Association in 2006. In 2009, he was awarded the Deutsche Bank Prize in Financial Economics. In 2010, he was named by *Foreign Policy* magazine as one of its top global thinkers. He remains ranked as one of the 100 most influential economists in the world according to the IDEAS ranking of the Federal Reserve Board of St Louis.[111] Bloomberg recently named him as one of the 50 most influential people in global finance.[112]

In 2006, Shiller was elected to the Fellows of the American Finance Association, a high honor now awarded to only one prominent finance scholar each year, which he shares with a number of finance scholars who have won the Nobel Prize. He has also received a Guggenheim Fellowship, numerous honorary doctorates, including from Georgetown University and Seattle Pacific University, and honorary professorships. He is a member of the American Philosophical Society and a fellow of the American Academy of Arts and Sciences. In addition, he is a member of the Competitive Markets Advisory Council of the CME Group, formerly known as the Chicago Mercantile Exchange, the Index Committee for the Standard and Poor's/Case-Shiller Home Price Indices, and the board of directors of MacroMarkets LLC, a financial risk management consultancy and financial products developer, where he was the chief economist until mid-2011.

The names of Shiller's books attest to both his theoretical perspective and his public policy prescriptions. He published *Animal Spirits: How Human Psychology Drives the Economy, and Why It Matters for Global Capitalism* with Nobel laureate George A. Akerlof in 2009,[113] *The Subprime Solution: How Today's Global Financial Crisis Happened, and What to Do about It* in 2008,[114] *The New Financial Order: Risk in the 21st Century* in 2003,[115] and *Irrational Exuberance* in 2000.[116] He also published his award-winning *Macro Markets: Creating Institutions for Managing Society's Largest Economic Risks* in 1993,[117] following his influential 1990 book *Market Volatility*.[118] His most recent book, *Reforming U.S. Financial Markets: Reflections Before and Beyond Dodd-Frank*, was published in 2011.[119] He also pens a regular column for *Project Syndicate* entitled "Finance in the 21st Century" and an "Economic View" column for the *New York Times*.

Shiller is currently the Stanley B. Resor Professor of Economics at the Cowles Foundation for Research in Economics, and at the International

Center for Finance, of Yale University. He and his wife still live in New Haven, where Virginia maintains her clinical psychology practice. Following their graduation from Hamden Hall Country Day School in Hamden, Connecticut, their two boys followed in their parents' footsteps. Ben graduated from his mother's alma mater, Brandeis, in 2004, and then earned a PhD in the economics of information from Wharton in 2011. He has returned to teach at Brandeis. Meanwhile, his younger brother Derek is completing a PhD in philosophy at Princeton.

Section 7
What We Have Learned

Unlike the contributions of the previous great minds in finance within this series, for which there is now broad acceptance, the contributors to the debate on the efficient market hypothesis in finance have each made contributions that have their supporters but do not garner universal acceptance among scholars. Instead, these great minds created a great debate that has pushed and prodded financial academics to better explain the value of its theories, especially when tested against financial reality. We conclude by summarizing and commenting on their collective contributions.

32
Combined Contributions

Modern finance today very much reflects how it began. Now, rocket scientists and advanced mathematicians, trained in our schools of science and finance, develop sophisticated models to price risk and returns. More than a century ago, in 1900, Louis Bachelier, a mathematical physicist who had earned an income to put himself through school at the Sorbonne in Paris by working at the Paris Stock Exchange, brought his mathematical prowess to an at that time obscure problem in finance. While his mentor, Jules Henri Poincaré, may have been chagrined by his academic blasphemy at that time, Poincaré saw flashes of brilliance in his idea.

Bachelier's idea was one of analogy. By the late 1800s, it was well understood that heat diffuses through an object according to a predictable pattern and dictated by a solvable differential equation. This equation used the Gaussian normal distribution that occurs frequently in nature when objects are subjected to the buffeting of random forces.

In fact, in financial markets, little is random. However, the compelling analogy that Bachelier's options on French government bonds may also be buffeted by random forces induced him to develop what we have subsequently known as the random walk process of securities movement. Five years later, Albert Einstein, in apparent ignorance of Bachelier's work, applied the same random walk process to particles and derived equations for Brownian motion that were essentially identical to those of Bachelier. In the 1970s, Fischer Black and Myron Scholes reinvented and refined Bachelier's work to produce their options pricing formula. All these theories demonstrate that various physical and financial phenomena propagate the same way as heat diffuses.

While such a workable and testable options pricing formula was revolutionary in 1900, the greater contribution by Bachelier was in his development of the analytic concept of a random walk. Others who followed him further refined this process, versions of which we now know variously as a martingale process or a Wiener process.

To reduce movements of stock prices to such a random process for which a change in one period is independent of a change in another means that all anticipated influences are priced into securities returns, leaving only unforeseeable and random forces. Paul Samuelson made this argument in his 1965 paper "Proof that Properly Anticipated Prices Fluctuate Randomly." In the same year, Eugene Fama stated the process somewhat differently when he defined an efficient market as one which fully incorporates information into the price of each security. While he qualified his statement five years later in his seminal review article of what we now call the efficient market hypothesis, this notion that prices fully reflect all available information became as central to finance theory just as the perfectly competitive ideal became central to economic thinking.

Compared to empirical work on the efficient market hypothesis, tests of the perfectly competitive ideal have received much less attention. Most economists take the competitive ideal as just that – an idealized extreme by which market imperfections are benchmarked. While some have conducted empirical studies in their attempts to establish the degree to which markets underperform vis-à-vis the ideal, there is no compelling need to show what everybody accepts. The market may get things right on average over time, but only on average once the degree to which it got it wrong, up or down, is averaged out.

However, finance markets also differ in a fundamental way from most other markets. A traditional market matches producers with consumers. The value from the flow of services one can expect is relatively understood, as are the costs of producing the item, and the difference between the two is an important signal as to whether or not there should be more production or consumption.

A financial instrument is not so clear-cut. It is a piece of paper promising the holder a right to a stream of future income that is contingent on various states of nature and valued based on our collective best guesses about the likelihood of these contingencies. James Tobin pointed out this fundamental difference in finance and economic pricing, and produced four measures of financial market efficiency, the first two of which coincide with Fama's weak and semi-strong efficiency, and the second two of which coincide with Arrow security prices and the pure consumption and production economies, respectively.

While Tobin's contribution to the meaning of market efficiency helped clarify the usefulness and appropriateness of the efficient market hypothesis, there still remained a great deal of interest in establishing the accuracy of the hypothesis. However, the establishment of the hypothesis is not straightforward. Whether security prices depart from their fundamental values depends both on the accuracy of the hypothesis and also on the accuracy of what the fundamental price should be. In fact, there are myriad models for pricing securities, and billions of dollars are spent each year on attempts to develop models that perform better than the others do. Ultimately, though, it is our perceptions that influence the probabilities and values that enter into these models, and hence the subjective side of financial theory cannot be ignored. Moreover, any proof of the hypothesis becomes a joint proof in the accuracy of the pricing model used to benchmark the hypothesis. At a philosophical level, the efficient market hypothesis is not provable.

A great deal of wealth is riding on such explorations. If we were to conclude empirically that arbitrage is effective and prices converge efficiently to their appropriate fundamental values, then it defies another empirical observation. Billions are spent each year on managing financial positions in the belief that such active management can consistently "beat the market." Practitioners, wedded to this belief for their very livelihood, simply do not agree with scholars who argue that these consistent profits could exist in theory.

For these reasons, arbitrage, efficient markets, and market pricing are much more significant and interesting questions than they are in traditional economics. This trio of related notions has been perfected in such pricing models as the APT of Stephen Ross. However, one looming question always remains. Do financial agents, arbitrageurs or otherwise, behave as if they are governed by rationality or is some other sort of behavioral model at work?

Just as the notion of the efficient market hypothesis divided academics and practitioners, finance theorists divided still further along the same fissure. On one side were the classical finance scholars who would impose on any market condition the notion of arbitrage as the invisible hand that guides the market back to efficiency. On the other side were all others who did not believe such rational arbitrageurs had the access to capital, superior information, or better models that would induce them, if they indeed existed, to risk their valuable capital to defy a market gone astray. These behavioral finance scholars and practitioners were united not in what they believed, but rather in what they did not believe.

A future volume of this series will survey the work of the behavioral finance proponents. This volume has explored whether markets are efficient, but does not describe the remedy if we discover they are not. Tobin offered some of these reasons why they may not be, but Robert Shiller is most associated with challenging the conventional wisdom of the efficient market hypothesis among academics and practitioners. Indeed, some believe he influenced the 1990s US Federal Reserve Chairman Alan Greenspan in a most notorious manner. A dramatic plunge in the value of the US information company-driven stocks in the late 1990s has been attributed to Greenspan's perhaps too glib use of the term "irrational exuberance" in his description of markets at that time. Shiller's book of the same name brought the behavioral approach to the attention of the public shortly thereafter.

This schism will not be resolved easily. No behavioral finance model can yet perform with the reliability and intuitive appeal of the more mature finance theories. In addition, there are no unifying and intuitively appealing paradigms in behavioral finance as there are in classical finance.

Until there is a unifying theory that can convince classicists and behaviorists alike, finance is likely to remain in a state of flux and to represent different camps, just as practitioners are divided between fundamentalists and technicians, or chartists. The first is driven by market fundamentals and expected future profits, almost regardless of patterns in the historical data, and the other is concerned with patterns, with little or no regard to fundamentals. Indeed, high-frequency traders and some day traders maintain that they do not need to know anything about the underlying fundamentals and purportedly attach no credence to these fundamentals. Instead, their strategy is to move in and out of positions with such speed that they are not vulnerable to day-to-day news and trends.

Significant debate is likely to continue on the twin premises of the random walk and the efficient market, and the greater premise of rationality. Lines will become blurred as the technicians ally themselves with the behaviorists who entertain an element of emotionalism and momentum in markets, while the fundamentalists have natural allies in the classical financiers who depend on fundamentals markets for their benchmark of where an efficient market should converge, either rapidly or conventionally. One premise remains true, though. Resources will flow to those approaches that have the greatest prospect of returning profits to these investors in the tools of finance.

33
Conclusions

The efficient market hypothesis has provoked more debate than any concept in the history of finance theory and practice. The previous three volumes of this series, on the life cyclists, the portfolio theorists, and the rise of the quants, uncovered no fundamental disagreements among scholars or practitioners, and described no dividing lines among financial theories. Each great mind built upon the foundations of his predecessors and each evolution added broadly accepted intuition into the discussion. However, the efficient market hypothesis is profound and intuitive to many, and dubious and distracting to others.

While this volume has documented the life and times of those who spurred the great debate, it also offers us a glimpse into how great minds are formed, how great ideas are created, and how disciplines evolve, sometimes very rapidly, and, at other times, remarkably slowly because ideas sometimes occur in isolation.

Most of the great minds in this volume, and in prior volumes, looked at a conventional problem in an unconventional way. They were often pioneers in their areas of finance, and hence they were able to look at problems without the blinkers and straitjackets of conventional wisdom. However, they were often not alone. Most of the great minds in this volume and many in previous volumes had married women who also had PhDs in economics for the more traditional theorists and in psychology for the behavioral theorists. Their lifelong partners understood the work to which their respective spouses had dedicated their lives. Their lives and times were intertwined in the endearing theories that flowed from these great minds.

From the evolution of thought described in this volume, we can conclude that the innovations of the random walk, the paradigm of the efficient market hypothesis, and the concept of arbitrage constitute a three-legged stool upon which classical finance sits. The advocates of this approach, the great minds of Louis Bachelier, Eugene Fama, Paul Samuelson, and Stephen Ross, among other classical finance scholars, have developed tools that appeal to those practitioners of finance who price securities based on models of market fundamentals.

Yet, periods of finance chaos, irrational exuberance and speculative bubbles, and extreme volatility have given some theorists pause to question each of these three legs of the classical finance stool. The challenges of James Tobin to the early orthodoxy of Fama's efficient market hypothesis demonstrated that Fama's semi-strong form does not satisfy the theoretical requirements of an allocatively efficient equilibrium. Then, Robert Shiller demonstrated that real markets perform with much more volatility than they should were they indeed governed by rational arbitrageurs who wring every iota of profit out of available market information until a security incorporates into its price all such information and is left efficient in Fama's strongest sense.

However, while it is always a useful academic exercise to test the integrity of the foundations of finance, the questions that constitute these challenges have not yet been answered. Until we resolve how we can either shore up classical foundations or replace the efficient market paradigm with a more appealing model that is also able to better predict the dynamics of financial markets, we cannot say that the story is complete. A subsequent volume of this series will present what we have learned so far in behavioral finance. The final chapter is far from ready to be written, though.

Glossary

Algorithms – programmable routines that control processes such as securities trading when certain criteria are met.

Allocative efficiency – the allocation of available production and resources in a way that cannot make any agent better off without making another worse off.

Anchoring – the psychological tendency to focus on a familiar approach or outcome in spite of available information that may commend a different approach or outcome.

Arbitrage pricing theory (APT) – a theory for the derivation of the value of a security based on its relationship with other predicate variables.

Arbitrageur – one who directs capital to purchase or sell mispriced securities in an effort to profit once the securities become accurately priced.

Asymptotic – the eventual convergence of a variable's value over time.

Auctioneer – a theoretical market construct that simultaneously matches all supply to all demand by the determination of the appropriate set of market prices.

Autocorrelation – the correlation of a variable with its past and future values.

Autoregressive – a pattern of relationships between past variable values and future variable values.

Bandwagon effect – the tendency to make decisions based not on fundamental analysis of their merits, but rather on the observed decisions of others.

Behavioral finance – a branch of finance that attributes decisions of agents to various psychological effects that typically depart from rationality.

Binomial options pricing model (BOPM) – a backward iterative discrete-time method that is used to price options based on their terminal time and price.

Black-Scholes equation – a continuous-time method to price options based on their terminal time and price, the security's price at a current time, and the pattern of volatility.

Bond – a financial instrument that provides periodic (typically semi-annual) interest payments and the return of the paid-in capital upon maturity in exchange for a fixed price.

Brownian motion – the seemingly random motion observed under a microscope by Robert Brown of pollen particles suspended in a fluid. This motion is used as an analogy for other phenomena, like securities prices, that are buffeted by seemingly random and unobservable forces.

Capital Asset Pricing Model (CAPM) – a simple model that is based on Modern Portfolio Theory and could be used to price an individual security based on the risk-free interest rate and the security's covariance with the overall market portfolio.

Case-Shiller index – a housing quality-adjusted home price index published monthly in the USA. The index was developed by Karl Case and Robert Shiller.

Center for Research in Security Prices (CRSP) – a center for research and the publication of data on securities prices that originated at the University of Chicago in the early 1960s.

Central limit theorem – a theorem which demonstrates that the distribution of random draws from a uniform probability distribution will asymptotically converge on a normal distribution.

Chaos theory – a mathematical method to analyze dynamic systems.

Chartists – proponents of a securities pricing analysis methodology that discerns patterns in price movements rather than the fundamental underlying value of a firm based on its flow of profits.

Chicago School – a reference to a school of academic thought, typically espoused by the University of Chicago, which believes that markets are competitive and ought to be unencumbered by regulation.

Circuit breakers – automatic trade-curtailing algorithms that are triggered by market volatility.

Classical model – a micro-economic-based approach to economic decision-making which assumes that all actors are rational and maximize their self-interest, and is driven by the principle that prices adjust to ensure that supply is equal to demand.

Cognitive dissonance – the process by which information is rejected if it clashes with one's expectations.

Competitive equilibrium – a theoretical construct for an equilibrium that results when there are no transactions costs or other market imperfections and prices reflect all available information.

Compustat – a competitor to the Center for Research in Security Prices database for securities prices.

Corporate finance – the study of financial decisions made by corporations to maximize shareholder value.

Correlation – the statistical relationship between two variables. It is typically measured by demonstrating that the movement of one variable is associated with the movement of the other.

Coupon rate c – the periodic payment to the owner of a bond.

Critically damped – a level of optimal feedback that allows a dynamic system to converge to an equilibrium.

Day traders – securities traders who mostly use the tool of technical analysis to capitalize on stock price movements during the day. These traders typically close out their positions at the day's end before the market closes.

Derivative – in mathematics, the instantaneous rate of change of one variable as a function of the change of another. In finance, a financial instrument that derives its value from another underlying asset or instrument.

Differential equation – an equation that specifies the relationship between the rates of change of a collection of variables.

Discount rate – the rate at which humans will reduce the value of future income in the determination of its present value. This term is also used to signify the interest rate set by a nation's central bank.

Discrete models – financial or mathematical models based on discrete time intervals rather than continuous time.

Dynamic – the analysis of a process as it changes over time.

Dynamic process – a mathematical or financial process that varies over time.

Econometric – a system of statistical analysis techniques that have been adapted especially to the time series inherent in economics and finance.

Efficient market hypothesis – the hypothesis that financial arbitrage quickly and efficiently incorporates all available and relevant information into the price of a financial security.

Enlightened capitalism – the collective actions of myriad independent economic decision-makers who nonetheless understand the cumulative effects of their decisions.

Equilibrium – a state in which a relationship converges upon a constant balance.

Event studies – the exploration of the evolution of securities prices following the announcement of a material event that affects the value of the underlying asset.

Face value F – the nominal value of a bond that is returned to the bondholder upon maturity.

Factor loadings – the estimated coefficients that influence the dependent variable as the independent variables fluctuate in the arbitrage pricing theory.

Fair game – a constant-sum game in which no player has an informational advantage.

Fat finger trades – trades that are made in error and can induce temporary and extreme market volatility.

Feedback – the process by which the evolution of a dynamic system feeds back on itself to influence its subsequent evolution. *See also* Critical damping; Negative feedback; Positive feedback.

First moment – a mathematical method of integration to determine the mean value of a variable.

Flash crash – the name attached to a rapid drop in the value of US stock markets on May 6, 2010.

Forward treasury bond – an option to purchase a US Treasury bond at a specified time and for a specified price in the future.

Fractal geometry – self-similar patterns that appear the same even if the scale of observation is changed.

Full insurance efficiency – an optimal competitive equilibrium when there are markets to insure against every state of nature.

Functional/operational efficiency – an equilibrium that is allocatively efficient and defined based on the supplies of producers and demands of end users, with the absence of speculation.

Fundamental analysis – the determination of the underlying value of a financial security based on the flow of future income that the security is expected to provide.

Fundamental valuation efficiency – the determination of the value of assets based on fundamental analysis.

Gaussian distribution – *See* Normal distribution.

Heat diffusion process – the process by which heat radiates in all relevant directions through materials.

High-frequency traders – extremely rapid and frequent algorithmic trading designed to capitalize on small movements and trends in securities prices.

Idiosyncratic risk – the inherent risk of a security based on the dynamics of its underlying asset. *See also* Systematic risk.

Inflation protected treasury – a US Treasury security that offers a rate of return that is adjusted based on an index of inflation.

Information arbitrage efficiency – the result of a process by which securities prices reflect all publicly and privately available information. This efficiency is equivalent to weak information efficiency.

Interest rate – the rate of periodic payments, as a share of the principal amount borrowed, to compensate for humans' inherent preference for the present over the future.

Intertemporal – a reference to decisions made across time.

Irrational exuberance – the term used by former US Federal Reserve Chairman Alan Greenspan to describe the process by which a speculative bubble is formed.

Itô's lemma – the derivation of the value of a stochastic variable over time as a function of its mean and its time-related drift and variability.

Least squares – a method to solve for the relationship between a dependent variable as a weighted sum of independent variables. This technique minimizes the squared difference between the dependent variable and the predicted amount from an estimate of a weighted combination of the independent variables. Before the recent advent of significant computing power, this readily calculable technique was used to estimate relationships between dependent and independent variables.

Lévy distribution – a continuous stable probability distribution for a non-negative number defined by Paul Pierre Lévy as a generalization of the Gaussian normal distribution.

Life cycle – the characterization of a process from its birth to death.

Life Cycle Model – a model of household consumption behavior from the beginning of its earning capacity to the end of the household.

Liquidity preference – a description of the amount of assets that a household or firm would prefer to keep in highly liquid form. This amount depends, among other factors, on the interest or other earnings sacrificed if assets are kept liquid.

Log-Gaussian distribution – a distribution of the logarithm of a variable that is distributed normally.

Martingale – a fair game process in which no knowledge of past events is useful in the prediction of future events.

Martingale independence property – a property which states that the change of a future value of a variable is independent of past values or changes.

Maturity – in reference to a bond or financial instrument, the time at which the instrument becomes due and the financial relationship ends.

Mean – A measure of the average value of a variable. *See also* First moment.

Modern Portfolio Theory – a theory developed by Harry Markowitz that shows how an efficient portfolio can be constructed through the use of a representative market portfolio. *See also* Separation theorem.

Modigliani-Miller theorem – a result derived by Franco Modigliani and Merton Miller which states that the market value of a firm depends solely on its ability to generate income and its risk, and not on the method of its financing.

Monte Carlo study – a simulation technique that derives how a stochastic system may evolve by simulating many possible runs of the system and tabulating the resulting distribution of outcomes.

Nanotraders – traders who execute rapid trades based on small changes in prices. *See also* High-frequency traders.

Negative externalities – the effect of one economic decision on the value of other decisions.

Negative feedback – the process by which the evolution of a dynamic system is induced upon itself to moderate its subsequent evolution.

Normal distribution – a continuous probability distribution that has the familiar bell-shaped probability density function. *See also* Gaussian distribution.

Option derivative – a security that is an option to purchase an underlying security or asset. Because its value is derived from the value of another asset, it is labeled a derivative.

Perpetuities – financial instruments that promise to pay a fixed amount each period indefinitely.

Personal finance – the study of the finance and investment of personal income and wealth.

Positive feedback – the process by which forces influencing a dynamic system are amplified by the system's evolution and further perturb the system.

Random walk – the description of a stochastic process by which its movement appears to evolve randomly. The expression was coined in the early 1900s by Baron Rayleigh who asked how one might measure the probability of the position over time of a drunk person who takes steps of fixed size in random directions each period.

Rational expectations – the characterization of the evolution of an economic system in which each agent behaves and anticipates rationally.

Reflection principle – a notion that all relevant information is reflected in the price of a financial security.

Regression – a technique used to fit a dependent variable as a weighted sum of independent variables.

Rent grabbing – a process by which wealth is not produced or created, but rather is exchanged between individuals.

Rente – the payment of perpetual bonds popular in France in the nineteenth and early twentieth centuries.

Rentier – one who invested in perpetual bonds.

Representative agent – a fictional characterization that reduces the actions of all market participants to a subset of representative participants in an effort to make models more tractable.

Residual errors – the difference between actual observations and a model's predictions.

Return – the expected surplus offered to entice individuals to hold a financial instrument.

Risk – in finance, the degree of uncertainty associated with exchanging a known sum for a larger future but less certain sum.

Risk neutrality – the characterization of decisions by one who is unaffected by risk and is affected only by returns.

Second moment – an integration method that measures the sum of squared differences between a variable and its mean as a measure of variance.

Security market line – a line of market efficiency along which an investor can choose an attainable combination of return and risk through the purchase or short selling of a risk-free asset and an efficient market portfolio.

Separation theorem – an interpretation of Modern Portfolio Theory offered by James Tobin which demonstrates that an investor can create an efficient portfolio for any risk preference through the combination of the market portfolio and a risk-free asset.

Serial correlation – a predictable relationship between a variable's evolution as a function of time.

Short sale – the sale of an asset one does not own with the intention of buying the asset back at a lower price later.

Simplifying assumptions – assumptions that make a financial or economic model easier to solve but that are not expected to change the overall conclusions of the model.

Speculative bubbles – cycles by which a broad portfolio of securities depart significantly, persistently, and systematically from their fundamental values.

Static process – a process that evolves in a way that is not a function of time.

Sub-martingale – a stochastic process in which the expected value next period, projected based on its current value, is greater than or equal to its value in the current period.

Systematic risk – the inherent risk of an entire financial market.

Technical analysis – a method of securities pricing based on the recognition of familiar and recurring patterns in the data and its representative charts. *See also* Chartists.

Tobin's q – the ratio of the market value of a firm's net assets and their replacement cost.

Uncertainty – the degree to which the value of future variables cannot be fully known today.

Variance – a positive measure of the spread of observed values from their mean. *See also* Second moment.

Volatility – a measure of the degree of uncertainty and unexplained movements of a variable over time.

Weak information efficiency – the result of a process by which securities prices reflect all publicly and privately available information.

Wiener process – named after Norbert Wiener, a continuous-time stochastic process that evolves in fixed mean-sized and independent increments.

Notes

1. http://ykabanov.perso.math.cnrs.fr/Bachelier2012/programmes%20angl/programme7_B3_ang.html, date accessed June 25, 2012.
2. http://en.wikipedia.org/wiki/Brownian_motion, date accessed June 25, 2012.
3. T.N. Thiel, *Sur la Compensation de quelques Erreurs quasi-systematiques par la Methodes moindres Carres*. Reitzel, Copenhagen, 1880.
4. Taqqu, Murad, "Bachelier and His Times: A Conversation with Bernard Bru," *Finance and Stochastics*, 5(1) (2001), 9.
5. http://en.wikipedia.org/wiki/Louis_Bachelier, date accessed June 25, 2012.
6. See his seminal work: Robert King Merton, *The Sociology of Science: Theoretical and Empirical Investigations*. University of Chicago Press, 1979.
7. John O'Farrell, *An Utterly Impartial History of Britain – Or 2000 Years of Upper Class Idiots in Charge*. Doubleday Press, London, 2007.
8. Jules Regnault, *Calcul des Chances et Philosophie de la Bourse*. Mallet-Bachelier et Castel, Paris, 1863.
9. Roger Mansuy, "The Origins of the Word Martingale," translated by Ronald Sverdlove, *Electronic Journal for History of Probability and Statistics*, 5(1) (2009), 1–10.
10. William Feller, "The Asymptotic Distribution of the Range of Sums of Independent Random Variables," *Annals of Mathematical Statistics*, 22(3) (1951), 427–32, at 429.
11. Steve Lohr, "Kiyoshi Ito, 93, Mathematician Who Described Random Motion, Dies," *New York Times*, November 23, 2008.
12. Benoit Mandelbrot and Richard L. Hudson, *The (Mis)Behaviour of Markets*. Basic Books, New York, 2004, p. 51.
13. Karl Pearson, "The Problem of the Random Walk," *Nature*, July 27, 1905, p. 294.
14. Louis Bachelier, "Theorie de la speculation," *Annales scientifiques de l'Ecole Normale Superieure*, 3rd series, 17 (1900) 21–86, at 64.
15. Alfred Cowles III, "A Revision of Previous Conclusions Regarding Stock Price Behavior," *Econometrica*, 28(4) (1960), 909–15, at 914.
16. Arnold B. Larson, "Measurement of a Random Process in Futures Prices," *Food Research Institute Studies*, 1(3) (1960), 313–24.
17. Holbrook Working, "Note on the Correlation of First Differences of Averages in a Random Chain," *Econometrica*, 28(4) (1960), 916–18.
18. Hendrick S. Houthakker, "Systematic and Random Elements in Short-Term Price Movements," *American Economic Review*, 51(2) (1961), 164–72.
19. Sidney S. Alexander, "Price Movements in Speculative Markets: Trends or Random Walks," *Industrial Management Review*, 2(2) (1961), 7–26.
20. Paul H. Cootner, "Stock Prices: Random vs. Systematic Changes," *Industrial Management Review*, 3(2) (1962), 24–45.
21. Arnold B. Moore, "A Statistical Analysis of Common Stock Prices," PhD thesis, Graduate School of Business, University of Chicago, 1962.

22. Clive W.J. Granger and Oskar Morgenstern, "Spectral Analysis of New York Stock Market Prices," *Kyklos*, 16(1) (1963), 1–27.
23. Louis Bachelier, *Le Jeu, la Chance et le Hasard*. E. Flammarion, Paris, 1914.
24. "La théorie du jeu et les équations intégrales à noyau symétrique gauche," *Comptes rendus hebdomadaires de l'Académie des Sciences*, 173 (1921), 1304–130.
25. Emile Borel, *Traite du calcul des probabilites et de ses applications, Tome IV, Applications des jeux de hasard*. Gauthier-Villars, Paris, vol. IV, 1938
26. A.N. Kolmogorov, *Selected Works*, vol. 2. Kluwer Academic Publishers, Dordrecht, 1991, p. 63.
27. P Erdös. and M. Kac, "On Certain Central Limit Theorems of the Theory of Probability," *Bulletin of the American Mathematical Society*, 52 (1946), 292–302.
28. M.F.M. Osborne, "Brownian Motion in the Stock Market," *Operations Research*, 7 (1959), 145–73.
29. John Maynard Keynes, *A Treatise on Probability*. Macmillan & Co., London, 1920, p. 351.
30. P. Wheeler Lynde, *Josiah Willard Gibbs – The History of a Great Mind*. Woodbridge, CT: Ox Bow Press, 1951, p. 173.
31. P. Samuelson, *Foundations of Economics Analysis*. Harvard University Press, Cambridge, MA, p. 3.
32. www.mosesrawlings.freeservers.com/davidselleck.html, date accessed June 25, 2012.
33. Norbert Wiener, "Differential Space," *Journal of Mathematics and Physics*, 58 (1923), 131–74.
34. Louis Bachelier, Mark Davis and Alison Etheridge, *Louis Bachelier's Theory of Speculation: The Origins of Modern Finance*. Princeton University Press, 2006, Foreword by Paul Samuelson.
35. Paul H. Cootner, *The Random Character of Stock Market Prices*. MIT Press, Cambridge, MA, 1964.
36. Paul Samuelson, "Proof that Properly Anticipated Prices Fluctuate Randomly," *Industrial Management Review*, 6(2) (1965), 41–9.
37. Edward O Thorp and Sheen T. Kassouf, *Beat the Market: A Scientific Stock Market System*. Random House, New York, 1967.
38. Robert Merton, "Interview with Paul Samuelson," www.afajof.org/afa/all/paul_samuelson_transcript2.doc, date accessed June 25, 2012.
39. Sanford Grossman, "The Existence of Futures Markets, Noisy Rational Expectations, and Information Externalities," *Review of Economic Studies*, 44 (1977), 431–49; Sanford Grossman and Joseph Stiglitz, "On the Impossibility of Informationally Efficient Markets," *American Economic Review*, 70 (1980), 393–408.
40. B. Graham and D.L. Dodd, *Security Analysis: Principles and Technique*. McGraw-Hill, New York, 1934, p. 17.
41. R. Lucas, "Asset Prices in an Exchange Economy," *Econometrica* 46 (1978), 1429–46.
42. S. Leroy, "Risk Aversion and the Martingale Property of Stock Returns," *International Economic Review* 14, (1973), 436–46.
43. "Proof that Properly Anticipated Prices Fluctuate Randomly," *Industrial Management Review*, 6(2) (1965), 41–9, at 48.

44. Foreword by Paul Samuelson, in Marshall E. Blume and Jeremy J. Siegel, "The Theory of Security Pricing and Market Structure," *Journal of Financial Markets, Institutions and Instruments*, 1(3) (1992), 3.
45. Robert Merton, "Interview with Paul Samuelson," www.afajof.org/afa/all/paul%20samuelson%20transcript2.doc, date accessed June 25, 2012.
46. "The Sveriges Riksbank Prize in Economic Sciences in Memory of Alfred Nobel 1970," Nobelprize.org, www.nobelprize.org/nobel_prizes/economics/laureates/1970/, date accessed June 25, 2012.
47. Paul A. Samuelson, "Lifetime Portfolio Selection by Dynamic Stochastic Programming," *Review of Economics and Statistics*, 51(3) (1969), 239–46.
48. Paul A. Samuelson, "Efficient Portfolio Selection for Pareto-Lévy Investments," *Journal of Financial and Quantitative Analysis*, 2(2) (1967), 107–22.
49. Paul A. Samuelson, "General Proof that Diversification Pays," *Journal of Financial and Quantitative Analysis*, 2(1) (1967), 1–13.
50. www.afajof.org/association/historyfinance.asp, date accessed June 25, 2012.
51. Benoit Mandelbrot, *The Fractal Geometry of Nature*. W.H. Freeman & Co, New York, 1982, p. xiii.
52. Benoit Mandelbrot, "Forecasts of Future Prices, Unbiased Markets and 'Martingale Models'," *Journal of Business*, special supplement (1966), 242–55.
53. Eugene Fama, "Efficient Capital Markets: A Review of Empirical Work," *Journal of Finance*, 25(2) (1970), 383–417.
54. Eugene Fama, "Random Walks in Stock Market Prices," *Financial Analysts Journal* (September/October 1965), 75–9, at 76.
55. *Ibid.*
56. Michael C. Jensen, "The Performance of Mutual Funds in the Period 1945–1964," *Journal of Finance*, 23(2) (1968), 389–416.
57. Eugene Fama, Lawrence Fisher, Michael C. Jensen, and Richard Roll, "The Adjustment of Stock Prices to New Information," *International Economic Review*, 10 (1969), 1–21.
58. Ray Ball and Philip Brown, "An Empirical Evaluation of Accounting Income Numbers," *Journal of Accounting Research*, 6(2) (1968), 159–78.
59. Burton Malkiel, *A Random Walk Down Wall Street*. W.W. Norton, New York, 1973.
60. Michael C. Jensen, "Some Anomalous Evidence Regarding Market Efficiency," *Journal of Financial Economics*, 6 (1978), 95–101.
61. Avraham Beja, "The Limits of Price Information in Market Processes," New York University Working Paper 78(19) (1977).
62. Paul Milgrom and Nancy Stokey, "Information, Trade and Common Knowledge," *Journal of Economic Theory*, 26(1) (1982), 17–27.
63. Sanford Grossman, "The Existence of Futures Markets, Noisy Rational Expectations, and Information Externalities," *Review of Economic Studies*, 44 (1977), 431–49.
64. Sanford Grossman and Joseph Stiglitz, "On the Impossibility of Informationally Efficient Markets," *American Economic Review*, 70 (1980), 393–408.
65. J. Michael Harrison and David M. Kreps, "Speculative Behavior in a Stock Market with Heterogeneous Expectations," *Quarterly Journal of Economics*, 92(2) (1978), 323–36.
66. Werner F.M. De Bondt and Richard Thaler, "Does the Stock Market Overreact?" *Journal of Finance*, 40 (1985), 793–805.

67. Andrew Lo and A. Craig MacKinlay, "Stock Market Prices Do Not Follow Random Walks: Evidence from a Simple Specification Test," *Review of Financial Studies*, 1 (1988), 41–66.
68. James M. Poterba and Lawrence Summers, "Mean Reversion in Stock Market Prices: Evidence and Implications," *Journal of Financial Economics*, 22 (1987), 27–59.
69. Myung Jig Kim, Charles R. Nelson, and Richard Startz, "Mean Reversion in Stock Prices? A Reappraisal of the Empirical Evidence," University of Washington Working Paper, May, 1988.
70. Andrew W. Lo and A. Craig MacKinlay, *A Non-Random Walk Down Wall Street*. Princeton University Press, 1999.
71. Burton G. Malkiel, *A Random Walk Down Wall Street*, 8th edn. Norton, New York, 2003.
72. Andrei Shleifer and Robert W. Vishny, "The Limits of Arbitrage," *Journal of Finance*, 52 (1997), 35–55.
73. Eugene Fama and Kenneth French, "Permanent and Temporary Components of Stock Prices," *Journal of Political Economy*, 96(2) (1988), 246–73.
74. John Cassidy, "Interview with Eugene Fama," *The New Yorker*, January 13, 2010, www.newyorker.com/online/blogs/johncassidy/2010/01/interview-with-eugene-fama.html, date accessed June 25, 2012.
75. Eugene Fama and Andre Farber, "Money, Bonds, and Foreign Exchange," *American Economic Review*, 69(4) (1979), 639–49.
76. www.chicagobooth.edu/faculty/bio.aspx?person_id=12824813568, date accessed June 25, 2012.
77. Eugene Fama and Kenneth French, "The Cross-Section of Expected Stock Returns," *Journal of Finance*, XLVII(2) (1992), 427–65.
78. Eugene Fama, "Market Efficiency, Long-Term Returns, and Behavioural Finance," *Journal of Financial Economics*, 49 (1998), 283–306.
79. www.afajof.org/association/historyfinance.asp, date accessed June 25, 2012.
80. "Steve Reflects on his Academic Career," video, Foundation for the Advancement of Research in Financial Economics, www.farfe.org/Videos/steve_on_academic_career.html, date accessed June 25, 2012.
81. Nai-Fu Chen, Richard Roll, and Stephen A. Ross, "Economic Forces and the Stock Market," *Journal of Business*, 59(3) (1986), 383–403.
82. G. Huberman and S. Kandel, "A Size Based Stock Returns Model," *Center for Research in Security Prices*, University of Chicago Working Paper 148, 1985.
83. Eugene Fama and Kenneth French, "Common Risk Factors in the Returns on Stocks and Bonds," *Journal of Financial Economics*, 33 (1993), 3–56.
84. Eugene Fama and Kenneth French, "The Cross-Section of Expected Stock Returns," *Journal of Finance*, 47 (1992), 427–86.
85. Eric B. Lindenberg and Stephen A. Ross, "Tobin's q Ratio and Industrial Organization," *Journal of Business*, 54 (1981), 1–32.
86. Richard Roll, interview with Stephen Ross as part of the History of Finance series of the American Finance Association, www.afajof.org/association/historyfinance.asp, date accessed June 25, 2012.
87. John Maynard Keynes, *The General Theory of Employment, Interest and Money*. Palgrave Macmillan, Basingstoke, 1936.
88. James Tobin, "Liquidity Preference as Behavior Towards Risk," *Review of Economic Studies*, 25(1) (1958), 65–86.

89. John Maynard Keynes, *The General Theory of Employment, Interest and Money*. Harcourt Brace & Co., New York, 1936, Chapter 12.
90. Arnold C. Harberger, "Monopoly and Resource Allocation," *American Economic Review*, 44 (1954), 77–87.
91. James Tobin, "How Dead is Keynes?" *Economic Inquiry*, 15(4) (1977), 459–68, at 468.
92. James Tobin, "On the Efficiency of the Financial System," *Lloyd's Bank Review*, 153 (1984), 14–15.
93. John Maynard Keynes, *The General Theory of Employment, Interest and Money*. Macmillan, London (1936) 1967, p. 160.
94. A. Kirilenko, A. Kyle, M. Samadi and T. Tuzun, "The Flash Crash: The Impact of High Frequency Trading on an Electronic Market," Social Sciences Research Network, 2011, http://papers.ssrn.com/sol3/papers.cfm?abstract_id=1686004, date accessed June 25, 2012.
95. Paolo Pellizzari and Frank Westerhoff, "Some Effects of Transaction Taxes under Different Microstructures," *Journal of Economic Behavior & Organization*, 72(3) (2009), 850–63.
96. Lanne Markku and Timo Vesala, "The Effect of a Transaction Tax on Exchange Rate Volatility," *International Journal of Finance & Economics*, 15(2) (2010), 123–33.
97. Willem Buiter, "Forget Tobin Tax: There is a Better Way to Curb Finance," *Financial Times*, September 1, 2009, www.ft.com/intl/cms/s/0/76e13a4e-9725-11de-83c5-00144feabdc0.html#axzz1mftdprWR, date accessed June 25, 2012.
98. "The Sveriges Riksbank Prize in Economic Sciences in Memory of Alfred Nobel 1981," Nobelprize.org, www.nobelprize.org/nobel_prizes/economics/laureates/1981, date accessed June 25, 2012.
99. www.google.com/patents/about/HEAT_TRANSFER_APPARATUS_UTILIZING_PARTIC.html?id=13J1AAAAEBAJ, date accessed June 25, 2012; www.prior-ip.com/patent/3540866/, date accessed June 25, 2012.
100. www.lawrencetech.net/page.aspx?pid=399, date accessed June 25, 2012.
101. www.detroityes.com/mb/showthread.php?6580-Redford-High-Site-sold/page3, date accessed June 25, 2012.
102. David Leonhardt, "Be Warned: Mr. Bubble's Worried Again", *New York Times*, August 21, 2005, www.nytimes.com/2005/08/21/business/yourmoney/21real.html?pagewanted=all, date accessed June 25, 2012.
103. Les, Shaver, "'Cover Story' Full Interview with Dr. Robert J. Shiller," *Big Builder Magazine*, January 10, 2008, www.builderonline.com/big-builder/cover-story--full-interview-with-dr--robert-j--shiller.aspx?printerfriendly=true, date accessed June 25, 2012.
104. Letter to Max Born (4 December 1926); *The Born-Einstein Letters* (translated by Irene Born). Walker and Company, New York, 1971.
105. Alan J. Friedman and Carol C. Donley, *Einstein as Myth and Muse*. Cambridge University Press, 1985, p. 119.
106. Robert E. Lucas Jr., "Asset Prices in an Exchange Economy," *Econometrica*, 46(6) (1978), 1429–45.
107. Stephen F. LeRoy and Richard D. Porter, "The Present Value Relation: Tests Based on Implied Variance Bounds," *Econometrica*, 49 (1981), 555–74.

108. Karl Case and Robert Shiller, "Is There a Bubble in the Housing Market?" *Brookings Institute*, 34 (2003), 299–362.
109. Sophie Roell, "Robert Shiller on Human Traits Essential to Capitalism," January 23, 2011, http://thebrowser.com/interviews/robert-shiller-on-human-traits-essential-capitalism, date accessed June 25, 2012.
110. David Loenhardt, Interview with Robert Shiller for the Yale Alumni Magazine, September/October 2009, www.yalealumnimagazine.com/issues/2009_09/shiller032.html, date accessed June 25, 2012.
111. http://ideas.repec.org/top/top.person.all.html, date accessed June 25, 2012.
112. http://topics.bloomberg.com/the-50-most-influential-people-in-global-finance/, date accessed June 25, 2012.
113. Robert Shiller, *Animal Spirits: How Human Psychology Drives the Economy and Why it Matters for Global Capitalism*. Princeton University Press, 2009.
114. Robert Shiller, *Subprime Solution: How the Global Financial Crisis Happened and What to Do about It*. Princeton University Press, 2008.
115. Robert Shiller, *The New Financial Order: Risk in the 21st Century*. Princeton University Press, 2003.
116. Robert Shiller, *Irrational Exuberance*. Princeton University Press, 2000.
117. Robert Shiller, *Macro Markets: Creating Institutions for Managing Society's Largest Economic Risks*. Oxford University Press, 1993.
118. Robert Shiller, *Market Volatility*. MIT Press, Cambridge, MA, 1989.
119. Robert Shiller, *Reforming U.S. Financial Markets: Reflections Before and Beyond Dodd-Frank*. MIT Press, Cambridge, MA, 2011.

Index

algorithms, 36, 128, 164–5, 187
Allais, Maurice, 89
allocative efficiency, 3
anchoring, 190
arbitrage pricing theory (APT), 2, 119,
  126, 127, 130, 131–3, 135, 136,
  137–8, 139, 203
arbitrageurs, 3, 85, 113, 135, 167,
  203, 206
Arrow, Kenneth, 39, 66, 90, 119, 124,
  126, 155, 171
Arrow-Debreu, 131, 133, 135, 139,
  157, 169, 184
asymptotic, 26, 99
auctioneer, 2, 110
autocorrelation, 39, 103, 114
autoregressive, 85

Bachelier, Louis, 1, 5, 8, 14, 16, 18,
  24–32, 33–7, 40, 42–3, 46, 47, 48,
  49–51, 55, 69, 74, 79, 82, 99, 184,
  201, 213n14, 214n23
Ball, Ray, 108, 189, 215n58
bandwagon effect, 42, 166, 167
behavioral finance, 2, 112, 118, 141,
  190, 191, 193, 194, 195, 203,
  204, 206
Beja, Avraham, 109, 215n61
Bernanke, Ben, 87
Bertrand, Joseph, 46
binomial options pricing model
  (BOPM), 140
Black, Fischer, 20, 26, 42, 51, 70, 78,
  83, 87, 107, 108, 114, 126, 129
Black-Scholes equation, 1, 5, 26, 42,
  78, 79, 80, 126, 129, 133, 137, 139,
  140, 141, 193
Böhm-Bawerk, Eugen von, 17
Bohr, Max, 186
bonds, 10, 12, 17, 19, 24, 37, 45,
  189, 201
Borel, Félix Édouard Justin Émile,
  10, 46

Bretton Woods, 161
Brown, Phillip, 108, 189
Brown, Robert, 11, 19, 34
Brownian motion, 11, 25, 26, 30, 34,
  35, 46, 47, 68, 69, 71, 75, 79, 80,
  184, 201

Capital Asset Pricing Model (CAPM),
  2, 5, 36, 96, 107, 108, 117, 127,
  128, 129, 130, 131, 132, 133,
  135, 136, 137, 142, 154, 156,
  170, 193
Case, Karl, 195
Case-Shiller index, 195, 196
Center for Research in Security Prices
  (CRSP), 104, 107
central limit theorem, 22, 42, 50
Chamberlin, Edward, 150
chaos theory, 96, 99, 184
chartists, 4, 83, 102, 106, 161,
  165, 204
Chicago School, 39, 58, 59, 60, 66,
  67, 79, 106, 153, 155, 172, 190
circuit breakers, 164
classical model, 186
Clinton, Bill, 90, 112, 143
cognitive dissonance, 190
competitive equilibrium, 3, 109–10,
  119, 127, 131, 135, 139, 184
Compustat, 104, 107
Conant, James, 150
corporate finance, 117, 133, 142
correlation, 24, 39, 42, 103, 113,
  134, 135
Cowles Commission, 38–40, 73, 100,
  151, 155, 170
Cowles Foundation, 151, 156, 170,
  196
Cowles III, Alfred, 38, 73, 100
Cox, John Carrington, 139
Crawford, Marion, 57, 62, 63, 64,
  90, 151
critically damped, 166

da Vinci, Leonardo, 14
Darwin, Charles, 79
day traders, 164–5, 166, 204
De Bondt, Werner, 112, 190
de Finetti, Bruno, 16, 31
Debreu, Gerard, 39
derivatives, 19, 24, 37, 51, 129, 143, 167, 168
differential equation, 9, 25, 71, 80, 123, 139, 155, 201
Dimeco, Sally Ann, 94, 95
discount rate, 17
discrete models, 140
Dodd, David, 83
Dow Jones Industrial Average, 101, 164
dynamic process, 2, 104
dynamics, 2, 3, 27, 75, 76, 78, 89, 99, 104, 130, 137, 183, 187, 192, 206

econometric, 30, 37–8, 39, 73, 88, 90, 96, 100–1, 103, 111, 112, 117, 135, 141, 143, 151, 171
efficient market hypothesis, 1, 29–30, 36, 39, 42, 43, 73–4, 85, 86, 90, 91, 106, 107–8, 109, 112, 114, 116, 119, 129, 139, 153, 156, 170, 175, 185, 186, 192, 193, 202, 205
enlightened capitalism, 178
equilibrium, 3, 26, 31, 39, 47, 60, 79, 89, 103, 104, 106, 109–10, 126, 130, 131, 133, 139, 151, 155, 156, 165, 166, 184, 206
Erdös, Paul, 50
event studies, 104, 117, 189

face value F, 17–18
factor loadings, 132, 135, 136, 137, 138
fair game, 28, 31, 36, 37, 102, 113
Fannie Mae, 142, 143
fat finger trades, 164
Faulstich, Virginia Marie, 181
Federal Home Loan Mortgage Corporation, 142
Federal National Mortgage Association, 142
feedback, 165–6, 194
Feller, William, 26, 40
Feynman, Richard, 53, 124

first moment, 31, 35, 153
Fisher, Irving, 17, 65, 87, 95
Fisher, Lawrence, 103, 108
flash crash, 164, 165
Ford, Henry, 178, 180
forward treasury bond, 132
Fourier, Joseph, 30
fractal geometry, 99
Freddie Mac, 142–3
Friedman, Milton, 67, 84, 87, 88, 136, 141, 152, 155
Frisch, Ragnar, 88
Frost, Carol, 124, 125, 126
full insurance efficiency, 160
functional/operational efficiency, 160
fundamental analysis, 36, 102, 105, 108, 131
fundamental valuation efficiency, 160

Galbraith, John Kenneth, 150, 181
Gauss, Johann Carl Friedrich, 10
Gaussian distribution, 11, 28, 29, 31, 36, 38, 40, 70, 75, 97, 99, 100
Gaussian normal distribution, 22, 201
Gevrey, Maurice, 48, 49
Gibbs, J. Willard, 61
Gibson, George, 102
Graham, Benjamin, 83
Greenspan, Alan, 183, 204
Grossman, Sanford, 82, 110, 187

Haavelmo, Trygve, 39
Haberler, Gottfried, 124, 150
Harberger, Arnold, 156
Harrison, J. Michael, 110–11
Hayek, August, 88
heat diffusion process, 10
high-frequency traders, 166, 204
Hilbert, David, 48, 65, 68
Huberman, Gur, 136

idiosyncratic risk, 134
inflation protected treasury, 132
information arbitrage efficiency, 160
information efficiency, 3, 106, 112, 187
Ingenhousz, Jan, 11, 34
interest rate, 17–18, 65, 78, 111, 135, 137, 185
intertemporal, 65, 129

irrational exuberance, 37, 113, 175, 183, 190, 192, 195, 204, 206
Itô, Kiyoshi, 27, 41, 71
Itô's lemma, 73, 77

Jegadeesh, Narasimhan, 190
Jensen, Michael, 87, 107, 108, 189

Kac, Mark, 50
Kandel, Shmuel, 136
Kendall, Maurice, 75, 100
Keynes, John Maynard, 46, 51, 73, 74, 87, 151, 154, 160–1, 163, 165, 171, 184, 187, 214n29, 216n87, 217n89, 217n93
Kim, Myung, 113, 216n69
Klein, Lawrence, 39, 103, 108
Knight, Frank, 31, 46, 58, 59, 155
Koopmans, Tjalling, 39
Kreps, Daniel, 110, 111
Krugman, Paul, 87

Least squares, 11
Leibniz, Gottfried, 15, 79
Leontief, Wassily, 60, 62, 150
LeRoy, Stephen, 84, 189
Levy distribution, 99
life cycle, 67, 89, 205
Life Cycle Model, 67
Lindenberg, Eric, 142
Lintner, John, 96
liquidity preference, 154
Lo, Andrew, 112, 113
Log-Gaussian distribution, 42, 43
Long Term Capital Management (company), 171
Lord Rayleigh, John Williams Strutt, 29
Lorie, James H., 103
Lucas, Robert, 84, 110, 186, 187, 214n41, 217n106

Mackinlay, Archie, 112, 113, 216n70
Maillot, Augustine Jeanne, 45
Malthus, Thomas, 16, 58, 59
Mandelbrot, Benoit, 96, 97, 98–101, 102, 103, 213n12, 215n51, 215n52
Marić, Mileva, 35
Markowitz, Harry, 5, 36, 39, 90, 96, 127, 128, 154, 155, 156, 170

Marquis de Laplace, Pierre-Simon, 10
Marschak, Jacob, 31, 35, 153, 155
martingale, 11, 22–3, 100, 113
martingale independence property, 73
Maxwell, James Clerk, 23
mean, 19, 22, 24, 113, 135, 190
Merton, Robert King, 15, 26, 27, 66, 75, 78, 80, 86, 108, 117, 119, 124, 129, 213n6, 214n38, 215n45
Milgrom, Paul, 109, 215n62
Miller, Merton, 96, 97, 98, 117, 133
Modern Portfolio Theory, 5, 90, 96, 128, 129, 133, 154, 156, 170, 171
Modigliani, Franco, 39, 66, 90, 96, 133, 143, 151, 155
Modigliani-Miller theorem, 117, 133, 191
Monte Carlo study, 76
Musgrave, Richard, 150

nanotraders, 166, 167
negative externalities, 167
negative feedback, 165, 166, 194
Nelson, Charles, 113
Newton, Isaac, 12, 15, 16, 21, 79

Okun, Arthur, 156, 195
option derivative, 19
Osborne, Matthew Fontaine Maury, 40, 41, 42, 50, 74, 75, 76, 98, 214n28

Pearson, Karl, 29, 213n13
perpetuities, 17, 18
Poincaré, Jules Henri, 9, 10, 12–13, 24, 25, 30, 35, 45, 201
Porter, Richard, 189, 217n107
positive feedback, 165, 166, 194
Poterba, James, 112, 216n68

Rae, John, 17
Raffia, Howard, 124
Ramsey, Frank Plumpton, 16
random motion, 10, 11
rational expectations, 103, 110, 111, 186
reflection principle, 31
Regnault, Jules, 19, 20, 21, 22, 23, 35, 213n8

regression, 132, 133
rent grabbing, 168
rente, 17, 24, 50, 51
rentier, 17, 19
representative agent, 154, 156
residual errors, 39
return, 17, 79, 80, 100, 102, 103, 107, 111, 112, 114, 117, 134, 136, 137, 159, 190, 201
Ringo, Elizabeth Fay, 151
risk, 28, 59, 108, 130, 137, 140, 154, 168
risk neutrality, 113, 134, 140
Roberts, Harry, 96, 101
Roll, Richard, 95, 108, 126, 134, 135, 136, 143, 189, 215n57, 216n81, 216n86
Rubinstein, Mark, 140

Savage, Leonard Jimmie, 31, 41, 42, 45, 48, 51, 67, 74, 75, 85, 158
Scholes, Myron, 26, 42, 51, 66, 78, 87, 96, 108, 117, 119, 126, 129, 139, 201
Schumpeter, Joseph, 60, 150
second moment, 31, 32, 35
security market line, 129, 133
separation theorem, 154, 170, 171
serial correlation, 39, 42, 103
Sharpe, William, 36, 87, 96, 107, 119, 127, 128, 154
Shiller, Robert, 2, 37, 111, 112, 113, 169, 175, 177, 181, 182, 183, 188, 189, 190, 191, 192, 193, 194, 195, 196, 204, 206
Shleifer, Andrei, 113, 194, 216n72
short sale, 131
Simon, Herbert, 39
Simons, Henry Calvert, 59
simplifying assumptions, 134, 156
Smith, Adam, 2–3, 168, 184, 190, 192
Solow, Robert, 151, 171
speculative bubbles, 37, 161, 163, 191, 192

Startz, Richard, 113, 216n69
static process, 89, 130
Stiglitz, Joseph, 82, 110, 175, 187, 215n64
Stirling, James, 21, 22
Stokey, Nancy, 109, 215n62
sub-martingale, 101
Summers, Larry, 90, 112
Sweezy, Paul, 150
systematic risk, 129, 134

technical analysis, 43, 84, 102, 108, 165
Tesler, Lester, 96
Thaler, Richard, 112, 190, 215n66
Thiele, Thorvald N., 11
Tinbergen, Jan, 88
Titman, Sheridan, 190
Tobin, James, 2, 39, 128, 141, 142, 145, 147, 148, 149, 150, 151, 154, 156, 157, 158–62, 163, 165, 167, 168, 169, 170, 171, 172, 175, 184, 202, 206, 216n88, 217n91
Tobin's q, 141, 142, 157, 159, 163, 172
Treynor, Jack, 107

Ulam, Stanislaw, 76
uncertainty, 28, 46, 59, 135

variance, 22, 113, 114, 128, 131, 135, 153
Ville, Jean, 47
Viner, Jacob, 59
Volatility, 31, 161, 163, 164, 167, 168, 206

Wallace, Alfred Russel, 79
Wiener process, 26, 40, 41, 69, 71, 73, 76, 77
Wiener, Norbert, 26, 27, 40, 62, 66, 68
Whitehead, Albert, 150
Wilson, Edwin Bidwell, 60
Working, Holbrook, 42, 75, 213n17

Printed and bound in the United States of America